Frontiers

OF THE

Soul

Frontiers OF THE Soul

Exploring Psychic Evolution

Michael Grosso

*This publication made possible with
the assistance of the Kern Foundation*

QUEST BOOKS
The Theosophical Publishing House
Wheaton, Ill. U.S.A.
Madras, India/London, England

The Theosophical Publishing House
P.O. Box 270
Wheaton, IL 60189-0270

A publication of the Theosophical Publishing House,
a department of the Theosophical Society in America.

Library of Congress Cataloging-in-Publication Data

Grosso, Michael, 1937–
    Frontiers of the soul : exploring psychic evolution / Michael
Grosso.
        p.   cm.
    Includes index.
    ISBN 0-8356-0676-7 (pbk.) : $12.95
    1. Parapsychology.   2. Evolution — Miscellanea.   I. Title.
BF1040.G69   1992
133.8 — dc20   91-58099
                                                                    CIP

Miracles happen, not in opposition to nature,
but in opposition to what we know of nature.
                                    Saint Augustine

Contents

Acknowledgments

Chapter 6, "Fear of Life After Death," originally appeared in *What Survives,* edited by Gary Doore (Los Angeles, CA: Jeremy P. Tarcher, Inc., 1990). Reprinted with permission.

Chapter 12, "The Marian Morphogenesis" originally appeared as "Visions of Mary and Psychic Evolution" in *Gnosis,* a San Francisco-based journal of the Western inner traditions. Reprinted with permission.

In addition to the many writers whose work I have referred to in the book, I want especially to thank Leslie Price for encouraging me to pursue the parapsychology of religion; David Pursglove and Kenneth Ring for useful comments on the text, and for being such great friends; my mate Louise Northcutt for our precious conversations; and Shirley Nicholson and Brenda Rosen for their superb editorial midwifery.

I
Return to the Beyond

Humankind lies groaning, half crushed beneath the weight of its own progress. People do not sufficiently realize that their future is in their own hands. Theirs is the task of determining first of all whether they want to go on living or not. Theirs the responsibility, then, for deciding if they want merely to live, or intend to make just the extra effort required for fulfilling, even on their refractory planet, the essential function of the universe, which is a machine for making gods.

Henri Bergson

Since the scientific revolution, the aspirations of religion have suffered one setback after another. Copernicus, Galileo, Darwin, Freud—to take four classic examples—all great scientists, were men whose breakthroughs to knowledge were at odds with traditional worldviews. By calling attention to a different kind of data, this book tells a different story. The gods gain a reprieve. A return to the beyond becomes possible. The beyond? The way beyond is the way within. The way back to the gods is through the frontiers of the soul.

1
Psyche and Religion:
Three Perspectives

Always he remains in the same place, moving not at all; nor is it fitting for him to go to different places at different times, but without toil he shakes all things by the thought of his mind.
Xenophanes

For a long time there has been a civil war in the human psyche between critical reason and spiritual imagination. The war first broke out among the ancient Greeks, a people wonderfully endowed with both reason and imagination.

Take Xenophanes, who lived six centuries before Christ, a pious thinker who attacked Homer's theology. "The Ethiopians," Xenophanes observed, "say that their gods are snub-nosed and black, the Thracians that theirs have light blue eyes and red hair."[1] In other words, we form our images of the gods in terms of ourselves. The gods are ourselves writ large. Xenophanes thus anticipates a view that Feuerbach, Marx, and Freud will elaborate centuries later.

The critical mind is negative, but the life-affirming soul craves wholeness. Here is the basis of the civil war within, the splitting of the self and the scattering of its energies. Since the rise of Greek rationalism, we have been trying to overcome this brokenness of self, this inward dis-ease.

The danger is to drift toward fundamentalism. By fundamentalism I mean a certain rigid cast of mind—a contracted style of cognizing the universe. It is a style that turns up in science as well as religion. In either case, it is self-defeating, because it is inflexible and mechanical. But people are not machines, and life is a process that flows and bends, grows and evolves.

To avoid this danger, this subtle drift toward lifelessness, we need

3

to recognize the claims of the whole person; all the voices within us need to be heard. Critical reason and transcendent spirit—each have their rights, their authentic domains of experience to explore. If we want to avoid the ills of psychic civil war, we need to learn to harmonize our inner powers.

Learning this is not easy, but trying to has value. For every attempt to deal with our inner conflicts gives us an opportunity to expand our consciousness. "Nothing can be sole or whole," said the poet William Butler Yeats, "that has not been rent."

We have been rent asunder, but are we making headway toward "soleness" and "wholeness"? Is the process of becoming a complete human being getting easier? It appears to me that every great attempt at synthesis is a station on the way to greater conflict—but also a challenge to greater synthesis. Consider a few examples from the history of thought.

In the Middle Ages, Thomas Aquinas used the "science" of Aristotle to bolster his theological program. Thomas used arguments about motion, first invented by Plato in the *Phaedrus,* to "prove" the existence of God. Some still put stock in such arguments, although most philosophers and theologians today find them of small use. Still, Aquinas made a bold, and for his time, controversial attempt to mate the latest science with a religion of eternal values.

The Thomistic synthesis could hardly be the last word; new scientific discoveries would drive thoughtful people to revision their metaphysical outlook repeatedly. So the crisis escalated in the seventeenth century, thanks to the rise of mechanistic science. The war between the new science of Galileo and the ancient soul desires as enshrined in the dogmas of the Church was a landmark in the evolution of Western consciousness. After all that was said and done, the two combatants, scientific reason and imaginal spirit, emerged undefeated and unreconciled.

The great German philosopher Immanuel Kant (1724-1804) tried a new tactic: ideas of God, freedom, and immortality, he argued, could never be objects of scientific knowledge. They were beyond anything we could know directly. Kant thus became an exponent of voluntarism: We could act as if there *were* a God and as if we *were* free. Spiritual truth could be willed, Kant said, but not known.

The long struggle to reclaim the transcendent has taken many twists and turns. What we find is a tortuous dialectic of reflection and imagination, the rational mind checking, critiquing the original productions of the spiritual imagination.

The attacks are invariably followed by imagination rising in revolt, reaffirming and reinventing its life-giving stories. A long view of the history of spirit shows that apart from events in the external world, and apart from all our scientific sophistication, inwardly we are still driven to reinvent the old stories again and again.

The Disappearing Act of the Gods

Xenophanes attacked the naive theology of Homer; but that was not the end of the gods. Gods are made of more resilient stuff. The attack on Homer gave rise in the long run to the Platonic school which reinstalled the gods under a sublimated disguise, which Plato called the Ideas.

A similar sublimation took place in the Near East. The Hebrew prophets savaged the polytheistic imaginings of their neighbors, then invented their own image of a supreme Deity. The history of the prophets is a history of the imaginal war of the gods. A general principle seems at work in the history of religions: every new formation in the imagery of the divine calls forth its criticisms and its complements. The one constant is a virtual instinct to forge images of divinity.

The conflict between reflection and imagination reached a peak with the rise of modern science. The new science of Galileo, Kepler, Newton, Descartes, and Hobbes struck hard blows against the traditional religious imagination. The poets recorded the impact of the new science on the psyche; John Donne, for instance, in his poem, "The Anatomie of the World," captured the mood of metaphysical angst:

> And new philosophy calls all in doubt,
> The element of fire is quite put out;
> The sun is lost, and th'earth, and no man's wit,
> Can well direct him where to look for it.
> And freely men confess that this world's spent. . .
> 'Tis all in pieces, all coherence gone.

The mechanistic philosophy of the seventeenth century destroyed the "coherence" of the traditional worldview. Since Donne's time a deep uneasiness has troubled the hearts of people, a deep need to recapture a coherent worldview—or, as we say today, a coherent "paradigm." Yet in spite of the rift between the two great powers of the psyche, the cunning of imagination always contrives to produce the antitype it needs to reassert its aims.

Three classic cases come to mind. The first is Darwin who piqued the vanity of humankind, as many like to say, by showing that our origins lie in the lower depths of nature, not as we had fancied, in the heights of God's creative will. Darwin, as we all know, challenged the old Western God story.

And yet Darwin's cofounder of the theory of natural selection, Alfred Russell Wallace, had already begun to tell a different story. Thanks, as he said, to having been "beaten by the facts,"[2] Wallace came to believe that there was an unknown psychic factor at work in evolution. He arrived at this view from his own investigations of Victorian spiritistic phenomena. Not surprisingly, this aspect of the history of evolutionary thought has been all but ignored by official science. Nevertheless, Wallace was Darwin's antitype and counterpart —his spiritual Shadow.

The second example is Freud. Freud argued on psychoanalytic principles that religion is nothing but a certified cultural neurosis, a symptom of humanity's adolesence, a soothing illusion. Freud called forth his antitype and complement in Jung, his most promising disciple. Unlike Freud, Jung took spiritual phenomena as proof for an expanded view of the human psyche. With Jung the gods return once more, as they did in the ancient world with Plato, newly christened as "archetypes of the collective unconscious."

A third example of type and antitype is Watson and Rhine. Watson, the behaviorist who wanted to annihilate consciousness, evoked his antitype in Rhine, the founder of parapsychology. Using Watsonian experimental methods, Rhine sought to demonstrate not only that consciousness exists but that it transcends physical reality.

And so it goes. The quelled gods return; they reaffirm themselves in novel, often unexpected ways.

The Reality Question

Is there an extraphysical order of being? That is a basic question. Is there anything *beyond?* Soul, god, demon, spirit, ghost, idea, archetype, spiritual energy—is anything *not* contained within the categories of physicalistic thinking? Is there a transcendent factor—an alternate category of being—anything we can use to get a handle on ideas such as God, Soul, Angel?

Answers to this question vary. Some scholars have found a common structure in our spiritual experience. This universal heritage is sometimes called the "perennial philosophy," an idea that goes back to Leibniz and the Renaissance thinker, Pico della Mirandola. More recently Helena Petrovna Blavatsky called it the "secret doctrine," which she found "scattered throughout thousands of volumes embodying the scriptures of the great Asiatic and early European religions, hidden under glyph and symbol."[3] The existence of a "secret" universal doctrine implies that spiritual explorers from different times and cultures have all discovered the same essential truths.

Still, there is the big, the inevitable question: can we justify the *ontology*—can we deal with the question of the *reality* of the objects of religious belief? If we can't, the skeptics are free to say that religion is illusory. It won't matter if the illusion is universally shared, or if it is comforting, therapeutic, or socially enobling. The skeptic can always insist that our high hopes are groundless, our spiritual ideals fictitious.

Psi and the Founders of Psychical Research

The English founders of psychical research understood this challenge and tried to find a new foundation for religious belief. For Frederic Myers, Henry Sidgwick, and William Barrett, the empirical psychic factor—more solid in their view than faith and hope—was the key to a new science of the transcendent.[4]

By psychic factor, or psi, I mean something whose field of activity is *beyond* the ordinary constraints of time, space, and matter. It is possible to distinguish two kinds of psi: extrasensory perception (ESP)—receptive psi, information received from the external environment apart from the known sensory channels—and psychokinesis (PK)—active or expressive psi, the mind's ability to influence physical reality *directly*.

I argue that the psi factor, so defined, is pivotal to traditional claims of transcendence. I believe it gives us an empirical foothold for appreciating the reality of such claims. Psi offers a kind of undifferentiated matrix out of which types of transcendence may crystallize: God, soul, afterlife, angel, grace, prayer, and so forth.

In order to build this beachhead on the shore of transcendence, it is not necessary to *explain* psychic phenomena; it is necessary only to establish their existence. Furthermore, it may be that psi is *un-*

explainable—it may be just a fundamental fact of nature. What can be said with confidence is that once the reality of psi is established, the range of the possible in nature increases enormously. Everywhere new and intriguing (and perhaps frightening) doors to reality are flung open.

For over a hundred years researchers have been gathering data on psi: telepathy, clairvoyance, precognition, psychokinesis; poltergeists, xenoglossy, materializations, apports; out-of-body flights; apparitions, hauntings, mediumistic phenomena; near-death encounters, reincarnation memories, and so on. Based on my own experiences,[5] on careful study of an extensive literature, and on discussions with countless firsthand experiencers, I find it very difficult to deny that psi is a fact of nature. This, at any rate, is the assumption I work from in this book.

The question I want to ask is this: if a psychic factor, dimension, or world exists, what does it imply for our understanding of religion? In my opinion, it implies a great deal. Let's consider three distinct (though not exclusive) ways religion and psychic phenomena may relate.

The Religion-Centered

One relation is religion-centered. In this instance, a seeker comes to psi studies with an already well-defined religious faith. For such a person, psi studies might serve several purposes. For example, they might, in a general way, validate the "supernatural." Psi—the realm of the paranormal—ratifies the reality of things that transcend scientific materialism. Psi studies point toward phenomena, perhaps laws, perhaps a whole order of being, which operate beyond the limits of ordinary physical existence. The psi dimension, it might seem to the person of faith, confirms what he or she has believed all along: that we inhabit a universe populated by forces, agencies, or beings beyond physical reality.

For the person of faith, psi studies might strengthen the belief that ours is the kind of universe that is friendly to the supernatural. The paranormal might be thought of as a kind of midpoint between the natural and the spiritual, a step on the ladder of the soul's upward ascent. As such, psi would be a welcome discovery—a breath of air after confinement in the claustrophobic box of mechanistic materialism.

Paranormal studies might offer a person of faith a strategic weapon. And they might do more. Within the world of religion are many beliefs likely to seem unacceptable to minds imbued with modern ideas and scientific sentiments. Paranormal studies might ease the path to particular beliefs, customs, and rituals that no longer speak to us. Many things that seem absurd, incredible, or even repulsive to modern sensibilities might, in light of psi dynamics, take on fresh significance.

Consider, for instance, the idea of "obedience." In many religious traditions, obedience is deemed a virtue. In the modern church of rational liberalism, whether of religious or free-thinking persuasion, obedience is more likely to seem servile, undignified, and authoritarian.

In an age that prizes individualism, what are we to make of a remark of Padre Pio? "I would," he once said, "jump out of a window, if I was so ordered by one of my superiors."

Padre Pio is one of the great mystics and thaumaturges of the twentieth century. (I look at his story in Chapter 10.) All I will say here is that there may be a link between Padre Pio's paranormal prowess and the virtue he makes of obedience. Research, in fact, suggests that anxious ego-involved effort impedes psychic functioning.

Padre Pio's readiness to jump out of a window at his superior's command, which some of us might deplore, may be part of an internal strategy useful in liberating his psycho-spiritual powers. The readiness to obey a higher principle may work as a device for helping people remain alert to their unconscious promptings. And it is via the royal road of the unconscious that the wonders of psi travel. There is more to the Christian virtue of obedience—it has to do with humility—than what I've said. Still, I think the psychic side is important.

Consider another example of something likely to appear queer and superstitious to us moderns: the concern for ritual purity. Recall the ablutions made in the house of Odysseus in Homer's *Odyssey* (Book 22). The halls have been splattered with the blood of the slain suitors. Blood, according to ancient belief, would taint the house and leave an evil stain on its walls and floors. Violently shed blood was thought in some obscure way to remember the deed, to carry a source of contagion or miasma from the original act. Hence the need for ritual cleansing.

A strange notion, to be sure. Yet hauntings and other phenomena suggest that physical objects may become linked literally with people's memories. Ancient rites of purification may have been based on this possibility. The ancients may have known many important things we have forgotten. Modern psi research might help people recover precious insights lost to the modern worldview.

Psi research favors religion in another basic way: by making a case for postmortem survival. Most great religions affirm a belief in some form of afterlife. Nowadays, thanks to an intimidating scientific materialism, even clerics play down, for want of confidence, belief in an afterlife. But the belief is at the heart of religion, and is the basis of religious optimism.[6]

The Science-Centered

A second perspective on the relation between religion and psychic phenomena may be called science-centered. For the parapsychologist there may be much to learn from studying psi in a religious setting. There are, to begin with, the big effects, so impressive that even hard-nosed skeptics cannot dismiss them easily. Examples that come to mind are the massive appearances of the (alleged) Virgin Mary in Zeitun, the levitations of Joseph of Copertino, or the materializations of Sai Baba (providing they stand up to scrutiny).

Aside from helping to establish, in dramatic and perhaps illuminating ways, the reality of psi, parapsychology might learn something of how psi works by studying it in a more natural setting: in the context of faith, symbol, and numinous experience. Experimental studies have demonstrated the importance of belief, expectation, and emotion in psychic phenomena. In a religious setting, these factors come powerfully into play. The study of psi in a religious setting might suggest experimental hypotheses or new conceptual frameworks for interpreting psi.

Thus, religion and parapsychology—each from its own guarded viewpoint—might meet and profitably interact.

The Soul-Centered

In a third model, religion and soul science would fraternize *freely.* Let me call this the soul-centered perspective.

Parapsychology has a role in the re-mythologizing of religion. So far in the war between science and religion, religion's turf has steadily shrunk. The project of de-mythology is a case in point. For example, theologian Rudolf Bultmann apparently accepts without question the scientistic dogma that New Testament miracles are impossible. Hence the project to *de*-mythologize Christianity, in which the supernatural element is carefully de-emphasized.[7]

Perhaps for the first time in its historic dialogue with science, the religious imagination, by means of psi research, has prospects of recouping, perhaps even of expanding, its domain of discourse. We may be able to reclaim and rediscover the transcendent meanings of ancient myths. With psi research it may be possible—perhaps in new and unforeseen ways—to *re-mythologize* the world of religion.

Coming Attractions

Let me pause here for a quick overview of what follows. In general, I select a few basic themes from the domain of religious narratives, with an emphasis on Western forms of theism, and in particular, on Christianity. (This is due to my greater familiarity with these themes.) Of the three relations between psi and religion described above, the focus in this book is on what I call the soul-centered. My main interest is the possibility of the evolution of individual human beings.

In Part One, I trace the role of psi in the rise of the God-Idea, the early Christian experience, and Saint Paul's conversion. I interpret these developments as aspects of the evolution of human psi potential. Certain psi-mediated events, I hold, are the experiential basis for people believing in God, the Holy Spirit, angels, and other entities rationalists discard as products of fantasy.

In Part Two, I look at the belief in an afterlife from the standpoint of psi—the transcendent soul factor. Belief in an afterlife is prominent in most religions. In Chapter 6, I argue that the fear of psi is part of the fear of life after death. In Chapter 7, I construct a model of life "after" death that stresses the transformative potential of psychokinesis.

My concern is a broad one: I want to exhibit the general potential for forming *any* transcendent belief-system. The modern view tends to undermine transcendent beliefs by reducing them to illusions; my aim here is to open up the transcendent horizon *in general*—to argue for the existence of a hyperphysical reality that underlies all such beliefs.

The perspective I adopt features an evolutionary view of religion. And so in Part Three I view transcendent psi as a force in the evolution of consciousness and the visionary component of religion as a blueprint for psychic evolution. The evolutionary outlook values the creative uses of time. Looking back in time, people may learn to see the earliest spiritual visions of the human race in a new light. They may come to see that the first products of the spiritual imagination were projected images of their own evolutionary future. From this perspective, all the gods and goddesses, indeed, the whole pantheon of spiritual powers, become images of super-evolved humanity. The following chapters explore this hypothesis.

Foreshadowings of our evolutionary future are shown in the first imaginings of the gods, in the behavior of extraordinary individuals, in ancient rituals and beliefs, in phenomena showing transcendence of the body, and in certain global patterns of transformative experience we can observe today—indeed, in a whole family of experiences I call *evolutionary accelerators.*

But now let us begin with a short description of the method to be followed in our explorations of psychic evolution.

2
Deciphering Signs of Transcendence

The world and the Gods are dead or alive according to the condition of our souls.

James Hillman

In contemporary intellectual life, there is a special term used for the art of interpreting religious texts—*hermeneutics.*

Hermeneutics is the art of interpretation. The word comes from the field of Bible criticism. In Greek, a *hermeneus* is one who interprets a foreign tongue. For Aeschylus the poet was a *hermeneus* of the gods. The gods speak through sacred texts, and they speak a language that has become foreign to most of us. Hence the need for hermeneutics—for an art to help us interpret the language of the gods.

How shall we interpret the contents of old religious writings? Should we focus on their historical settings? On the sociological issues? The existential pathos? Should we view the text as the inerrant deposit of God's word? Or should we, in a "deconstructionist" style, engage the text in whatever way we wish, as if it had no rights of its own, but drew all its meaning from our subjective responses? The answer, of course, is that in practice, what we stress when we interpret a text is always a matter of choice.

One thing seems clear. It's impossible to interpret any sign or text without making assumptions. The philosopher Karl Popper once pointed out that even everyday words—common nouns like *stone* or *glass*—contain theoretical assumptions. Indeed, every thought passing through our minds is theory-laden. We don't just think and talk—we think and talk with a point of view—using our hidden conceptual baggage.

The word *hermeneutics* comes from the Greek *Hermes*—the god of messengers. There is always a "god" presiding over the act of

13

interpretation—always a set of assumptions guiding the translation of ancient signals into current meanings. This is true whether the signals are words, images, paintings, temples, or inscriptions. There is always the influence of the god: the hermetic messenger—in other words, the slant, the bias, the way we decode the message.

Something else is worth noting. The Greek god Hermes was a thief. Indeed, every hermeneutic is a thief; every act of interpretation "steals" something from the text. I am reminded of Dryden's advice to authors. When you steal, he said, steal like a monarch! In other words, appropriate, integrate, make the text your own. All interpretation is theft; we are thieves who ransack the banks of meaning. Theft is here a metaphor for assimilation—for spiritual nutrition. Hermeneutics, then, is a technique of spiritual nutrition.

Religious texts—the Bible, the Upanishads, the Tao Te Ching, The Tibetan Book of the Dead, and so on—all are open to interpretation. There are as many types of interpretation as there are people or schools of thought. For our purpose, let us mention three types of hermeneutics, three approaches to interpreting religious texts: the reductionistic, the literalistic, and the transcendent.

Freudian hermeneutics tends toward reductionism. The Freudian for the most part interprets a religious text as signifying something operative in the dynamics of the lower psyche. For example, for Freud, as he explains in *The Future of an Illusion,* to talk of God is, at bottom, to talk of a father surrogate. Freud reduces religion to personal concerns. The transcendent is treated as a special type of psychic illusion.

At the other end of the spectrum, literalistic hermeneutics takes the sacred text at face value. The literalist accepts assertions, descriptions, and references exactly as they appear. God is literally the King of heaven, sitting on his throne, delighted with servants, angry with sinners, promising paradise, terrifying with brimstone, and so on— just as the words of the text declare. For me this is another form of reductionism, another way of killing the living ambiguity of the sacred word.

Neither way seems adequate to the contemporary challenge of interpretation, so we are prompted to use a third—a transcendent hermeneutics. In short, we are going to look at sacred texts in a way that attempts to bring out and develop their transcendent meanings.

We shall not automatically assume that every extraordinary or supernatural claim is reducible to the ordinary or the conventional. But neither are we going to fall into the opposite trap of swallowing all claims literally and uncritically.

What, then, do we mean by transcendent? The word is often used to suggest something vaguely uplifting and edifying. Etymologically, it derives from a word that means "to climb over or beyond." In this book, I use the word *transcendent* in three distinct but overlapping senses.

1) The first and theoretically strongest sense refers to the transcendence of space, time, and matter—the *psi*-related side of transcendence. Psi refers to those occurrences in nature that violate what the philosopher C. D. Broad called the "basic limiting principles" that rule the thinking of the average educated person in an age of scientific materialism.

Extrasensory perception involves receiving information in ways that violate these basic limiting principles. In telepathy, for instance, a person acquires information about another person's thoughts without using the known channels of sense. In psychokinesis, to take another example, a person exerts an influence on physical reality, independent of his or her muscular apparatus or any known energy transaction. The possibility of this type of transcendence, and thus of a transcendent hermeneutics, rests on a mass of empirical data—experimental studies and spontaneous case histories.[1]

A point to stress is that the limits of psi-influence remain unknown. If we are willing to entertain the idea of group or collective psi, for example, where psi may work additively, those limits widen considerably. More important, everything we know suggests that what limits our psi capacities are psychological variables, belief and expectation, for example.

Another point we should make now is that psi may be a fundamental fact of nature, an irreducible datum. In that case, we might have to accept psi as not having any explanation. In other words, psi may be an unanalyzable fact of nature, just as life and the existence of mind may be.[2] The point is that we don't have to understand the ultimate nature of mind to accept as real and to use our minds—the same is true for psi.

But we can describe psi; we can study its behavior, how it manifests in nature. My aim in this book, at any rate, is *not* to try to explain psi but rather to use the fact of its existence to broaden the empirical and theoretical base for revisioning religious realities.

2) The second sense in which our hermeneutical stance is transcendent is that it avails itself of the findings of archetypal or imaginal psychology. The immediate source here is the work of C. G. Jung, whose view of religion contrasted sharply with Freud's. For Jung the phenomena of religion play a major and positive role in human psychology. A key concept is *individuation*. Jung uses this word to refer to a natural development in human beings, a process in which opposing psychic functions such as feeling and thinking, intuition and sensation, fuse in a seamless dynamic of the whole self.

In this development, Jung claimed to find certain universal psychic constants at work. At turns he called them archetypes of the collective unconscious, primordial images, or psychic dominants. These "a priori forms of the imagination" shape our psychological evolution. Jung's archetypes are a legacy from Kant and from the master of Western imaginal philosophy, Plato.[3]

In the *New Science* (1744), Neapolitan scholar Giambattista Vico also described certain universal psychic constants he called "imaginative universals." Vico spoke of a transcultural "mental vocabulary" that appears spontaneously and guides the development, integration, and individuation of whole cultures.

For Vico, as for Jung, these psychic constants were vital to the health of a culture or civilization, although Vico stressed a corrosive trend at work in the evolution of civilizations. (As the rational impulse comes to dominate, according to Vico, the creative imagination declines.) What Jung called individuation was for Vico a more cyclic or spiral phenomenon. We never achieve total balance, and all development is restless and self-transcending.

Vico was one of the first and perhaps the most original critic of and antitype to Descartes and is hence of special interest to new paradigm builders. Vico represents a relatively undeveloped strain in Western thought based on the synthetic power of the imagination rather than on the analytic power of linear rationalism.

By drawing on these sources, in exploring the transcendent meanings of texts, I attend to the creative power of the religious imagination. Vico's philosophy, a type of Renaissance deification of man, reinterprets divine power as expressing itself in human ingenuity and makes of imagination (*fantasia*) a force that gives form to the gods, to the arts, and to all historical institutions. Similarly, Jung's psychology sees in the archetypal imagination a power that shapes human personality and helps us adapt to the cosmic environment.

Thus combining psychical research and imaginal psychology forms a basis for a hermeneutics of transcendence.

3) A third sense of transcendent—namely, the evolutionary—flows from the first two I have described. In this exploration I stress the evolutionary aspect of religious texts. Whether or not current thinking agrees with Darwinism on every point—and much is debatable—it is now clear, not only from biology but also from modern physics and cosmology, that we inhabit an evolving universe. Becoming, not being, is the logo of the contemporary worldview. Time is of the essence: energy, change, creativity, extinction, process, history, novelty, chaos, mutation, catastrophe, transformation—these are the words that fill today's metaphysical lexicon.

Not all evolution means progress, however. Whether evolution has a benign or upward drift depends upon what view we adopt or what value we choose to stress. Still, we inhabit a universe in which, as Whitehead said, "there is no nature at an instant." An instant of nature is like a snapshot of a rushing waterfall. It is an abstraction, in a sense, a falsification of the real. Every actual moment of reality is pregnant with future change. Every particle of becoming is a novel synthesis of its predecessors. Heraclitus said it long ago: We never step into the same river twice.

An evolutionary cosmology has implications for religion. Many say that religious ideas, texts, and personages are out of touch with the world of science. Belief in other worlds, miracles, extraordinary forms of consciousness and communication, higher forms of embodied life, divine joy and ecstasy—the scientific materialist rejects all these as too fantastic to take seriously.

My aim is to turn this bias on its head and to look at the extraordinary claims, the reports of superhuman potential, not as relics of a bygone era, but as harbingers of our evolutionary potential. The words, deeds, and visions of mystics, shamans, saints, artists, prophets, and philosophers,[4] in the present system of interpretation, assume greater, not lesser, meaning. Once freed from dogmatic assumptions, and grounded in the *whole* range of available empirical data, religious experiences become signposts of the future, images of humankind's possible evolution.

To summarize, the method of interpretation I follow is transcendent in a threefold sense. First, it looks for evidence of function that operates beyond the ordinary constraints of space, time, and matter; second, it alerts us to the archetypal meanings of religious imagery; and third, it is sensitive to the evolutionary outreach of religious symbols and images.

I realize that the idea of psi is riddled with controversy. In my opinion, however, controversy is not justified over whether paranormal claims are based on matters of fact. The philosopher Henry Sidgwick, writing in the late nineteenth century, spoke of the "scandal" of failing to acknowledge the reality of psychic function. That was over a hundred years ago. The situation is no less scandalous today. One is startled to find, for instance, the following remark in a state-of-the-art textbook on the subject: "None of us considers psi to be an established fact."[5]

The four authors of the book that makes this statement are deeply involved in the scientific study of the paranormal; they have written a careful account of the best experimental evidence for psi, and yet they feel driven to preface their book with the timid disclaimer quoted above. Why? The key word is "established." The idea that psi is not an established fact may mean that 1) psi cannot be produced on demand and 2) that the scientific community at large doesn't accept psi as an established fact.

Much could be said about this, but I will confine myself to a few remarks. First, lack of repeatability *on demand* is no argument against the existence of psi. Many disciplines that pretend to scientific status cannot produce their effects on demand. This is true of the behavioral sciences, of astronomy and cosmogony, and of parts of biology. Scientists, for example, study the origin of the universe, an event we can hardly reproduce on demand in the lab. Every science adapts itself to its subject matter; there is no one way to study all subject matters.

Psi has been demonstrated repeatedly in the laboratory, though not on demand, and repeatedly observed in spontaneous or quasi-experimental situations. There may be no accepted theory to account for the phenomena, and they may not be reproducible on demand, but that in no way takes away from their status as "established" facts.

The second scruple that causes the writers to hedge their claims about the reality of psi is, I would guess, political. Maybe they hope to gain acceptance from the scientific community by toning down their claims. A ploy like this has merit, but facts are facts, however nettlesome to the established paradigm.

The history of the paranornal is an open book; you have only to take the trouble to study it. Unfortunately, psi research is languishing today. Funding is at a new low, and centers have been dismantled. There's a huge gap between popular interest and rigorous study of the subject. Nor is the field aided by the professional debunkers and self-appointed watchdogs of orthodoxy.

Still, the data exist. In my opinion, it's time to quit being defensive about the reality of our psychic abilities and to start exploring their full significance. In this book, I use psi research as a tool for revisioning the relation between religion and evolution. The British founders used psi research to explore the soul and its place in nature. For Frederic Myers, it led to the frontiers of spiritual evolution. On the threshold of a new millennium, let us remember Myers' call to explore our evolutionary potential.

11
Psyche and God

II
Psyche and God

All the gods that antiquity painted in the heavens to account for any benefit conferred upon human society—all these gods are none other than you yourselves.

Vico

Western thought has learned to think of divine reality as an either/or proposition—either absolute transcendence or total illusion. But the truth about God may lie at neither extreme of being or nonbeing—but at the cutting edge of becoming. The saviors of God have turned to many sources for help: to the criteria of pragmatism, to the idea of healing fictions, to the great lessons of comparative religion, and to the insights of the new physics.

Part II of this book turns to another source. In particular, I examine three topics—the life of the God-Idea, the origins of Christianity, and the conversion of Saint Paul—from a psychic perspective. I argue that the living core of these aspects of divine encounter is a transcendent psychic factor. The spotlight is on psyche and God—partners in a dance of cocreation.

3
The God-Idea:
A Psychic Perspective

It is not God who will save us—it is we who will save God, by battling, by creating, and by transmuting matter into spirit.

Nikos Kazantzakis

Since the dawn of history people have believed in an unseen world—a world of gods and goddesses, demons and spirits, angels and elementals. And since the dawn of history the forms of divine power have evolved. Belief in nature spirits evolved into tribal gods; tribal gods became the one great god. Some say monotheism is the climax of this development, though Hinduism courts a single divine reality while at the same time allowing a polytheism of divine forms. Religions like Buddhism and Jainism drop the God-Idea altogether and see the divine not as *a* being but as *a state of* being—*nirvana,* for example.

However we name or describe this object of "ultimate concern,"[1] it has been a constant feature of human history. Yet in our age of science, many proclaim or secretly feel that God is dead, that nothing exists corresponding to the idea of God.

Yet despite modern science and skepticism, God—the idea of God—continues to live, breathe, and wield great power. The forms of belief shift and change, but the longing for God seems undying, and there is no uprooting the divine element from our inner environment.

Why then do people persist in believing in God? Didn't Nietzsche's madman announce the death of God? In recent times theologies have been built on dirges for the "death of God." The God-Idea revives and returns, and people go on believing, seeking, sacrificing, meditating, praying—sometimes dying, sometimes killing—for their idea of a Supreme Being.

23

Those in power exploit the religious needs of ignorant people, say
the Marxists, and no doubt this has been true from time to time, but
I doubt if it explains the whole of religious aspiration and experience.
Plausible psychological hypotheses also try to account for the longevity
of the God-Idea, and many *do* hold religious beliefs in ways best
described as neurotic or childish. But again I doubt if this sort of
psychological reductionism explains the true vitality of religious belief.
Not everyone embraces religion as a father surrogate. Does it really
seem like Mother Teresa has a hard time coming to grips with reality? Or is it the opposite? Maybe her religious convictions help her
face grim realities that most of us prefer not to think about.

At the turn of the century, William James in his classic study of
religious experience wrote, "The uses of religion, its uses to the individual who has it, and the uses of the individual himself to the world,
are the best arguments that truth is in it."[2] The right to believe is
here justified on pragmatic grounds.

More recently writers like Mircea Eliade and Joseph Campbell have
shown how the God-Idea and its variants speak to us through the
world's myths, fables, and fairytales. Studies in comparative religion
show that the God-Idea is a durable feature of our inner environment.
One cannot make the sacred, the mystical, the numinous dimension
of experience disappear by rationalistic sleight of hand; they express
something too deeply entrenched in human thought.

Some even urge us to embrace religious beliefs as healing illusions.
Learn to live *as if* gods and other spiritual entities were real, they
say. The Spanish philosopher Miguel de Unamuno wrote a story about
a priest who served his people well but for one dark secret which
he took with him to the grave: he didn't believe in God! Leopardi,
Italy's great nineteenth century poet, had a view of religion that was
bleaker than Freud's. In his ironical fable, *The Story of the Human
Race,* he depicts history as a struggle between Truth and the "phantasms" of civilization: love, justice, fame, the gods, and so forth.
Without these "phantasms," sheer unadorned Truth would make life
unbearable. In the end, Leopardi thought, the human race would suc-
cumb to the corrosive influence of soul-killing Truth. Hence the need
to cultivate healing fictions.

Jean-Paul Sartre was heir to this tradition. Sartre wrote of the "project to be God." Sartre was a turning point in the evolution of the

God-Idea; in Sartre's thought, the boundary between fiction and philosophy dissolves, and humanity discovers its project to become God. Militant atheists never fully escaped the lure of the God-Idea. God was recognized as the supreme value, the supreme idea, and these thinkers, far-seeing in their denials, knew that human beings are compulsive meaning makers, and that without goals around which our energies can focus, life becomes unlivable. Sartre placed his bet on a loser, the Communist Revolution; Nietzsche's visionary superman was discredited because of the Nazi distortions.

The Parapsychology of God

God as social cement, as a technique for manipulating the lower classes, as neurotic illusion, as pragmatic belief, as collective archetype, as healing fiction and phantasm, as secular project of self-transcendence, as object of comparative studies and goal of perennial philosophy—all these are aspects of the universal persistence of belief in God. But how deeply do they touch the soul of religion? Is there something more basic to the secret life of the God-Idea? I believe that there is—something that can be called the psychic factor.

I want to look now at the God-Idea from a psychic perspective. My concern is with the parapsychology of God. My contention is that the God-Idea takes on renewed life when viewed from this perspective. I have no wish to discuss in this chapter the existence of God from a philosophical or theological point of view. Hence the chapter's title—the "God-Idea." God as a psychic fact, as an experience, is my concern. The metaphysical nature of the being called God is something else.

I believe that studies of psychic abilities can help us understand the persistent life of the God-Idea. Once we agree on the reality of the paranormal, we will, I think, be in a better position to understand the self-generating, self-verifying power of belief in God. We will see that the creative power we impute to divine agency may be the result of our own transcendent soul powers.

This is not to say that the psychic is the ultimate level of religious discourse or that the philosophy of religion and theology can be replaced by the parapsychology of God. But I believe that the parapsychology of God can open us to new dimensions of religious meaning. What follows are some examples.

Petitionary Prayer

"Ask and ye shall receive," said Jesus. Human beings ask favors of God. This sort of favor-asking is called "petitionary prayer." (There are other, less self-serving, forms of prayer.) People ask for favors from God and often feel they receive them. Let us then consider petitionary prayer in light of our potential paranormal abilities.

From what is known about psi, I can imagine our prayers producing desired changes in the minds of other people or even in external events and material processes. Take a simple but important example. Suppose I pray to God to help a sick friend or ailing loved one. Perhaps by thinking certain thoughts—by, for example, entreating a higher power—I succeed in influencing my friend's or loved one's mood, emotions, even his or her cells, glands, or hormones. Living systems are labile, or readily open to change, and parapsychologists say that labile targets are more open to psi influence. As a matter of fact, there is a fair bit of evidence for what is called psychic healing. Laboratory studies, for instance, show that people can accelerate the healing rate of wounds and the growth rate of plants. Other studies show that healers can influence the behavior of enzymes, hemoglobin, and anesthetized organisms. Field studies support more spectacular claims of traditional healers from Brazil, the Philippines, Native America, and elsewhere. *The Realms of Healing,* by Stanley Krippner and Alberto Villoldo (1986), is one of the best accounts of the whole range of psychic healing. Deepak Chopra's *Quantum Healing* (1989) is another up-to-date source of information on the role of mind in the healing process. Some experimental studies of psychic healing in the context of prayer have also been reported. For example, physician Randolph Byrd published a study showing the positive therapeutic effects of intercessory prayer in a coronary care unit population.[3]

The possibilites of petitionary prayer go far beyond healing. But for our present purpose, the example above will serve to make the following points. Suppose that after praying to God, a sick person's condition noticeably, perhaps dramatically, improves. If we are believers, or even half-believers, these positive, sought after results will hardly seem coincidental. Success at intercessory prayer will most likely tend to strengthen belief in God.

Now notice the next step. The more frequently we pray, the more often we are likely to experience positive results, which in turn strengthens our confidence in the power of prayer. Our confidence, or as it is called, our faith in the power of prayer will then increase the probability of meaningful responses to our prayers. And so a circle of self-confirmation develops: as we know from research, belief increases the probability of psi occurrences.

Of course, this process is apt to work both ways. Those who reject the power of prayer will likewise confirm the truth of their nonbelief. They do not pray, and therefore their prayers will not be answered. The psychology of unbelief is as self-validating as the psychology of faith and committment.

The philosopher H. H. Price has explained how petitionary prayer might work by telepathy.[4] Price suggests that if telepathy is a fact, our minds may all be linked in what he calls a "common unconscious." Prayer may work like a telepathic "broadcast"—we broadcast our appeal in the common unconscious. Our appeals may be "heard" unconsciously by people with whose minds we have an affinity. The whole interaction takes place below the surface of conscious awareness, and the response to our prayers sometimes comes about in unexpected ways.

Price doubts if the telepathic theory of prayer would satisfy the theist:

> [The theist] will insist that prayer is not just thinking, nor even wishing; it is *asking*. An 'I-thou' relation is an essential part of it. In petitionary prayer we are *addressing* one whom we love and trust, and we are sure that he loves us.

This description seems correct, but it doesn't strengthen the case for theism, although it does strengthen the case for a telepathic theory of prayer. The reason is that by addressing "one whom we love and trust," we place ourselves in a state of mind most likely to expedite a psi response. In fact, in Kenneth Batcheldor's important table-levitating experiments,[5] the table levitated more readily if the subjects addressed it, just as Price says, in an "I-thou" relation.

The work of Batcheldor and his associates is important for the parapsychology of religion, and since I refer to it several times, I should describe it in further detail. Batcheldor was interested in the psychology of psychokinesis and modeled his experiments on Victorian séances. The old séances were conducted in the dark, in a group situation; participants carried on in a spontaneous and jovial, yet attentive and expectant manner.

Batcheldor conducted table-levitation experiments in a similar way. Technical issues of controls and measurement aside, the British researcher found that ordinary people without any known psychic talents could develop a special psychological skill of producing various paranormal effects. The critical factors were unwavering belief and confidence. Batcheldor found that a deep resistance to and fear of the paranormal had to be overcome, and that even the emotions of surprise or astonishment could upset the right mindset.

In particular, subjects performed best when they did not feel they were personally responsible for the effects; hence darkness, the sense of group responsibility, and other devices for overcoming "ownership" inhibition aided results. Batcheldor also found that "false-feedback" would stimulate subjects' paranormal capacities; in other words, introducing an illusion that a table moved would awaken real levitational power. Belief that the source of power was external to the subject evidently liberated the subject's own psychic power. The implications of this for religion are apparent, since in the religious attitude, one surrenders oneself to a higher power, a psychological attitude Batcheldor's work shows as leading to psychic manifestations. The British work led to further research in America and Canada, which often produced startling results.

Coming from a different but confirming angle, archetypal psychologist James Hillman cites "personification" as a metaphoric device for engaging the deeper levels of psychic reality.[6] The religious thinker Martin Buber has taken the "I-thou" relation as virtually definitive of the human-divine encounter.

One reason that addressing a "thou" may work is that by acting as if an outside power were causing the result, we become less anxious about personal failure. Batcheldor speaks of "witness" or "ownership" inhibition. When we let go and don't interfere, the psi process, the evidence shows, occurs "unconsciously." Researcher Rex Stanford has devised a PMIR model, where PMIR stands for "psi-mediated instrumental response." What this means is that we sometimes unconsciously use psi to detect ways of satisfying our needs. Prayer may facilitate a "PMIR" or unconscious use of psi.

More directly related to the parapsychology of God, a group of researchers in Toronto, using methods developed by Batcheldor, invented an imaginary personage, Philip, whom they addressed in an "I-thou" relation. They sought in effect to personify and thus create what theosophists call a "thought-form" or the Tibetans a "tulpa"—in short, a psychic entity with a life and power of its own. The experiment was a success to the degree that it helped produce "abundant PK phenomena—regularly reproducible, seen repeatedly by innumerable witnesses, and recorded in full light many times on film, vidcotapc, and audiotapc."[7]

By inventing and personifying an imaginary entity, the researchers aroused the psychic potential of the group and gave it a focus. The Philip experiment, in my opinion, sheds a great deal of light on the parapsychology of God. In the procedures that "conjured up Philip" the experimenters have produced a model of how we may "conjure up" a variety of "supernatural" entities—from gods to elementals. The important thing is unwavering belief in an imagined entity and an unforced but steady confidence that this entity can accomplish the desired effects. Somehow this belief and group expectation awakens the psi process.

What the evidence shows, and what Price's explanation reinforces, is that the psychological condition of belief and the custom of addressing a loving and trustworthy being are the conditions most likely to produce paranormal results. In other words, the evidence suggests not that traditional theism is true, but that practical theism will generally confirm itself by generating paranormal results.

Theism is therefore a self-confirming belief system—not, let me stress, as some skeptics would say, one that is self-deluding. The believer may be more attuned to this aspect of nature than the skeptic or materialist. This is shown by the history of the saints. The strongest believers, the saints, as the evidence shows, also produce the greatest "miracles."[8]

OBEs and NDEs: Psychic Roots of the God-Idea

A man in his late thirties, Robert T., suffered a massive head injury in a car accident and almost died. The following is an excerpt from his account of the experience:

> I remember being in a darkness that is so vast and so pure and com-
> pletely indescribable. . . . All of a sudden in the distance there was
> this light and I started heading towards the light. It was kind of
> like a communion, and it was instantaneous, but it was experienced

in a completeness, like travelling eternity. And the closer I came
to the light, the closer I came to peace and well being, harmony,
serenity, unconditional love and acceptance.

The pattern of the near-death experience is a general one, similar
to the traditional mystical experience. People report feeling detached
from their bodies; they have OBEs, or out-of-body experiences. They
see luminous beings, enter realms of ineffable bliss, and have panoramic recollections of their whole lives. They encounter beings such
as deceased loved ones or otherworldly messengers. Near-death experiencers feel certain they have visited another world; they often
feel convinced they've had direct contact with divine reality.

Raymond Moody has touched on the religious implications of the
NDE.[9] He notes the resemblance between NDEs and Saint Paul's
conversion—a resemblance examined in Chapter 5. One of Moody's
near-death experiencers said: "I didn't ever see a person in this light,
but to me the light was a Christ-consciousness, a oneness with all
things, a perfect love." Descriptions of exalted states like this are
not uncommon among ND experiencers. A oneness with all things?
A perfect love? An NDE is clearly a tremendous experience, and a
deeply spiritual one.

The experience is modified by culture. Dying Hindus have slightly
different experiences than Christians.[10] Buddhists see the light of
Buddha just as Christians see the light of Christ. The NDE triggers
an experience each person may interpret in light of his or her own
belief-system and cultural glyphs. Moody's Christian experiencer
states, *"To me* the light was a Christ" (emphasis added). The important point is this: in NDEs we find a psychic experience that forms
the basis of claiming one has experienced God.

The more systematic researches of Kenneth Ring confirm the
religious side of the NDE. In *Life at Death,* Ring describes the
"qualitative changes in religiousness among core experiencers." Says
one person: "My faith in there being a higher power and greater that
is somehow controlling my life has been heavily reinforced." "In
his will is our peace," is the way Dante put it. Ring cites another
witness as saying, "Well [afterward], I felt closer to a—a God. Which
I had not for years. [Before] I was agnostic." The language is revealing here—"a God." The construction reminds me of the ancient Greek
theos, godlike, a divine manifestation. Less a thing than a way of

being. Another person reports: "I rely a great deal more on God. I know that very definitely He's there."[11]

In Ring's next study of the near-death experience,[12] he found more evidence for spiritually transformative NDEs. Ring contrasts religious and spiritual aftereffects; "religious" for Ring connotes dogma and institution—the letter not the spirit. NDEs awaken the spirit. The NDE is a gnostic encounter, a natural uprush of higher consciousness.

The examples I have mentioned make the point. An NDE is a natural psychological experience with paranormal elements[13]—an experience that creates belief in God, Christ, or other divine beings. The form this awesome potential takes depends on chance factors such as belief-systems and cultural frames of reference. An NDE might have slight impact or trigger a deep transformation. In the case of Saint Paul, the NDE—if Moody is right—helped give birth to a new religion.[14]

A regular feature of near-death episodes is the sense of being out of one's body. The out-of-body experience (OBE) is also associated with experiences of divine reality. To illustrate the religious overtones of the OBE, consider the religious experiences of the early Greeks.

Two strands of religious experience were common among the early Greeks, the Olympian and the Dionysian. In the Olympian Greek religion, immortality was the earmark of divinity. In the Homeric epics, the gulf between mortals and immortals was impassible, and the human was forever closed off from the divine.

But there was another, less patriarchal strand of Greek nature mysticism, the Dionysian. As a result of ecstatic experiences brought on by Dionysian dance orgies, the Greeks transcended the limitations of the Olympian worldview. The Dionysian revel led to the discovery that the *human* soul contained within itself the seeds of immortality. The human soul could soar, in a manic dance frenzy, out of the mortal body. For the Greek this spoke to the godlike in humanity.

"In *ekstasis*," writes Irwin Rhode, "the soul is liberated from the cramping prison of the body; it communes with the god and develops powers of which, in the ordinary life of everyday, thwarted by the body, it knew nothing."[15] The word *ecstasy* (*ekstasis* in Greek) literally means "standing outside" [oneself], in other words, having an OBE. By means of specially induced out-of-body experiences, the Greeks discovered and defined for themselves the reality of the God-Idea and of the immortal soul.

The Thracian cult of Dionysos cultivated the power of *ekstasis*; by means of this ability to project oneself beyond the body, participants induced intense awareness of divine forces. The belief that it was possible to contact divine forces spread in Greek culture. The Orphic idea that the body was a tomb *(soma sema)*, the Pythagorean belief in the transmigration of souls, and even Plato's belief in immortality all look like branches of the same tree of Dionysian ecstasy.

Dionysian ecstasy was a type of OBE that gave "state-specific" knowledge of the soul's divinity and immortality. The religion of Dionysos was based on ecstasy, rapture, possession—the products of special psychic experiences. The Western idea of the immortality and hence of the divinity of the soul can thus be traced back to a special psychic experience, one we are learning about today in greater detail, thanks to psychical research.[16]

Internal Attention States

So far in our examination of the idea of God from a psychic perspective, I have suggested psi-mediated petitionary prayer, NDEs, and OBEs as possible psychic roots of conceptions of deity. Coming at the question from another starting-point, I now look at how altered states of consciousness increase the possibility of detecting psi "signals."[17]

Based on a review of eighty experimental studies, parapsychologist Charles Honorton concluded that by shifting attention inward, subjects were more likely to detect a psychic impression[18] or have a psychic experience. Our focus is inward when we dream, meditate, are hypnotized, and during the "ganzfeld" state (perceptual uniformity).[19] In all these situations, sensory input is minimized and attention is focused on the inner plane. The more inwardly absorbed, the less distracted by outer things, the more likely that we "pick up" ideas, images, or feelings paranormally.

This tendency has great significance for religion. It may, for example, show an important link between mysticism and experimental parapsychology. The techniques found by modern parapsychologists that promote psi are similar to techniques of introversion used by mystics of all ages. The great mystics would probably agree with the findings of parapsychology: spiritual discipline involves shifting attention to the inner life. Whether we wish to experience divine consciousness or increase our extrasensory perception, the evidence suggests a common method.

For example, Saint John of the Cross says: "The goods of God, which are beyond all measure, can only be contained in an empty and solitary heart." The words "empty and solitary heart" are metaphorical ways of describing the reduction of attention to external or sensory data. Or consider the words of another great mystic, Meister Eckhart: "Become pure till you neither are nor have either this or that; then you are omnipresent and, being neither this nor that, are all things."

The Hindu Shankara expresses the same idea: "I shall reveal to you that very method by which sages have reached the other shore . . . [t]o detach the mind from all objective things. . . . Of the steps to liberation, the first is declared to be complete detachment from all things which are noneternal." Similarly, according to the Arab mystic-philosopher, Al Ghazzali: "In the state of sleep, when the avenues of the senses are closed, this window (of the spiritual heart) is opened and man receives impressions from the unseen world and sometimes foreshadowings of the future." Finally, note how Patanjali defines yoga: "Yoga is the inhibition of the modifications of the mind."

In these examples, descriptions of spiritual disciplines call for a shift in awareness from the external to the internal world. According to modern psi research, this shift increases the probability of psychic experiences. So the parapsychological evidence here meshes with traditional spiritual wisdom. The great mystics routinely recommend withdrawing attention from the external world; by thus shifting attention inward and minimizing distractions—by reducing the "noise" from the external and the internal world—it becomes easier to detect "signals" from the unseen. In effect, modern research supports Saint Augustine when he said: "If you want to know the Truth, go within."

The Role of the Will

Most psi researchers agree that the wrong sort of effort foils the psi task. The old textbooks on hypnosis and suggestion spoke of the "law of reversed effort." More recent work gives fairly exact descriptions of the optimal internal strategies for producing paranormal effects.

A landmark study in methods of response in ESP experiments was written by a leading archivist in the field of exceptional human abilities, Rhea White.[20] Based on a review of descriptions of old and new methods of response in ESP experiments, White describes a model of the stages of inner preparation for heightening human psychic receptivity.

The gist of her findings is that the respondent must develop a rather paradoxical skill. According to White, "although the steps in this method are *conscious,* i.e., deliberate, the aim is to produce a spontaneous and *unconscious* response, i.e., one not initiated by the conscious mind." Everything in the psi-liberating model "throws [a person] back upon the deeper, non-rational resources of his being."

In this method, a person begins by relaxing, then engages without strain or effort the conscious mind, then waits patiently until a certain tension is broken. Finally, the right response bursts spontaneously into consciousness. White underscores the paradox of using conscious will to produce an unconscious response when she says: "Perhaps we shall never be able to produce ESP at will, but by means of the 'will' we can put ourselves in the proper frame of mind to receive psi impressions." Batcheldor confirms the sense of this paradox when he urges in a similar way that sitters in group PK experiments learn to intend without concentrating or striving.

The psychology of the will in psi experiences is similar to the psychology of the will in spiritual experiences. In both we find the paradoxical idea that we must voluntarily turn things over to a higher power. A kind of surrender, a release of egocentric striving, is recommended in most of the great spiritual disciplines. The word *Islam,* for instance, means "surrender." The Hindu *Gita* teaches the art of conforming the human to the divine will, of learning to live on a day-to-day basis in such a way that one is not burningly intent on success or obsessed with results. The Taoist idea of *wu wei,* or nonaction, is also about the art of releasing oneself from the grip of the hypertense ego. I have already quoted the laconic Dante: "In his will is our peace," words which echo the admonition of the Lord's Prayer: "Thy Will Be Done."

Again, it would be easy to multiply examples. One thing stands out: the right kind of deployment of the will is common to psychic and spiritual discipline. Whether the goal is to guess cards or to unite with the Godhead, the critical point is the reformation of the psychology of the will. So once again psychic research supports the great spiritual traditions. The art of transcendence seems to have a common psychodynamics, and modern experimental methods confirm the great religious classics.

The Creative Power of Belief

Belief is yet another variable that links the psychodynamics of psi and spirit. The so-called "sheep-goat" effect is said to be "perhaps the most thoroughly studied relationship in the field of parapsychology."[21] A persistent research finding, it states that belief, confidence, and expectation that one will succeed in a given psi task increases the likelihood of success. As shown in hundreds of experiments with ungifted subjects, the "sheep-goat" effect is marginal.[22] (The term "sheep-goat" was introduced by parapsychologist Gertrude Schmeidler. "Sheep" refers to believers in psychic ability; "goat," to skeptics.)

The studies point in the direction of an important pattern. To see the truly powerful implications of the "sheep-goat effect," researchers should look not at random experimental subjects with vague beliefs in ESP but at the geniuses of religious faith—the athletes of god consciousness. Nevertheless, the findings of parapsychology support the claims of traditional wisdom.

What do "belief" or "faith" really mean? Is there something that can be called creative belief—as distinct from belief as correspondence? Let me give an example to demonstrate the difference: I believe that the Pythagorean theorem is true. I can justify my belief by demonstrating at will that the theorem is true. Even if I didn't believe the theorem was true, or was convinced it was false, the theorem would still be demonstrably true. The truth of this type of belief is thus logically independent of the believer.

The case is different with creative belief. The "truth" of a creative belief depends on the believer. For example, consider belief as it works at a table-tilting experiment, a Victorian parlor game. As I have been saying, people need to be in the right state of mind to produce psi effects. Part of the right state of mind involves having the right beliefs. If, during the experiment, people are assailed by doubts, the table won't move. If people believe, on the other hand, that the table will move, it is more likely that it will.

Note the curious epistemology. I believe that if I lay my hands lightly on top of a table and expect it to levitate, it will levitate. In this case, my belief—indeed, if Batcheldor is right, my *unwavering* belief—is a *condition* for demonstrating the belief to be true. A slight doubt, a tremor of hesitation will inhibit the effect.

In the example of the Pythagorean theorem, belief corresponds to an existing state of affairs—the demonstrability of the theorem. However, in the second example drawn from the realm of psychic studies, belief helps bring about a state of affairs. A belief of this type may rightly be described as *creative*.

What, then, of belief in God? (Or, as I ask in Chapter 8, what of belief in angels or other "supernatural" entities?) Is the belief in God creative or correspondent? Or is it perhaps a mixture of both?

To answer these questions, it is necessary to decide whether belief in God is a condition for making God manifest. In other words, does belief in God work more like belief in table-tilting, ESP, or psychic healing or more like belief in the Pythagorean theorem or the fact that Mikhail Gorbachev was arrested by Communist hardliners in the summer of 1991?

We, of course, have been taught that God created us. But may there be a critical sense in which it is we who create God? According to this model of belief, what we call God is a being—or rather a process—that depends on our creative contribution.

This idea, heretical to most Westerners, has a history in theosophical and Eastern schools of thought. The writings of theosophist E. L. Gardner, for instance, stress the creative function of belief in the idea of God.[23] Let me quote from his discussion of the "cult of god-making" and the "worship of God-Elementals." Writes Gardner:

> A congregation of worshippers, sincere in belief and devotion, who are led to the adoration of a 'GOD' as an exterior being, will create the figure of a 'God' in their midst. The form, thus built on the mental plane, is ensouled by the eager elemental essence, throbbing with emotional vibrations of the worshippers. The strength and vitality of the God-Elemental, thus made, is the measure of the worshippers' aspirations.[24]

This suggests that the mind interacts with super-physical entities that can embody or partially materialize human thought. Such entities, Gardner writes, acquire a will to "live on their own."

A similar creative function of belief and imagination is apparent in Mahayana Buddhism. Jung has commented on this psychic approach to "god-making" in The Tibetan Book of the Dead. Westerners have a hard time thinking of the divine forms as both subjective *and* objective, psychic *and* real. The *Bardo Thodol* (The Tibetan Book of the Dead), says Jung, contains the essence of Buddhist psychology:

> Not only the 'wrathful' but also the 'peaceful' deities are conceived as *sangsaric* (phenomenal) projections of the human psyche, an idea that seems all too obvious to the enlightened European, because it reminds him of his own banal simplifications. But though the European can easily explain away these deities as projections, he would be quite incapable of positing them at the same time as real.[25]

Both theosophist and Tibetan seer affirm the reality of the forms of the religious imagination; but Jung and more recent archetypal psychologists like James Hillman encourage a deeper insight, in which we learn to "see through" the relativity of these manifestations. In this liberating insight we learn to identify ourselves with the root of creative consciousness—the fertile source within, in which we are one with all humanity.

But What of Love and Justice?

Let us pause now to look at the argument. Against the reductionists who see in the life of the God-Idea mere ideology and pragmatic illusion, we say that idea is grounded in a basic creative psychic power—in our deliberately flat and colorless phrase—a transcendent psi factor. One thing is sure: the idea of God is an idea that *works*. It works, according to what we have said, because of the transcendent psi factor.

Psychical research thus helps us to understand the power of the God-Idea. Power is important, but this is only a part of the God story. The God of the great religious traditions is not merely powerful. In Amenhotep, in Xenophanes, in Zoroaster, in Lao Tze, in the Buddha, in Plato, in the Upanishads, and in the prophets of the West, there dawned a consciousness of a Supreme Being that was just, loving, compassionate. God, in the biblical tradition, for example, is a being said to intervene in history on behalf of the *powerless*.

How does all this relate to psychic ability?

Let me try to clarify my view with a thought experiment. Imagine a being with infinite PK (omnipotence) and infinite ESP (omniscience). Such a being would possess only some of the qualities attributed to the Supreme Being in higher spiritual traditions. Such a being would be awesome, but would lack the qualities of love, justice, and compassion. Such a god would be a psychic monster, a dangerous demi-god. This result would be fatal to any attempt to derive the entire idea of God out of the data of psychical research.

This shortcoming also points to a potential danger of psychic science. Psychic science, at least in principle, holds the promise of creating tremendous godlike power, but it guarantees nothing about the way this power will be used. Large scale success in psychic science might compound the problem. The idea of an amoral technology of the psyche, one that ignored the spiritual ideals of love and justice, would only make science more dangerous than it already is. Soul science may bolster the reality status of the God-Idea, but it could leave us at the mercy of an amoral god.

An Imperfect God?

Following this line of reasoning, it may not be possible to salvage the traditional deity. The God derived from human psi abilities may be imperfect. Humanity may have to adjust its vision, as Jung stressed, to a God with a Shadow—an incomplete, an evolving God. It would be a God who is a partner, coequal and imperfect, an incomplete brother to evolving humanity. Such a God would need us—as much as we needed God.

In losing the traditional God, however, we would gain something. No longer would we need to torment ourselves with theodicy—with the problem of reconciling evil with the alleged good will and om-nipotence of God. In the revised view, God is our collective psyche struggling to evolve, struggling to achieve new and more comprehen-sive levels of consciousness.

This God would represent the ideal potential of psychic humanity. There would be no God who knows and can do all—only a potential in humanity to transcend itself. The God that appears through the lens of parapsychology is therefore a struggling God, a God in need of the whole of humanity to incarnate the highest divine potentials.

I could halt here, but I think the argument can be carried a step further. Consider what might trouble the person of faith. "You still haven't touched on the essence of higher religions," he or she might say. "You haven't explained our ideals of higher love, our longing for justice, truth, mercy, and so on. These things aren't psychic phe-nomena; they're spiritual realities."

To answer this objection, I could, to begin with, point out that spiritual values and activities are themselves "paranormal" phenomena, in that they cannot be explained by current physical theories. In this way of thinking, spiritual love, spiritual joy, spiritual courage are as "paranormal" as telepathy, clairvoyance, and precognition. Such noble impulses cannot be accounted for by present ideas of biology and physiology. The unselfish behavior of a Mother Teresa, in this sense, is as "paranormal" as a poltergeist or an out-of-body experience.

Telepathy and Spiritual Values

But I think it is possible to say more. I want to suggest a model of how the higher spiritual values such as love and justice may have emerged as a *byproduct* of the evolution of human psi potential.

A little telepathy may be a dangerous thing, but a lot might speed the evolution of spirit. Let me clarify with a down-to-earth example. Suppose I find I can read an opponent's mind in a poker game. I have just enough telepathy to tell what hand he has. I have a full house; he has a straight. I can bet to the limit, knowing I have him beat. There is nothing very spiritual about this, of course.

But now let's intensify the faculty. My telepathic vision suddenly widens; I see not only that my opponent has a straight when I have a full house, but by an increase in clairvoyant power, I see his outer and feel his inner life unfold into the future. I see and feel the consequences of his loss. By a kind of precognitive telepathic impression, I feel his chagrin when he has to face his wife and confess he has squandered a month's salary in a poker game. Now the eye of my soul grows keener, more sensitive, and I begin to sense more of his immediate environment. I form an impression of his children, that they are ragged and unhealthy. I feel their hunger, their discomfort, their humiliation.

What effect would all this information have upon me? I think it would necessarily change my perception of the person I was tempted to cheat. The more able I was to enter his world sympathetically, the more sensitive I would become to his long-range plight.

But this new attitude would not arise in me in a mechanical way. Nothing would coerce, compel, or push me in any particular direction. Nothing would compel me not to exploit my poor poker opponent; but thanks to my deeper capacity to sense, intuit, and imagine what would happen to him if I did, I might find myself less disposed to cheat or take advantage of him.

Out of this psychic matrix, a sense of justice and love might come more readily into play. I might still be tempted to follow a selfish path, but I also might, thanks to episodes of expanded telepathic consciousness, enjoy a wider sense of the options. I might, in short, naturally evolve a more sympathetic transpersonal identity. An increased capacity for love and justice could flow more easily from my enlarged capacity to feel.

The word *telepathy* literally means "feeling at a distance." Frederic Myers, the classical scholar who invented the word, once defined love as a form of "exalted and unspecialized telepathy." In this statement Myers shows the link between spirituality and parapsychology. An intensification and widening of the capacity to empathize with other beings offers a model for developing our spiritual values.

It doesn't follow from this that a person has to be psychic in a conspicuous way to be capable of love. The psi involved in our higher spiritual capacities may be inconspicuous and may mask itself behind more mundane capacities such as intuition or sensitivity. It is important to make the distinction between conspicuous and inconspicuous psi, for it is plain that people capable of love are not necessarily psychic (in a conspicuous way). Nor are psychically gifted people necessarily rich in spiritual love.

Psychical research calls attention to the pathos of knowledge. It reveals another side of the enterprise of knowledge, a side that needs stressing in a time when mechanistic habits of thought, combined with the literal proliferation of machines, threaten to overwhelm living nature. To stress the telepathic side of knowledge is to stress the pathos in cognition, the capacity to enter into the object, in other words, to overcome the dualism that separates the subject as knower from the object as known. Telepathy, the hidden side of knowledge, reflects an older type of knowledge—a gnosis of the soul.

The Saviors of God

In conclusion, the data suggest there is a primitive psychic capacity latent in all human beings. In the course of human evolution, this unspecialized capacity or "latent faculty" (to use Myers' words) gradually, fitfully, reveals itself in our consciousness and behavior.

I hold that our higher spiritual powers are the fruits of this original psychic faculty. This faculty, I believe, pervades our mental life under the cloak of luck, intuition, inspiration, creativity, sympathy, empathy, imagination, and extraordinary feats of will.

Great artists, great saints, great prophets—these are people who by nature, accident, or discipline enter more deeply than most into the inner life of things. They are great in pathos. As for belief in a divine reality. I conclude that the stronger the belief—the greater the frequency of the right inner gestures—the greater is the probability that one's idea of God will be empirically confirmed. Believers verify their beliefs; skeptics confirm their disbelief.

So we are free to make the God-Idea an experimental hypothesis. God is the great experiment in cocreation, and support for this ultimate hypothesis lies in the outermost limits of our creative spirit. Understood in this way, we can agree with Kazantzakis that it's not God who saves us—it is we who must save God.

4
The Psychic Origins of Christianity

He that believes in me, the works that I do, he shall also do; and greater than these shall he do.

John 14:11-12

Religious communication is basically psi communication, pure and simple: it is neither sensory nor motor; it is unequivocally extrasensorimotor. . . . All the physical miracles, whether in the healing of disease, the miraculous movement of objects, or the control of the elements, had to be manifestations of PK.

J. B. Rhine

In the last chapter we examined the psychic side of the God-Idea. I tried to show that skeptics leave out something essential in their story of religion: the paranormal—the transcendent factor. In this chapter, I look at the paranormal as a factor in the origins of Christianity.

"One of the most amazing and significant facts of history is that within five centuries of its birth Christianity won the professed allegiance of the overwhelming majority of the population of the Roman Empire and even the support of the Roman state," writes Kenneth Latourette.[1] A tiny group of poor, uneducated people in an eastern outback of the Empire, the followers of Christ made claims that were blasphemous to the Jews and absurd to the Romans. In the end, however, the movement they started redefined the religious imagination of the Western world.

Many scholars have puzzled over this extraordinary turn of events and have given different explanations. I want to highlight a neglected factor, in Jung's terminology, a factor that still lies in "the Shadow"—the controversial and repressed psychic or paranormal factor.

The Conspiracy against Miracles

The main point I want to make in this chapter is that to discount the "miraculous" in the origins of Christianity is to discount one of its vital forces. My definition of "miracle" is minimal: a miracle is any apparent paranormal event that occurs in the context of religious experience, symbols, and beliefs. I expect talk of miracles will arouse resistance. Scientific materialists will certainly disclaim the miraculous. Religious people will also resist, but for different reasons. For example, liberal interpreters of the New Testament play down talk of miracles because they agree with Rudolf Bultmann that in an age of science, miracles aren't acceptable.[2]

Besides, miracles are an unedifying ground for faith, as underscored by the story of the Roman centurion who believed without seeing. Saint Paul complained that the Jews sought too much for signs. They wanted "proof"; hence they were inferior in faith. Liberal Christians recoil from miracles and beg off from making faith rest on tangible proof.

I was in a Christian bookstore in New York and asked for a book on the Virgin of Guadalupe. (There is a famous painting of her with some anomalous properties.[3]) The proprietor eyed me suspiciously and mumbled her disapproval. I had to demand that she look for the book (it was stocked in the cellar). On another occasion I was having dinner with a well-known Protestant minister and civil rights activist. When I raised the question of evidence for miracles, he said that to do so was somehow "self-serving." Why he felt this was so remains unclear to me.

Catholic and Protestant fundamentalists do not deny the reality of the paranormal. Phenomena outside established belief may be authentic, they admit, but are likely to be of diabolic provenance. For example, some fundamentalists identify the Being of Light described in the near-death experience as Lucifer. (*Lucifer,* they point out, means "bearer of light.") People who have near-death encounters, of course, disagree.

Why the aversion toward the paranormal? Shouldn't religious people welcome evidence for phenomena that seem to challenge the dogmas of materialism? It would seem that they should, but apparently they feel concern. I grant that some of their misgivings are well founded.

For example, there are dangers of ego-inflation and the delusions that could arise from powerful psychic experiences.

Consider also the political angle. People with psychic charisma threaten Church authority. The Catholic Church is suspicious of gifted psychics, even if they are saintly; powerful psychics might found destabilizing cults. The Church puts miracle workers like Padre Pio through fierce tests of loyalty; it sometimes overdoes it.[4]

Another reason for anti-miracle prejudice is the liberal idea of faith. Modern Christians understand that science competes with faith. Therefore, they try to place their faith—Luther and Kant were proto-types—*beyond* such competition. Faith, they say, has nothing to do with reason, science, or empirical reality. Faith is its own way of seeing the world. Don't base it on anything so fragile, they say, anything so easily sabotaged.

Take the Shroud of Turin. Cautious Christians underplayed the importance of the famous relic. People who felt their faith bolstered by its mysteries were disappointed when carbon tests proved it—not, as alleged, a fake—but as having the wrong date to be the burial cloth of Jesus.

A certain type of religious faith is indeed cautious; it does its best to avoid collision with matters of fact. Should faith be so cut off from empirical tests? Was true faith meant to be so solid, so impervious to risk and uncertainty? Such a view of faith seems almost like a trick to guarantee security from doubt. What such faith seems to crave is certainty. But the craving for certainty seems to me the very opposite of faith.

Jesus the Magician

Morton Smith, Columbia University historian, has called attention to the role of miracles in the ministry of Jesus. But *Jesus the Magician* is not, I am afraid, a book that will appeal to devout Christians.[5]

What's the true story of Jesus? The man was arrested by Roman occupiers of Palestine, and he was executed. He was charged with sedition, blasphemy, sorcery—vague charges, prompted by political expediency. The few notices in Roman history were not favorable. How different it was for believers! They arrived at an altogether different view; to the converts, the crucified Jesus was the Messiah, the Christ, the God-Man, the Son of Man, the Lord of History, the Savior of the World.

We know how believers saw Jesus, says Morton Smith, but how did opponents see him? A fair question. Smith's book, a piece of brilliant detective work, comes up with an answer. Smith concludes that the opponents of Jesus saw him as a *goes,* a *magos*—a magician or sorcerer. "And by extension," according to Smith, "a deceiver." In a detailed appendix, Smith argues that Jesus was unlike the typical Hebrew prophet. His "social type" was shadier, a type fairly common in the ancient Levant. According to Smith, Jesus was more like the Samaritan Simon the Magus or the Greek Apollonius of Tyana than the Hebrew Isaiah or Ezekiel. He was a man who practiced magic and claimed self-deification.

To make his point, Smith examines the miracles in the career of Jesus, especially exorcisms and healings. The ancient Near East lacked asylums and psychiatrists, so mad folk were thrown into the streets and left to wander, beg, and rave. In those days people knew nothing of hysterical paralysis and other psychosomatic disorders.

Today we know better. We can understand how an intuitive psychologist, working with a primitive system of symbols, and playing on the credulity of the needy and the uneducated, might have given the appearance of possessing divine power. Jesus was a sensitive with great charisma, perhaps like Mesmer, with a gift for dealing with troubled souls. Jesus appealed to faith and hope, radiated love and authority, and worked therapeutic "miracles."

Smith sees Jesus through the lens of Charcot and Freud and sheds light on Jesus the magician. But Smith's argument can be carried further. A new and important layer of meaning is revealed if we look at these same reports in light of knowledge of not just abnormal but of paranormal psychology.

Smith accents the miraculous and the magical in the Jesus narratives; yet, apart from the psychosomatic connections, he thinks the miracles are all bunk. The rationalist historian reasons that since Jesus couldn't have done all the miracles ascribed to him, he had to be a quack, a trickster, a charlatan. Smith never quite comes out and says so directly, but the reader senses that this is his view. Professional skeptics and debunkers treat contemporary psychics the same way; *all* are dismissed as flim-flam artists.

According to Smith, the phenomena ascribed to Jesus, apart from ones Smith can explain as hysterical, are "obviously inventions." Smith has no doubts: "Walking on water, multiplying food, and the like are best explained not as 'misunderstandings,' but as fictions."

However, a more complete knowledge of facts established in modern times suggests a different view of these biblical reports.

For example, there is eyewitness testimony of complete levitation of the human body.[6] If Joseph of Copertino, Teresa of Avila, and D. D. Home levitated, why couldn't Jesus have walked on water? Complete bodily levitation is admittedly rare; but the evidence, especially in the case of Joseph of Copertino is very strong. Joseph's levitations, which have been described as aerial flights, were witnessed by numerous people over a period of thirty-five years. Many witnesses were prominent people—for example, at least three Cardinals; the Archbishop of Avignon; Prince Leopold of Tuscany; Juan de Cabrera, Duke of Medina and an Admiral of Castile, together with his wife (who fainted when the monk flew over her head); Johann Friedrich, Duke of Brunswick and patron of the great philosopher, G. W. Leibniz (after witnessing the monk levitate, the Duke converted to the Catholic faith); and the surgeon Francesco Pierpaoli who attended Joseph during his last illness in 1663 and watched him levitate from his deathbed.

Joseph's supernormal manifestations were not isolated, freakish oddities but aspects of a pattern. For example, his levitations expressed his ecstatic flight toward God. Ecstasy and levitation were, in the case of Joseph, aspects of an overall pattern of psychophysical transformation. If we accept this evidence, our view of biblical accounts of levitation becomes open to revision. We're no longer entitled to dismiss such claims as preposterous.

The other obvious fiction Smith mentions is multiplying food. Thurston has reviewed more recent cases suggestive of this prodigy.[7] And if the reports on Sai Baba hold up (see Chapter 11), people today are apparently multiplying food. Why not Jesus then? The fact is that for many types of Jesus' reported phenomena, we have good contemporary evidence; this increases the probability that at least some of the ancient miracle stories, which Smith admits enchanted the first Christians, may have been based on fact after all. My point is a modest one. A careful study of all the evidence shows that we have no right to dismiss all the miracle stories out of hand.

My concern in this chapter is not with any particular miracle. Direct evidence for New Testament miracles is lacking. I want to stress the general idea that we inhabit the kind of world in which "miracles" like those reported in the New Testament can and do occur.

My aim is neither to de-mythologize nor re-literalize the Gospel narratives but rather to develop a view I call "evolutionary catholicism." According to evolutionary catholicism, the alleged supernormal phenomena of Christianity express universal aspects of human potential; they help us form a hypothesis about our possible psychophysical evolution.

Miracle Stories

The rise of Christianity was filled with stories of psychic phenomena. The four Gospels, which tell the story of Jesus; the Acts of the Apostles, our best guide to how the movement spread to Europe; and Paul's letters, where we see the historical Jesus evolving into the psychic Christ, make frequent reference to angels and other paranormal entities and contain vivid accounts of miracles.

Begin with Mark, probably the oldest Gospel, written about a generation after the death of Jesus:

> Passing by the sea of Galilee, he saw Simon and Andrew, Simon's brother, casting a net into the sea, for they were fishermen. And Jesus said to them, 'Come after me and I shall make you be fishers of men.' And at once, leaving their nets, they followed him (Mark 1:16-18).

The way Mark tells it, the two men responded instantly to the summons; the "authority" of Jesus was absolute. Jesus' command over Simon and Andrew seems like testimony to his supernatural power. Thus Jesus began his career with miracles of personal magnetism.

Later in Mark, Jesus is said to cast out a demon, and then the "news of him went out everywhere into all the Galilean countryside" (1:23-26). Eventually Jesus began to perform healings:

> [T]hey brought him all the sick and those possessed by demons, and the whole city was assembled at the door [of the house where he was staying]. And he cured many sick with various diseases and cast out many demons (Mark 1:32-34).

The healings caused crowds to come from everywhere. They came from Jerusalem and Sidon when they heard of the things he did:

> [F]or he healed many, so that all who had afflictions fell on him, trying to touch him, and those possessed by unclean spirits, when they saw him, fell before him and cried out, saying, 'You are the Son of God' (Mark 3:10-11).

Reading these accounts, one thinks of crowds flocking around
modern miracle men like Padre Pio and Sai Baba. The detail about
trying to touch Jesus is telling. In their desire for bodily contact with
the force they sense emanating from him, people have tried to rip
off Padre Pio's clothes.

Matthew and Luke wrote their accounts eighty or ninety years after
Jesus' death, basing them on Mark and another older source, known
to scholars as Q.[8] In these Gospels, miracles also play a central part.
In Matthew, the disciples decided that Jesus was the Son of God
because he could walk on water. When the disciples saw Jesus walking on the sea, they were frightened, thinking he was a "ghost." When
he said "Come!" Peter, too, walked on water, but after a few steps
lost his nerve and had to be saved. When the two got into the boat,
the wind stopped. "And those who were in the boat worshipped him,
saying 'You are certainly God's son'" (14:33). Again, an apparent
miracle braces belief in Jesus' divinity.

At the end of the ministry in Galilee, Matthew also describes Jesus
as a healer:

> And crowds upon crowds came to him, bringing with them their
> lame, deformed, blind, mute, and many others, and they laid them
> at his feet and he cured them, so that the crowd marvelled (Mat-
> thew 15:30).

In his Gospel, Luke also accents the psychic side of Jesus' ministry.
After netting a huge catch of fish, Simon Peter "fell down at Jesus'
knees, saying, 'Depart from me, for I am a sinful man, O lord!' For
amazement had seized him and all his companions because of the catch
of fish they had taken" (5:8-9). Such seizures of amazement are
reported throughout the Gospels. "Amazing" psychic phenomena
always draw the crowds from great distances.

In Luke a paralytic was lowered from a roof so Jesus could heal
him (this was the only way to get past the crowd). The man was cured:
"And they were all seized with astonishment and began glorifying
God, and they were filled with fear, saying, 'We have seen remarkable
things today'" (5:26). Psychic marvels awaken fear as much as
amazement.

John's Gospel also stresses miracles. The story of Nathanael is
revealing:

> Jesus saw Nathanael coming to him, and said of him, 'Behold, an
> Israelite indeed, in whom is no guile.' Nathanael said to him, 'How

do you know me?' Jesus answered and said to him, 'Before Philip called you, when you were under the fig tree, I saw you.' Nathanael answered him, 'Rabbi, you are the Son of God; you are the King of Israel' (John 1:47-49).

A demonstration of paranormal cognition is here taken as a sign of divinity. Rather than play his powers down, Jesus assures Nathanael that he will see "greater things than these" (1:50).

At Cana, Jesus turned water into wine with the effect that "his disciples believed in him" (2:11). Before long the crowds in Jerusalem "believed in his name, seeing his signs that he performed" (2:23). Nicodemus, a Pharisee, came to Jesus by night and declared: "We know that you have come from God as a teacher; for no one can do these signs that you do unless God is with him" (3:2). The demonstration of psi ability seemed a sure "sign" of God's agency.

Psychic Pentecost

In a similar vein, the Holy Spirit is a powerful presence in Acts of the Apostles. Acts, written apparently by Luke, traces the story of how the apostles brought the Good News from Jerusalem to Rome. Thus it is a valuable document on the origins of Christianity. The Christian "new age" began with the first outpouring of the Holy Spirit:[9]

> When the day of Pentecost came, all the believers were gathered together in one place. And suddenly there came from heaven a noise like a violent, rushing wind, and it filled the whole house where they were sitting. And there appeared to them tongues as of fire distributing themselves, and they rested on each one of them. And they were filled with the Holy Spirit and began to speak with other tongues, as the Spirit was giving them utterance (Acts 2:1-4).

Witnesses were duly "amazed and marvelled" at this strange spectacle of paranormal lights.

Some said the apostles were drunk, but Peter invoked Joel's prophecy of the last days, in which the Lord will pour forth his spirit on all humankind and people will dream dreams and see visions. Peter thus rebuts the charge of drunkenness by linking the psychic phenomena with the end of the world and the outpouring of God's spirit.

The picture of what happened on that day is remarkable. A power in the form of a sound, resembling a strong wind, comes down from the sky, and a lightform in the shape of tongues hovers over the apostles' heads. Then comes the phenomenon of glossolalia—speaking in tongues. Each person present thought he heard his own language being spoken. And, of course, people were "amazed and unable to explain it."

Psychic Terrorism

Clearly, the author of Acts wanted to show that supernatural power inspired the early Christian community. Nor is he averse to demonstrating the fearful side of this power.

The importance of psychic terrorism in religion merits some attention. The stories in Exodus detailing the way Moses liberated his people are examples of psychic terrorism in the Old Testament. (See, for example, the account of the plagues inflicted on the Egyptians in Exodus (7-11). The story of Elisha is suggestive:

> The brother prophet of Elijah was in Bethel, when some small boys came out of the town and jeered at him. 'Hurry up, baldy,' they shouted. He turned round and looked at them; and he cursed them in the name of Yahweh. And two bears came out of the forest and savaged forty-two of the boys (2 Kings 2: 23-25).

Similar events abound in the Acts: "And fear came upon every soul; and many wonders [terata] and signs [semeia] were done by the apostles." The economic implications of this psychically induced fear (phobos) are revealed in the next verses: "And all that believed were together, and had all things in common; and sold their possessions and goods, and parted them to all men, as every man had need" (2:43). In other words, frightening psychic phenomena apparently induced the first Christians to part with their private property and become "communists."

In another story the Holy Spirit sent Paul and Barnabas to Paphos where they met a Jewish magician, Bar-Jesus, Elymas Magos in Greek. The apostles were trying to convert a proconsul, Sergius Paulus. Elymas Magos tried to interfere and Paul cursed him. By invoking the Lord, Paul blinded Elymas temporarily. Observing this, the proconsul became a believer. In this skirmish between warlocks, Paul, by mixing psi and suggestion, won another convert to the new religion (13:4-12).

The story of Ananias and his wife is the most shocking case of psychic terrorism in the New Testament. Told in some detail, readers are obviously meant to take the lesson to heart. The couple sold a possession and kept part of the price for themselves. Peter somehow discerned this and confronted Ananias with his deception:

> Ananias, why did you let Satan take control of you and make you lie to the Holy Spirit by keeping part of the money you received for the property? Before you sold the property, it belonged to you. . . . You have not lied to men—you have lied to God. As soon as Ananias heard this, he fell down dead (Acts 5:1-5).

Maybe the thought that he had fallen under the spell of Satan terrified Ananias, or he may have thought that he had been caught lying to God. He may have had a weak heart, or he may have just fainted, which legend gussied up into death. In any case, the story in Acts shows what we're supposed to believe, and what probably was believed by the faithful. Comparable stories exist today of people having their secret sins laid bare by Padre Pio, especially during confession. Such experiences have a way of "encouraging" faith.

After Ananias expired he was carried away by some young men and promptly buried. We are not surprised that "great fear came on them that heard all these things." Then followed a deadly sequel. About three hours later, Sapphira, the wife of Ananias arrived. Peter put her to the same test, and the hapless woman fell into the snare and perjured herself.

Then we are told that Peter uttered these remarkable words: "Why did you and your husband decide to put the Lord's Spirit to the test? The men who buried your husband are at the door right now, and they will carry you out too!" It seems clear from this that, voodoo-like,[10] Peter meant the woman to die by the power of suggestion. If we believe the narrative, he succeeded:

> At once she fell down at his feet and died. The young men came in and saw that she was dead, so they carried her out and buried her beside her husband. The whole church and all the others who heard of this were terrified (Acts 5:6-11).

Again, the formula speaks about great fear. For this is how "believers were the more added to the Lord."

In this look at the dawn of Christianity, what we see are abundant psychic signs and paranormal wonders. Signs and wonders are a big

part of what captivated the first Christians; as the texts repeatedly
show, such events caused their numbers to grow.

There is no use getting squeamish about the frequent mention of
fear and terror. As Rudolph Otto has shown, sacred power is "numinous"—it has an awe-inspiring, uncanny, and terrifying aspect—which
explains why some prefer *not* to believe in psychic power. The prospect of our private thoughts being exposed to public scrutiny is unsettling; the idea of voodoo death is even less appealing.

Matthew tells a strange tale of Jesus cursing a fig tree. The Lord
was hungry, we're told. He came upon a fig tree but found no fruit
upon it. So he cursed the tree: "'No longer shall there ever be any
fruit from you.' And at once the fig tree withered" (21:18-19).

This tale is reminiscent of something parapsychology has demonstrated, called "psi-missing." Psi-missing is negative psi. Bernard
Grad found that depressed patients retarded the growth of barley seeds
in one of his experiments in psychic healing.[11] Apparently, we can
both hasten and retard vital processes by paranormal means. This
evidence has important implications. In a burst of concentrated psychic
power, a person might be able to do just the sort of thing Jesus is
said to have done to the fig tree.

Psychic Healing

We shouldn't exaggerate the importance of psychic terrorism. I think
it played a part in galvanizing the early Christian movement, but a
minor part. The terror was a latent possibility, but the real power
lay in the appeal to hope. The healing powers of the early Christians
drew the crowds. What could be more natural? The appeal of Jesus
must have been the same appeal that's behind such best-selling books
as Bernie Siegel's *Love, Medicine, and Miracles.* For example, in
Acts 5 crowds of sick people try to place themselves in the shadow
of Peter (in the ancient world, a person's shadow was thought to be
part of the soul). What mattered was the power of belief, as we know
from modern placebo studies. We moderns believe in pills; the ancients believed in the shadows of holy men. In either case, we're
watching the healing power of mind at work.

Nearly one-fifth of the Gospel narratives refer in some way to Jesus'
healings. The healed were people possessed by unclean spirits; the
deaf, the dumb, the blind; victims of dropsy, leprosy, paralysis, im-

potence. The healing methods were faith, touch, words, prayers, and exorcisms.

The people who responded to Jesus as healer were poor and ignorant. Perhaps these people—just because they *were* ignorant—responded more vehemently to the "placebos" as well as to the "voodoolike" suggestions. The more vehement responses may have caused effects more marvelous than anything we're likely to find in our culture.

For example, the apostles were imprisoned because of their healing activities; the angel of the Lord freed them during the night, and they went back to teaching in the temple (Acts 5: 18-25). Is it possible that the vehement belief of naive and spontaneous people created an entity they called an angel—an entity that somehow helped them in a miraculous escape? Later, in the chapter on angels, I shall try to explain how this might indeed be possible.

The Two Stages of Initiation

Acts gives another clue to the importance of psi in early Christianity. The following account shows there were two stages of initiation in the primitive church:

> When the apostles in Jerusalem heard that Samaria had accepted the word of God, they sent Peter and John to them, and they went down there, and prayed for the Samaritans to receive the Holy Spirit, for as yet he had not come down on any of them: they had only been baptized in the name of the Lord Jesus. Then they laid hands on them, and they received the Holy Spirit (Acts 8:14-17).

The first stage of initiation was baptism; the second stage was psychic—the Holy Spirit "came down" on you. This experience can be observed at contemporary charismatic meetings. I once watched the charismatic priest Father di Orio walk up and down a church aisle and lightly tap people who were instantly "slain in the spirit." They fell to the ground in a state of ecstatic trance, oddly enough, never hurting themselves.

Acts shows that prayer and the laying on of hands were preparations for receiving the Holy Spirit. The idea of a universal healing energy is widespread in world cultures and goes under many names. Again, modern psychic science supports ancient intuition. Experiments back the hypothesis of a healing force; Bernard Grad and others have shown that people can exert an unknown healing force on wounded mice, plants, and other living organisms. Apparently it is possible to "charge" water with this healing power. (The "charged" water is used to speed plant growth.) It is possible that the healing energy studied by parapsychologists is related to what Christians call Holy Spirit. Great Spirit, Animal Magnetism, Chi, Prana, Orgone, and so on—all these names, like the name of the Holy Spirit, point to an unknown healing force that science is only now beginning to investigate.

Another story in Acts says something about psychic power and belief in gods. Paul and Barnabas cured a cripple in a town near Lycaonia. The crowd was so astonished, they shouted: "These people are gods who have come down to us disguised as men" (14:12). The crowd called Barnabas, Zeus, and Paul, Hermes, and were prepared to offer them sacrifices. The apostles, of course, disclaimed any divine status. Nevertheless, their actions gave an impression suggesting divine power.

A renaming of the gods had begun. Zeus, Marduk, Yawheh, Aphrodite, and countless other deities had monopolized the collective imagination of the Mediterranean world for thousands of years. The time had come for a new name and form. Still, behind this changing of god forms was the ever fertile psyche, the power that made Barnabas appear to glow with the splendor of Zeus and Paul with the majesty of Hermes.

Icons of Miraculous Meaning

Stories of healings and exorcisms, telepathy and prophecy are plentiful in the New Testament. One can hardly read a verse without coming across something that proclaims the marvelous and the superordinary. Among the hundreds of references to miracles,[12] several stand out as uniquely archetypal in the Christian story.

Consider a few of these icons of miraculous meaning. The possibilities are many: the Virgin Birth, the Baptism of Jesus and Descent of the Dove, the Calming of the Storm, the Turning of Water into Wine at Cana, the Temptation in the Wilderness, the Transfiguration, the Crucifixion and Resurrection, the Meeting of Thomas with the risen Christ, the Ascension, and so on.

All these put their stamp on the origins of Christianity. A family of archetypal images, they became part of the mental vocabulary of the new religion. Through art, liturgy, and theology, they have shaped and inspired Christian society for centuries.

Jung called these stories archetypes of transformation. In them, the narrative, the spiritual, and the miraculous are interwoven. A story is told, a vision is enshrined, a path to action is opened. The archetype becomes a doorway to an alternate reality. Archetyes of miraculous meaning become visible to the eye of the soul in statues and paintings, in symbols and stories. Encoded in the collective imagination, they speak to our transcendent psi powers.

According to Vico, the rise of Christianity marked the beginning of a "new humanity."[13] The origins of this new humanity lay in a new order of "miracles" and a new type of courage in the face of death. Miracles or psychic phenomena in the New Testament thus promise, in effect, the birth of a new type of human being. Among the world faiths, Christianity promises total newness of being; it pictures a renovated cosmic environment where want, pain, and discord are abolished, and previews a world where human and divine come together in close communion. Consider several images from the Gospels that evoke the emergence of Vico's "new humanity."

Multiplication of loaves and fishes. According to Matthew (14:15-21), Jesus fed a crowd of five thousand with two fishes and five loaves; after this serendipitous repast, twelve baskets of leftovers were gathered up. Of course, the idea that we can generate food from nowhere is too outrageous to merit serious thought. It flouts our sense of the way the world works. The tale must be either sheer fiction or based on delusion that mushroomed into legend.

Nevertheless, when I consider the variety of PK effects that have been documented, the idea that Jesus may have paranormally produced food seems a little less fantastic. Piecing the bits of information together, we can begin to imagine how the multiplication of food may be more than a tall tale.

Consider, for example, the fine-grained selectivity of psychokinesis. The work of physicist Helmut Schmidt shows how selectively one-pointed psychic influence can be. Radioactive particles behave as randomly as anything in nature, impervious to gravity, heat, or electricity; yet experiments show they are psychokinetically open to the influence of human intentions.[14] That a thought could bias the behavior of the smallest, least accessible unit of physical reality known in nature enlarges our idea of what is possible.

In fact, there is some reason to believe that human thought can bend metal,[15] charge water with vital energy,[16] cause objects to pass through solid matter,[17] create a variety of living phantoms,[18] lift heavy objects,[19] manifest as physical lightforms that can be photographed,[20] imprint images on light-sensitive film,[21] create recordable auditory effects,[22] and so on.

With the help of a little extrapolation, I can stretch my mind to imagine tangible loaves and fishes erupting apparently out of nowhere. In combining these various reports of paranormal physical action, it appears there resides in—or through—human beings an unrecognized capacity for direct transformation of natural law. Thus, if a thought can move an object, it can create energy. Why then couldn't a thought rearrange a sufficient amount of atoms to produce a new object? Even a living object? Perhaps the creative power traditionally ascribed to divinity resides in some spark-like capacity in all human beings. In fact, we are told by the Bible that "man" is made in the image of God. Indeed, the idea of God's omnipotence may be an idealization of an evolutionary potential in humanity. From time to time extraordinary beings like Jesus may be born who more fully embody that evolutionary potential and thus manifest those powers we think of as tokens of divinity.

Multiplying food, so seen, might simply be an example of the superdevelopment of our paranormal latencies. In fact, there is evidence for specific cases of the paranormal multiplication of food. We have already cited Thurston's examples from the annals of Catholic sainthood. There are, in addition, eyewitness accounts of Don Bosco's multiplication of food in the nineteenth century.[23] The most recent case for miraculous food production has been reported by Howard Murphet and Erlendur Harraldsson in their studies of the contemporary miracle worker Sai Baba. (See Chapter 11.)

Calming the storm. Jesus calming the storm is an astonishing image—an image of mastery, and of communion, with the turbulent forces of nature. Jesus walks on water, subdues the storm waters, changes water into wine. Water is a symbol of the unconscious. Perhaps, then, the story of calming the storm contains another great promise, namely, that we shall subdue the unconscious powers of nature and transfigure them.

Something yet more subtle may be meant. Perhaps the idea is that the only way to truly master the powers of nature is first to master the powers in our unconscious. Inner must precede outer mastery—a model pretty much the opposite of scientific materialism. Through modern science we have learned to master the powers of nature, the powers external to us; meanwhile, we remain enslaved to the nature within. In the New Testament vision, we first master the powers within. In other words, the real storm that needs to be calmed is the storm within.

On the other hand, there is still the literal content of the image, direct power over the elements. Some contemporary observations support the claim that people can influence the raw elements. American anthropologist David Barker had the disconcerting experience of watching an African shaman stop a rainstorm. The converse was observed by John Neihardt, who describes in his book on the Indian medicine man Black Elk how he saw Black Elk call rain out of a clear sky. The Tibetan yogi Milarepa was reputed to have wrecked crops by mind-caused hailstorms. Witnesses in the twentieth century say Padre Pio stopped rain and commanded the behavior of animals.

All this plus the experimental data helps us imagine the possibility of direct control of the elements. In the "new heaven and the new earth" envisioned by prophets of all faiths, a critical mass of human consciousness may be achieved that will temper the violent and destructive extremes of nature.

The resurrection. Lazarus is said to have lain in the grave four days and, when summoned by Jesus, came forth. What's remarkable about the Lazarus story is the paucity of details. Such a prodigy seems to merit a little more descriptive detail. All one can say here is that if the story were true, it would indeed imply a very remarkable ability.

However, my purpose here is to search for the unity of the pattern of our potential psychophysical evolution. It is not the isolated incidents that count in the narrative but the form and pattern they weave, the total image they reveal and unfold in time. The details, in short, are part of a pattern, and the pattern reflects a process. The process, I am suggesting, may be one pointing to the birth of a new species of humanity.

In the overall pattern, Lazarus and other stories of raising the dead prefigure the resurrection. In fact, *all* the promises, the supernormal archetypes and paranormal manifestations seem to converge and coalesce as prefigurings of the resurrection. How are we to take the resurrection story?

In the story I am trying to tell, the resurrection is an image of the outer reaches of our PK potential—that is, the power of the soul to reform the habits of physical reality. The resurrection, in this view, would be a visionary—and in some sense literal—anticipation of possible developments of future humanity. To sustain this vision, we must keep before our minds the array of psychophysical phenomena that come under the misleading term "psychokinesis."

The resurrection anticipates Blake's eternal imaginal body and Vico's new humanity. One must pause to take in the enormous range of this thought. The resurrection is only a sign, a beginning—as Paul says, the "firstfruits"—of a vast cosmic transformation that is yet to come. The evolutionary implications of the resurrection, though present in the writings of Paul, have by and large been ignored. An exception is philosopher Patrick Sherry in *Spirits, Saints and Immortality* (1984), who recommends that we view the saints as living "images" of the life to come—as forerunners of our evolutionary potential.

According to the Christian vision, nature itself is becoming increasingly malleable to the intentions of the higher will. All wonders and signs converge on this promise of a new body—and if a new *body,* a new *world.* The vision we are trying to decode into contemporary language anticipates a new epoch in the organization of the universe.

Tracking the Hidden Pattern

Multiply food? Calm the storm? Resurrect the dead? Definitely, as Charles Fort would put it, wild talents! What promises are encoded in these stunning images? Whatever they are, they are part of a pattern. But to get at the full pattern, it is necessary to look at all the pieces in the puzzle. And many pieces are still missing. Still, it appears that the emerging pattern foreshadows basic changes in the mode of our possible existence.

Are these phenomena isolated freaks of nature, or are they signs of a comprehensive evolutionary trend, aspects of a total capacity for psychophysical development? In Chapter 7, I take up this question. The idea here is the possibility that we are evolving an *imaginal* body.

Jesus as a Psychic

I hope I have begun to show the importance of the psychic factor in the morphogenesis of Christianity. Jesus was a remarkable psychic;

that much should be plain. I want now to conclude with some comments that further bring out the psychic dimensions of his personality:

(1) the revealing type of insults he suffered;
(2) his use of metaphor;
(3) the mysterious authority he exerted over people;
(4) his extra-vivid sense of psychic reality;
(5) the lifestyle he promoted.

Evidence from insult. The reality of Jesus' psychic phenomena may be deduced from remarks made by people who rejected him. His opponents taunted him on the cross: "He saved others, himself he cannot save." They don't deny his powers; they insult him because he failed to use his powers to save himself.

There is a story of Jesus visiting his hometown. When he began to preach in the synagogue, listeners were surprised to recognize "the carpenter, the son of Mary," and took offense (Mark 6:1-6). Mark says that Jesus was unable to perform any impressive miracles there because of the people's unbelief. This tallies with what we know of psi function. The setting, the atmosphere of belief and heightened expectation, need to be just right. Jeering skeptics kill the miracle-making dynamic.

Moreover, modern studies show that placebos work better when figures of authority administer them.[24] In his hometown, Jesus was perceived as just the carpenter. The saying "familiarity breeds contempt" seems especially fitting in the realm of psychic phenomena. Unable, perhaps, to project his usual air of authority, the delicate group dynamic failed, crippling Jesus' healing powers.

The use of metaphor. Research indicates that psychic function is blocked by literal-mindedness and mechanistic habits of thought. Consequently, people with artistic ability often make the best psychics. A contemporary example is Ingo Swann, a gifted psychic and a talnted visionary artist. The psychic mind moves less in linear than in metahoric patterns.[25] The connection between psychism and so-called "right-brain" thinking is often discussed today. Unusually gifted psychics exhibit a more than common "right-brain" or metahoric sensibility. The poet William Butler Yeats is another example. Yeats was one of the great poets of the twentieth century; he was also involved in theosophy, magic, automatic writing and other psychic practices.

William Blake said that "Christ's apostles were artists" and that true "Christianity was art." Jesus did seem comfortable with poetic, metaphoric modes of thought. Take the story of the woman of Samaria. Jesus met a Samaritan lady at a well and asked for a drink; she refused him because he was a Jew. Jesus confounded the woman by reading her mind, revealing that she had been divorced many times. He didn't condemn her. Instead, he offered *her* a drink—a drink, he said, that would quench her thirst forever. The woman missed the point of the metaphor and asked where she had to go to get such unusual liquid.

Of course, Jesus wasn't talking about anything you can buy in the supermarket. He was referring to the water of spirit, the metaphorical water he spoke of to Nicodemus—the life-giving water that quenches spiritual thirst. Jesus used a metaphor to convey his thought to the woman of Samaria. He often expressed himself with hyperbole, jokes, parables, aphorisms, stories. The poet, the visionary, and the psychic share the metaphoric mode of consciousness with children, who use metaphors because they haven't mastered conventional expressions to describe experiences. This may explain why Jesus was partial to children, why he told his disciples to become like children if they wanted to enter the Kingdom of God.

The authority of Jesus. Another indication of the psychic side of Jesus is his charisma. Jesus spoke and acted with authority—with *exousia*. In Greek the word means "from his own being." It was this authority that caused problems with middle-class scribes and pharisees who were committed to the status quo. Conflict with them was inevitable.

How, for instance, would the medical establishment feel about someone said to cure cancer by touch? How would corporate executives view a man who inspired workers to quit their jobs with a single commanding glance? "And they left their nets at once and followed him," says Matthew (4:20). Nor would typical academics take to a fellow who, as Matthew said, "taught with authority, not like their own scribes" (7:29).

"Here is a teaching that is new," witnesses said, "and with authority behind it" (Mark 1:27-28). In Jesus we have a man whose authority came from an immediate consciousness of inner power. By external standards, he was a man without credentials. His ethics, his teaching, his healing power came *from his own being—exousia.* The authority of Jesus was based on self-knowledge. He knew the depths of his own soul—not only the powers that lay there, but also the weaknesses. *The extraordinary reality of the psyche.* The psyche for Jesus was extraordinarily real. Not all people experience the reality, the depth of their psyches with equal clarity and intensity. Most people build walls to shut out experiences. "Humankind," said T. S. Eliot in a much quoted line, "cannot bear too much reality." Truth for Jesus lay in the realm of passionate subjectivity. But of course such passion can be dangerous! For if the sense of truth is ruled by inner states, and if one is true to these inner states and what they dictate, cognitive dissonance—mortal conflict with outer authority—is inevitable.

A story about how Jesus viewed ritual cleanliness may clarify this point. In a speech recorded by Mark, Jesus discoursed on the "clean" and the "unclean." He got quickly to the heart of the matter: "Nothing that goes into a man from outside can make him unclean; it is the things that come out of a man that make him unclean" (7:14-23). What this shows is a man who forms his sense of reality on the basis of his inner sense, and not on the basis of what he has heard or been taught by rote. With Jesus, intentions are what count—motives, feelings, inner realities.

The stress on intention is also seen in this example: "If a man looks at a woman lustfully, he has already committed adultery with her in his heart" (Matt. 5:27). This is a very strange thing to say. We normally ascribe moral predicates to actions. Can I be blamed for merely thinking about or desiring something? I may desire a woman, I may even fantasize enjoying her. Am I thereby guilty of wrongdoing? Normally, of course, the answer is no.

From the standpoint of rational common sense, the imagination of a deed is not the same as the deed itself. Apparently, however, for Jesus, imagination *was* reality. This might be so for a man whose inner life is as intense as we can surmise Jesus' to be. For such a man the letter of the law would be of secondary importance. For Jesus, it must have been a terribly real thing to experience a desire. This was a point brought out in Martin Scorsese's disturbing movie *The Last Tempatation of Christ.* Nor should we forget that Jesus was fond of women. Scripture shows that women played a significant part in his ministry.[26]

A passionate man with a vivid imagination, a man whose dreams and visions already felt like solid reality, would have a distinctive moral sense. The remark of Jesus about looking at women lustfully, and the wrongness of doing so, implies a remarkable belief in the reality of inner life. It implies, in my opinion, an awareness of the psychokinetic potential of mere intention.

A Psi-Liberating Lifestyle?

Was Jesus a superpsychic? It is hard to avoid the conclusion that he had extraordinary psychic power. The last question I want to ask is whether there was anything in the lifestyle he urged upon his followers that was especially psi-conducive. I think several things show that the early Christian lifestyle, if authentically lived, would, on the basis of what we know today, probably contribute to freeing psi potential.

The features of this lifestyle are interwoven and mutually reinforcing. The first I would mention is the expectation of the end of the world. As Albert Schweitzer has painstakingly argued, the essence of early Christianity was apocalyptic. Jesus and the first Christians expected the world to end. A person who lived in earnest expectation of the approaching end of earthly time would hardly behave as normal people do. Expecting the end, expecting total transformation, might well have created a mindset disposed to induce those leaps of function called psi.

Two aspects of endtime mentality would contribute toward this effect, radical trust and radical spontaneity. Jesus showed extraordinary confidence in the power of belief:

> [I]f anyone says to this mountain, "get up and throw yourself into the sea," with no hesitation in his heart but believing that what he says will happen, it will be done for him. [And he adds B]elieve that you have it already, and it will be yours" (Mark 11:23-24).

If we trust in the right way, there is virtually no limit to what can be achieved.

Is such extraordinary power latent in human beings? Mark's words paint an exact portrait of the inner attitude conducive to psychic liberation. "With no hesitation in his heart but believing that what he says will happen" well describes the inner strategy that most modern reports say will free our psi potential.

Moreover, Jesus preached the end of the world and the coming of the Kingdom of God. The Good News was that we could place our lives trustingly in the hands of divine providence. This turning oneself over to divine providence may also be seen as turning oneself over to unconscious powers. Again, it is an attitude known by modern researchers to liberate psychic ability.

The more rigid we are in thought and behavior, the more we inhibit the manifestation of psi. By contrast, when we are spontaneous in thought and behavior, we are more likely to use our latent psi abilities to serve our needs. In Matthew, Jesus explained this connection:

> That is why I am telling you not to worry about your life and what you are to eat, nor about your body and how you are to clothe it. . . . Look at the birds in the sky. They do not sow or reap or gather into barn; yet your heavenly Father feeds them (Matthew 6:25-26).

A Freudian might see such talk of the father as neurotic and regressive. Yet a different view is possible. Evoking the father image may be a strategy that liberates paranormal powers. Decoded into the language of psychic function, "trust in our heavenly Father" may be a way of talking about removing the burden from our conscious striving selves and thus liberating powers latent in the unconscious.

The early Christians lived a communal lifestyle. In my opinion, the intense sense of community was probably important to the success of its psychic life. We know from modern research that psychic interactions take place between people who are intimately and emotionally related. A mother is likely to sense danger to her child. Apparitions of the dead appear to people who have been long married, mentally as well as literally.

In Matthew (18:19), Jesus proclaimed, as do many New Age oracles today, the unlimited nature of our psychic potential. Success depends on mutual support and deep mutual trust: "If two of you shall agree on earth as touching anything that they shall ask, it shall be done for them of my father which is in heaven." This is a rather remarkable assertion. In one way it sounds like magic. Or is it an intuition of the psychic science of the third millennium? Jesus promises that if two people enter a state of mind called agreement, they may invoke a supreme principle that will respond lovingly to their needs, and in a manner that is virtually unlimited.

The Greek word for "agree" is *symphonein,* from which we get our word *symphony.* Thus, if we choose to agree and ask for aid from God, we have only to "sound together"—to vibrate subtly in unison.

Jesus the psychic offers here a musical metaphor—a practical suggestion of how to develop group PK. Modern psi research I have cited previously supports this ancient intuition. We can all acquire this special psychological skill by practice. Consciously "agreeing" can help us produce paranormal effects.

One final point about spontaneity as a liberator of our miracle potential. The primitive Christian habit of sharing goods is one way people cultivated a type of spontaneity. The power of the early Church depended on openness, trust, and generosity. Any stinting, calculating, or holding back would have wrecked the group dynamic. This may explain the harsh treatment of backsliders like Ananias and Sapphira, who were accused of sinning against the Holy Spirit.

Psychic Christianity

Christianity is a religion that makes enormous demands on the nonrational—the faith and imagination side of our nature. It asks us to make a clean break with our human limitations, to throw ourselves at the feet of a greater reality, to trust in an ultimate benevolence. To commit ourselves to such a worldview means plunging into the mysterious depths of our psychic existence.

Whatever else it was, original Christianity was a training ground for liberating supernormal powers. As a general way of constructing reality, it forced people to discipline the inhibiting side of the rational intellect; it expanded their (shall we coin a phrase?) "belief quotient." The wilder, the more absurd, the greater the defiance of commonsense rationality, the greater, I would say, the potential for freeing our psi powers. And in this, original Christianity was unexcelled. Anyone who embraced this myth with unwavering passion might very well have unleashed extraordinary powers.

5
Paul's Conversion and the Near-Death Experience

The first man is from the earth, earthy; the second man is the Lord from heaven.

1 Cor. 15:47

Scholars generally agree that Paul was a crucial figure in the evolution of Christianity. He began as a rabid persecutor of early Christians but ended by becoming the missionary that brought the new faith to Europe. The Acts of the Apostles and Paul's own letters report the experience that transformed him. An unusual visionary encounter resulted in his deeply changed spiritual personality.

What happened to Paul on the road to Damascus that fateful day long ago? Of course, we will never know for sure. Still, it may be possible to gain fresh understanding of Paul's transformation, thanks to recent findings of near-death studies and psychical research. I don't claim that the psychic side of Paul's conversion explains all; but I do say that his spiritual evolution was related to psychic experiences. Psyche and spirit are subtly interwoven; for this reason, Paul's psychic experiences may offer clues to his spiritual mystery.

What follows, then, is a speculative reconstruction of Saint Paul's *metanoia*—his conversion or psycho-spiritual transformation. The word *metanoia* in New Testament Greek means "repentance"—literally, "afterthought." *Metanoia* implies a radical reorientation in goals, values, perceptions; it marks a giant step in a person's personal evolution. Paul's own *metanoia* led to major historical changes.

Raymond Moody was the first to notice the resemblance between Paul's conversion and the pattern of the near-death experiences he was studying. The mystical connections with near-death experiences had already been noted by researchers. In a series of studies, the pre-

65

sent writer presented a Jungian interpretation of the near-death experience.[1] The NDE seems to be an example of a psychic mechanism I label the "archetype of death and enlightenment" (ADE). The near-death crisis appears to awaken what Jung calls archetype of transformation. Saint Paul's experience, I hold, fits this archetypal pattern.

Like the Hellenistic age of Saint Paul, ours is an age of soul in transformation, an age, as Jung would say, in which the archetypes—the psychic dominants or primordial images—are stirring uneasily in the collective depths. Signs of this are many: exotic neo-pagan cults, Protestant evangelists, Catholic charismatics, Islamic fundamentalists, popular New Age spiritualists—all manner of soul-questing is afoot.

Likewise in Paul's day, the individual was adrift in the empire, looking for spiritual roots amid a glut of exotic beliefs and esoteric practices. Paul's spiritual evolution took shape in a world rife with inner ferment and turmoil. Paul was on the borderline between civilizations—a marginal man, who ended by defining a new universalism. We, too, are on the borderline between civilizations, struggling to forge a new spiritual identity—a new myth of transcendence.

Paul's Conversion

Information on Paul's conversion is sparse. What we know comes from the Acts of the Apostles and the Letters.

Evidence from the Acts of the Apostles. The Acts, probably written by Luke, depict the rise of the early Christian movement. This key document is full of references to supernatural forces, the most important and the most active being the "Holy Spirit." The Acts reflect the larval stage in Christian history before the first organs of the Church hierarchy evolved, the period when disciples still lived in expectation of the Second Coming.

Paul's *metanoia* is highlighted in these writings. We know from Corinthians that Paul the Pharisee was opposed to the new Nazarene sect: "I am not worthy to be called an apostle," he wrote, "because I persecuted the Church of God" (1 Cor. 15:9).

The author of the Acts describes Paul, en route to Damascus, as "breathing menace and slaughter against the disciples of the Lord" (9:1-2). Paul's intention, authorized by the chief priests, was to drive Christian blasphemers from the synagogues and bring them back to

Jerusalem. A change of heart took place on the road. The Acts tells the story three times.

Paul was approaching the city, we read in the first account, when "suddenly a light from heaven flashed around him" (9:3). He fell to the ground and heard a voice: "Saul, Saul, why are you persecuting me?" The voice also said: "I am Jesus whom you are persecuting."

Paul—or Saul, his Hebrew name—was told to rise and enter the city. Paul's companions saw nothing of the invisible entity he was addressing. Paul stood up, blinded by the light, and was led by the hand into the city. He remained without sight for three days, neither eating nor drinking. In Damascus a certain disciple, Ananias, himself guided by visions, laid hands on Paul, restored his sight, and baptized him, filling "him with the Holy Spirit" (9:17-18).

Note that in this account, it isn't said that Paul had a vision of Jesus. This is similar to the near-death experience, in which a person typically sees an extraordinary light and then identifies or interprets it as Jesus, God, or some other supernatural being.

The second account (22: 6-21) appears in Paul's address to the Jews of Jerusalem. It is pretty much the same, except that this time his companions are said to have also seen the light, although they heard nothing.

The third account of Paul's conversion is found in his defense before King Agrippa. A few new points emerge. Again, a light, brighter than the sun, shone around Paul but also around his companions, who themselves are now said to have fallen down (26:14). In this account, the Lord also explains the purpose of his appearance. Paul has been called to witness and to bring God's message of light and forgiveness to the "Gentiles." There is no mention of the light blinding Paul.

At the core of all three accounts is a light with transforming aftereffects. Stories of men transformed by a supernatural light were commonplace in antiquity. The imagery and language of Paul's experience, as told in the Acts, is in some ways typical of the time. For example, the author of the Acts uses the word, *exaiphnes,* "suddenly," to describe Paul's illumination; Plato used the same word in the Seventh Epistle to describe the moment of philosophic conversion. Paul's refusal to betray his "heavenly vision" calls to mind Socrates' sworn allegiance to his post as divinely appointed gadfly of Athens.

The Acts thus reflects the conventional language of divinely inspired *metanoia*. What is the source of the convention? It may, as biblical exegete Charles Guignebert says, reflect a fantasy with no basis in objective reality.[2] Or the convention may be a residue from a typical psychic experience. The latter is the working assumption of the present chapter.

What comes through the minor variations of the three accounts of Paul's conversion is clear. Here is the story of a man whose view of the world has been overturned by a sudden, powerful experience. He undergoes a dramatic reversal of loyalties and affections, based on a meeting with a luminous entity—with a voice that asks him: Why are you persecuting me?

The core elements of the experience are: 1) a transforming light form or energy; 2) a voice that addresses the innermost Self; 3) a total reorientation of one's value system and psychic energies—all features of the archetypal near-death experience.

The picture as it emerges from the letters. Paul himself spoke of his experience. Three times he said he had been called to a mission. Two main points emerge: first, Paul's conviction of direct contact with a divine force, and second, his conviction that he had been directed to announce the Good News revealed by this contact.

People with powerful near-death experiences also feel they have been in contact with a divine force that gives a new direction to their lives. Near-death converts proclaim their healing visions on TV talk shows and news programs. They write books and often enter the helping professions. In essence, many people today are having Paul-like transformation experiences.

Paul wrote in a letter to the Galatians (1:12-17) that the Good News he was proclaiming came not from any man but from an *apocalypse*—a direct "uncovering" or revelation. Like people gripped by the archetypal near-death process, Paul claimed direct experience with divine reality: "For I neither received it from man, nor was I taught it, but I received it through a revelation of Jesus Christ." Paul's conviction of divine contact, as with modern NDEers, was based on his own immediate experience. And like the typical NDEer, few details of the apparition are given; we hear mainly of dazzling light, sacred presence, and numinous energy.

In 1 Corinthians Paul asks: "Am I not free? Am I not an apostle? Have I not seen Jesus our Lord?" (9:1). The direct seeing of the divine form frees Paul from dependence on previous, tribally sanctioned mores. It gives a new direction to his life; it makes him "sent"—an apostle.

In the first letter to the Corinthians (15:8), Paul listed himself as the last of more than five hundred who had seen the Lord with their own eyes: *ophthe kamoi,* he said, "he was seen by me also." Paul's tone indicates total confidence in the authenticity of his vision—his "apocalypse." Clearly, he had a striking encounter with something he took to be the glorified Jesus.

Then there is the famous ecstatic flight reported in 2 Corinthians:

> I know a man in Christ, who, fourteen years ago, was caught up—whether still in the body or out of the body, I do not know, God knows—right into the third heaven . . . into paradise and [who] heard things which must not and cannot be put into human language (2 Cor. 12:2-4).

This, too, fits the near-death model. But there are some problems. Was the "man in Christ" actually Paul himself? Most commentators think so; for my part, it seems clear from the context that Paul is speaking of his own vision and revelation.

Paul's statement is shaped by the need to do two things that seem to conflict. On the one hand, he wants to defend himself, justify his authenticity to the Corinthians. To do so he is forced to boast and call attention to himself. But there is also the risk of appearing proud instead of humble. Paul speaks of two grounds for boasting: "If I have to boast, I will boast of what pertains to my weakness" (11:30). This allows him to boast of his numerous trials and tribulations, the sufferings he endured as a servant of Christ. But when he comes to boast of his visions and revelations, he switches from the first to the third person: "I know a man in Christ. . . ."

Says one commentator: "He speaks of himself in the third person as if to emphasize more strongly the gift quality of his experience. . . ."[3] And another, commenting on the same verse: "Certainly Paul himself. If he was to 'glory' about himself, it could not be the self who was in Christ."[4]

There is another reason for Paul's irony. He says this of the man in Christ who was caught up in paradise:

> On behalf of such a man will I boast; but on my own behalf I will not boast, except in regard to my weakness. For if I do wish to boast I shall not be foolish, for I shall be speaking the truth; but

> I refrain from this, so that no one may credit me with more than
> he sees in me or hears from me (2 Cor. 12:5-6).

Paul here seems to be saying that if he did choose to boast about his
visions directly, he (perhaps in contrast to others) would be telling
the truth; but he prefers not to, choosing to establish his "credit"
on the basis of his observable behavior. Paul, of course, had a point:
his visions were private affairs, whereas his public ministry was
observable, thus providing surer ground for certifying his "credit."

However, there is another point to consider. Even if the passage
in 2 Corinthians refers to Paul's experience, are we sure this experience is the event of his conversion? The dates of Paul's birth,
conversion, letter writing, and death are not known with certainty.
Probably the key dates are 35 A.D. for his conversion and the 50s A.D.
for 2 Corinthians. In 2 Corinthians Paul mentions that it has been
fourteen years since his paradise experience. That isn't a bad fit with
the postulated dates. Still, it is possible that the paradise experience
was distinct from his initial conversion experience in Damascus.

Even this distinction, however, would not be fatal to my view of
Paul's conversion. The total pattern—all the elements of the archetype
—are rarely experienced in a single near-death episode. Elements may
emerge piecemeal, depending on circumstance. Some people see light;
some divine beings; some deceased relatives; some leave their bodies;
and so on: the mix varies from case to case. People often report more
than one near-death experience, and the total pattern may unfold
gradually, in a series of related experiences. However we arrange
the elements of Paul's visionary experiences chronologically, viewed
together, they fit the archetypal pattern of the near-death experience.

Another common component of the near-death crisis is out-of-body
experiences. Paul's allusion to paradise and the third heaven sounds
like the celestial landscapes reported in NDEs. As for hearing things
that cannot be put into language, this resembles the transcendental
sounds and music NDEers often rapturously report. The "unspeak-
able" nature of the experience is a constant in near-death and, for
that matter, in all mystical experiences.

Aftereffects of Paul's Conversion

Paul's bringing the Good News to the gentile world was critical for
Christianity. His transformative experience inspired him to surmount

tribalism and move toward Hellenistic universalism. A move toward universalism is a known aftereffect of the classic NDE. In the blaze of authentic vision, concern for the external in religion is burnt away. The passion for a specific sect vanishes, and one reaches toward a wider human sympathy.

Paul's missionary fervor tallies with the expansive nature of the NDE. This fervor is fueled by an unusual psychic energy. The scientific pedigree for such "energy" remains obscure; it may be thought of as a life force and is sometimes referred to as *kundalini,* which Gopi Krishna called an evolutionary force.[5] The awakening of the kundalini life-force may awaken the passion to proselytize.

In the wake of the near-death experience, people often report an increase in their psychic sensitivity.[6] The Acts of the Apostles describe Paul's psychic powers at length. For example, the people in Lycaonia were so impressed by his healing ability that they addressed him as the Greek god, Hermes (Acts: 14-13). In my account of the psychic origins of Christianity, I discussed this episode as demonstrating the effects of psychic initiation (see Chapter 4). Here my point is different. I want to stress that Paul's conversion follows the pattern of the archetypal NDE, after which so many claim increased psychic sensitivities as well as increased healing abilities.

In Paul's case, however, all charisms—all psi powers—are treated as being of secondary importance. The following passage is one of the most famous from Paul's letters:

> Though I speak with the tongues of men and of angels, and have not charity, I am become as sounding brass, or a tinkling symbol. And though I have the gift of prophecy, and understand all mysteries, and all knowledge; and though I have all faith, so that I could remove mountains, and have not charity, I am nothing (1 Cor. 13:1-2).

This is perhaps the classic statement in the West about the relationship between the psychic and the spiritual. Similar statements have been made in Eastern traditions. Without charity, love, wisdom, or insight, psychic power, like any type of power, may become an obstacle or a danger to spiritual progress. This, of course, is in line with my argument. All along I have been stressing the need to discover the total pattern of psychospiritual development, and not to be concerned only with isolated anomalies for their own sake. This is, in fact, just what we mean by an *evolutionary* interpretation of psychic phenomena. What, I am asking, is the complete developmental picture of our inner potentials?

The supreme value, the guiding principle, for Paul is love. Now the remarkable thing about the near-death experience is that, in its most developed form, it expresses a pattern of development that culminates in the celebration of spiritual love. An NDE is not a single anomalous occurrence, but a complex of mutually enforcing experiences, a pattern with an apparent purpose. It frees one from the fear of death, awakens spiritual consciousness, enlarges one's sense of cosmic and human communion—as well as stimulating one's paranormal faculties. In particular, and in harmony with Paul, it typically involves one in an experience of total, all-embracing love. This focal experience of "unconditional love," noted by different researchers,[7] is what makes the NDE an especially apt model for interpreting Paul's conversion.

On "Weakness"

An oddity of Paul's personality is interesting in light of this hypothesis. Paul speaks of a certain "thorn in the flesh" (2 Cor. 12:7) that dogged him and that he asked the Lord to rid him of. His request was denied, but for a good reason. "For my strength is made perfect in weakness," the Lord said. "The Spirit too comes to help us in our weakness," Paul wrote in Romans (8:26). Jung has made a similar psychological point. Once we drop the delusion of the all-powerful ego, our unconscious healing powers are free to come to our aid. This may be how the NDE works—by forcing one to become receptive to the healing powers latent in the unconscious.

Paul traveled widely, knew hunger and solitude, had adventures at sea, was beaten and imprisoned. He probably spent much time hovering in states of consciousness on the verge of death. Thus he writes: "I have been sent to prison more often, and whipped so many times more, often almost to death" (2 Cor. 11:24-26). Paul may have had many visionary experiences, hovering for long periods of time on the threshold of alternate realities, his normal egocentric hold on himself continually weakened by these harrowing experiences.

The Problem of Sex

Paul made several remarks about sex and women that raise hackles in these post-Freudian times. Statements like "A woman who will not wear a veil ought to have her hair cut off'' (1 Cor. 11:6) won't find much favor today. "Better to marry than to burn," Paul also said, implying that sex is an evil we should minimize by containing it within married life. Wilhelm Reich regarded Paul as a bringer of the dreaded "armor" and "emotional plague." However, several things put Paul's attitude toward sex in perspective.

To begin with, Paul was probably reacting to the excesses of his day. Pagan antiquity knew depravity on a scale that dwarfs that of the modern world. Paul was troubled by debauchery in the Church; in particular, he was worried about incest in Corinth (1 Cor. 5). Historian Robin Fox Lane discusses the opulent, often decadent eroticism of pagan Rome and describes the Christian ideal of chaste sexual life as a defiant attempt at "living like angels."[8] Moreover, the first Christians lived in expectation of the world coming to an end. What then would be the point of procreating?

Paul also thought single life preferable to married life because it freed him for his mission. Marriage—normal, binding sexual relations —would only get in the way. There is a parallel with modern NDEers who find it hard to tolerate ordinary, less than divinely fulfilling, relationships after having glimpsed more sublime forms of love.

Finally, Paul's experience may have released a surplus of hypersexual or "kundalini" energy. Gopi Krishna has described the painful side of awakening this life force. Perhaps the "thorn in his flesh" was some physiological oddity aggravated by the ardors of repressing a powerfully awakened sexual vitality.

For a new, divinely inspired society to flourish, the energies of sex would have to be properly harnessed, properly redirected. Paul likened the Church to a single mystical body. This idea of a mystical group body bears on sex—or, rather, on fornication. Thus, in 2 Corinthians Paul says: "Your bodies are members making up the body of Christ" (6:11-22). Paul wanted to make sexual energy sacred, to use it to create a new type of collective spiritual organism.

A New Humanity

Is talk of the mystical body of the Church just a metaphor, or did Paul's experience lead him to believe in a new type of psychosocial organism? Paul believed in the possibility of a "new man." "If then," he writes in 2 Cor. 5:17, "any man be in Christ, he is a new creature: the former things have passed away: behold, all things are made new." And: "The first man is from the earth, earthy; the second man is the Lord from heaven" (1 Cor. 15:47). As we have borne the image of the earthly man, "we shall also bear the image of the heavenly man" (1 Cor. 15:49).

Paul understood this image or archetype of the new heavenly human from the model of the resurrection. Because of the resurrection, he knew that:

> [A]ll flesh is not the same flesh, but there is one flesh of men, and another flesh of beasts, and another flesh of birds, and another of fish. There are also heavenly bodies and earthly bodies (1 Cor. 15:39).

The resurrection thus forms the model for understanding a new mode of bodily organization. The new human being will have a new body. Speaking of the resurrection, Paul says:

> It is sown a perishable body, it is raised an imperishable body; it is sown in dishonor, it is raised in glory; it is sown in weakness, it is raised in power; it is sown a natural [psychikon] body, it is raised a spiritual [pneumatikon] body (1 Cor. 15:42-44).

In Paul's language, the new humanity is pneumatic-heavenly, not psychic-earthy. The psychic-earthy state is marked by internal conflict and slavery to the "body" of death (Rom. 7:25). The chief mark of the pneumatic-heavenly state is liberty—liberty from bodily death.

Paul's Damascus experience must have been the basis of his vision of the "new man." For in that vision he believed he saw the resurrected Christ. "He was seen by me also," he proclaimed (1 Cor. 15:8). It was this vision that formed the basis of his thinking about the general process of resurrection, the process of the Old Adam becoming the New Adam, of the earthy, psychologically bound individual evolving into the heavenly, spiritually free one.

In my view, Paul's visionary experience—its effects and aftereffects —was the empirical model of his eschatology: the model of his vision of humankind's evolutionary goal. The Damascus experience achieved two things: Paul came to believe he had direct evidence of the resurrection of Christ; and he experienced a kind of resurrection in himself. In short, Paul's archetypal near-death experience became for him a paradigm of the "new man."

Although he says he learned nothing from philosophy, Paul does quite a bit of speculating:

1) He extrapolates from his own visionary experience that the whole of creation is in the throes of rebirth.

> From the beginning till now the entire creation, as we know, has
> been groaning in one great act of giving birth; and not only crea-
> tion, but all of us who possess the firstfruits of the spirit, we too
> groan inwardly as we wait for our bodies to be set free (Rom.
> 8:21-34).

The whole universe is in process of giving birth to this new reality,
this new form of "glorified" embodied existence. In the near-death
experience, people also experience a "glorified" existence. Paul came
to believe that the "paradise" he glimpsed in his vision was the omega-
point toward which the whole creative process of the universe was
heading.

2) A second extrapolation is that Paul understood that the "resurrection" of the creation—the new age of a new pneumatic humanity—
had already begun. In his visions, our eyes are already beginning to
open, the signs and wonders of the new creation are already in our
midst. We have begun to enjoy the "firstfruits" of a new spiritual
order. So it may have seemed to the first converts. Miracles were
being performed. Gifts from heaven were being showered on earth.
For Paul the outpouring of Spirit, the "charisms" or gifts of the spirit
were evidence of these "firstfruits." They were the signs of a new
order of reality breaking in on the old.

The Rapture

The NDE model also sheds light on Paul's idea of the "rapture."
Paul describes what is to happen to the faithful on the Day of the Lord.
He wrote to the Corinthians:

> Behold, I tell you a mystery; we shall not all sleep, but we shall
> all change. In a moment, in the twinkling of an eye; for the trumpet
> will sound, and the dead will be raised imperishable (1 Cor. 15:51).

And this:

> For our citizenship is in heaven, from which also we eagerly wait
> for our Savior the Lord Jesus Christ; who will transform the body
> of our humble state into conformity with the body of his glory (Phil.
> 3:20-21).

But the most startling passage about the rapture is in 1 Thessalon-
ians 4:15-18:

> At the signal given by the voice of the Archangel and the trumpet
> of God, the Lord himself will come down from heaven; those who

have died in Christ will be the first to rise, and only after that shall
we who remain alive be taken up in the clouds, together with them,
to meet the Lord in the air.

How did Paul arrive at this idea of Endtime rapture? He may have
been thinking of Elijah (2 Kings 2:11) and Enoch (Gen. 5:24) who
were taken up into the presence of God without dying.

More vivid, I venture to say, was the memory of his own rapture
on the road to Damascus. His own out-of-body experience may well
have provided the empiricial model. If he could be raptured out of
his body in the twinkling of an eye, why not all the faithful on the
Day of the Lord?

Modern reports describe what out-of-body "rapture" is like: the
sudden sense of freedom, of being unconfined in space, of being elated
in ways that beggar description. Teresa of Avila, who had such experiences, described their irresistable power in her autobiography:

> [W]ith rapture . . . it comes like a strong, swift impulse, before
> your thought can forewarn you of it or you can do anything to help
> yourself; you see and feel this cloud, or this powerful eagle, rising
> and bearing you up with it on its wings.

Paul's rapture-fantasy may have been a spinoff from the memory of
his ecstatic out-of-body experiences. This psychic experience probably
shaped his view of the "last things." Christian ideas of the End take
on fresh meaning here. They seem like extensions and embroideries
of psychic experiences common to all of us.

Revisioning Paul

I have tried to reconstruct Paul's conversion experience by means
of the archetypal NDE. Paul saw his psychic experience as an encounter with the resurrected Christ. In so doing, he gave voice to
a model of the higher Self for much of the Western world that has
held up for two millennia.[9]

Christian history has two tendencies: One is to revert to legalism,
literalism, and fundamentalism. The other is to advance toward in-
clusion, dialogue, and universalism. When Paul said in Galatians: "No
more Jew or Gentile, no more slave and freeman, no more male and
female; you are all one in Christ" (3:28), he spoke in the spirit of
evolutionary catholicism. Faced with the need to overcome all that
divides the human family, our job today is to stress the inclusive trend
in the Pauline legacy.

On the other hand, it is also necessary to reject the exclusive trend. For example, modern society has inherited from Paul an antagonism to the feminine principle. John Dourley, a Catholic priest and Jungian therapist, has boldly addressed this problem in his book, *The Illness That We Are* (1984). Feminism, Marian visions, the revival of the Goddess—all these witness to a return of the repressed feminine. If contemporary believers want to carry on the work of evolutionary catholicism, if they hope to develop Paul's vision of the "new man," they will have to reintegrate the feminine. Paul's New Adam needs to embrace a New Eve. I will take up the problem of the "New Eve" again in some detail in Chapter 12.

I conclude this discussion of Paul with some considerations about conversion as a mystery. The Romans destroyed the Jewish temple in Jerusalem in 70 A.D.; the first community of Christians was thereby scattered. This community, which grew from the twelve disciples, knew Jesus personally and believed he was the Messiah. In accord with Jewish expectations, they awaited his Second Coming.

The Good News then spread among the dispersed Hellenized Jews. It was here in the wider pagan world that the historic form of Christianity took shape. This second Christianity—with Paul as the model convert—wasn't based on personal acquaintance with Jesus but on a psychic vision of Christ. The cosmic Christ, no longer the Jewish man-messiah, became the Savior-God, the life (*zoe*) and light (*phos*) of humanity (John 1:4).

The idea of a resurrected Savior God with whom initiates ritually unite was widespread in the Graeco-Roman mystery schools. For example, the Egyptians worshipped Osiris, also a resurrected God-man who inspired hope in believers. Paul adapted his Gospel to the form of a mystery which was familiar to the gentiles of the Mediterranean world. In this way, the failed messiah-ship of Jesus evolved into a world religion.

The psychology of the ancient mysteries—based on ritual union with the deity—overlaps with the psychology of Paul's conversion. I believe this inner psychic affinity explains why Christianity spread so easily in the Graeco-Roman world. Paul created a new form for an ancient experience. And we, too, can still respond to this ancient vision of a new humanity, for the same powers of transformation lie within us.

III
Psyche and Survival

The answer to human life is not to be found within the limits of human life.

C. G. Jung

In Part Two the God-Idea and the origins of Christianity were considered. The evidence indicated that a transcendent psi factor lay at the living core of religious experience.

In Part Three the focus is an attempt to rethink the prospects for an afterlife, to work out a new "survival" model. The previous section stressed a more intimate relation between God and humanity and spoke of their mutual need and cocreative partnership; Part Three suggests ways to overcome the dualism between this life and a possible life to come. As the divine needs the human to realize its goals—perhaps even to discover them—so the reality of an afterlife may best be proven by the creative manifestations in *this* life.

Skeptics delight in challenging us to face our illusions. For example, they say that belief in an afterlife is caused by psychological immaturity. (This was Morton Smith's way of dealing with belief in the resurrection of Jesus.)

Chapter 6 looks at the other side of the story and argues that there is a fear of life after death, which, on closer examination, turns out to be a fear of our own psychic depths. I try, in short, to unmask the motives for *disbelief* in an afterlife.

Because of the fear of life after death many, spellbound by modern science, refuse even to look at evidence suggestive of life after death. Scholars have reviewed that evidence, and I have no intention of going over old ground. Instead, I try to look at the evidence we have in a new way.

The gist of my view is this: Eastern and Western traditions speak of the spiritual body, a body of light, a subtle body. (My word is *imaginal* body.) I propose that we think of such a body as part of our evolutionary potential. In doing so, we shift the emphasis from evidence for life *after* death to evidence for extraordinary capacities observed *before* death. According to the survival model explored in Chapter 7, the ultimate experiment in survival research is focused on the here and now—in the liberation of earthly life.

6
Fear of Life after Death

Fear is the expectation of the unknown. We fear only the new,
and death is for us, the absolutely new and unknown.

Wilhelm Stekel

Talking about life after death with an educated person can be difficult.
"Let's admit," I might say, "that the prospect of death can be
depressing—even, on occasion, terrifying." My friend, who may be
a bright academic, nods in agreement.

"As it happens," I say, "I've looked into certain facts suggestive
of an afterlife."

"Facts?" my friend asks.

I reply that there is a significant literature dealing with evidence—
not necessarily proof—of life after death.

"Just think, if there *were* a life after death," I say, "we could go
on with the adventure of consciousness and evolution, the quest for
more knowledge and higher experiences. Wouldn't it be worth our
effort to look into the queer facts of apparitions, mediumistic phenomena, out-of-body experiences, reincarnation memories, and other
occurences that point to the possibility of an afterlife?"

"It might," answers my friend, joylessly.

My next move is to offer articles or books on the subject. "Read
this," I say, "and then we'll discuss."

However, the type of person I have in mind will come up with weak,
if not irrational, excuses for not reading the literature I place in his
or her hand. In one case, the reasoning ran, "It's only words on paper;
there's no reason to take any of it seriously." Another said he just
didn't have the time.

"You mean you can't find a few hours to read a book that might
change your basic outlook on life and death?" I ask, incredulous.

81

How strange that intelligent people should be not just indifferent but resistant to the prospect of an afterlife. It's as if there were a conspiracy against this information, a need to make it harmless, irrelevant, if possible, nonexistent. This resistance is notable, and I suspect it's part of a deep-seated fear of the irrational—a fear, in Jungian lingo, of the Shadow.

Of course, that isn't how the typical, educated believer in modern scientific materialism sees it. He or she will assume that people who believe in life after death are indulging in magical or wishful thinking. However, I think it can be shown that some people are as motivated to *disbelieve* in life after death as others are motivated to believe in it.

The Primitive Fear of the Dead

Sir James Frazer found that among tribal peoples "immortality has a certainty which the individual as little dreams of doubting as he doubts the reality of his conscious existence." Early people spontaneously believed in life after death. How come? Scientific materialists invoke wishful thinking as the explanation. With Freud, for instance, belief in God and immortality was a product of infantile wish-fulfillment, a symptom of neurotic rebellion against the harsh reality principle. Otto Rank maintained similarly that the fear of death inspires us to invent the idea of a double—that shadowy replica of ourselves said to survive in a phantom "next" or "other" world. In Rank's view, doubling the image of the self is a narcissistic denial of our personal extinction.[1]

Do these psychological explanations of belief in a life after death tally with the evidence of anthropology? Not really. The facts indicate that the first people feared not extinction, but beings from an after-death world; they feared not death but the dead themselves.

Frazer collected accounts from missionaries and anthropologists attesting to a primitive fear of the dead. Tribal peoples everywhere, in Melanesia, Polynesia, New Guinea, the Indian Archepelago, Asia, Africa, and North and South America, believed that the spirits of the dead were capable of inflicting all kinds of mischief on the living, the spirits of close relatives regarded as the most lethal.

While spirits were thought to give good counsel occasionally, for the most part native people viewed them with fear and apprehension.

The spirits were a constant but elusive source of harm, before which the living were driven to cringe, to beg for favors, to try to deceive or to coerce, because of their unseen power. To say, as psychologists like Otto Rank do, that belief in these powers is the product of narcissistic wish-fulfillment just doesn't ring true. If the unconscious were merely forging a dream world to placate the narcissistic ego, why would it not forge a more agreeable one?

Throughout the world, tribal people believed that during the time immediately after death, spirits hovered about their former earthly abodes and did the greatest harm at this time. For instance, among the Tarahumara Indians of Mexico, "a mother says to her dead infant, 'Now go away! Don't come back anymore, now that you are dead.' And the father says to the dead child: 'Don't come back to ask me to hold your hand. I shall not know you anymore.'"[2] Here the fear of the dead outweighed the usually strong bonds of parental love.

Frazer cites strategies for dealing with the dangers of departed souls. For example, tribal peoples often believed that a person's soul "sticks," as it were, to his or her personal belongings. Thus, one strategy was to destroy a dead man's house and personal effects. The Araucanian, Puelche, and Patagonian Indians of South America went a step beyond and wrecked a dead man's entire village. The economic effects of fear of the dead were plainly ruinous. Therefore, to say that belief in survival is "consoling" seems facile; it would have been a great deal more consoling *not* to believe in an afterlife.

The primitive fear of the dead and the enormous paranoia it presupposes is still part of the heritage of our collective psyche. Depth psychologists have shown that humans are walking psychic museums. Each of us carries inside the psychic archaeology of the race. The nameless terrors that plagued our ancestors have been repressed but not uprooted.

From the standpoint of our psychic evolution, the invention of scientific materialism was a powerful fetish for banishing, at least from our conscious minds, the primitive fear of hostile spirits. The primitive mind was hemmed in by a deep fear of the *other*. For instance, the age-old fear of the "evil eye" shows how disposed we are to project our dark impulses onto another agent of consciousness. Sartre has given us a modern analysis of the "evil eye" in his discussion of "the look.''[3] We fear that behind the physical eye there is an invisible subject of consciousness, which, like Medusa, threatens to turn us to stone or make us into a mere thing.

In this context, it is easy to understand the appeal of scientific materialism. A materialist belief system deanimates nature, wiping out mind, soul, and consciousness by reducing them to mere by-products of biochemical reactions, which are doomed to annihilation with the death of the body. Thus science makes our fear of the other go away. There's nothing in the dark to frighten us, science reassures us—no disembodied souls out there with uncanny powers to enchant, glamorize, or spy on us; no spirits with power to inflict mischief on us. Annihilation is the ultimate talisman against the evil eye—against the fear of the objectifying consciousness of the other.

The Depths of Hades

The pagan conception of life after death was rooted in the primal fear of the dead. In classical times, however, fear of the dead shifted to fear of an unappealing form of life after death. Ancient writings amply attest to this. The most famous example is from Homer's *Odyssey*. During Odysseus's descent into Hades, Achilles says to Odysseus: ''Better by far to remain on earth the thrall of another . . . rather than reign sole king in the realm of bodiless phantoms'' (11.488). Likewise, the poet Anacreon wrote: ''Death is too terrible. Frightening are the depths of Hades.'' The Greeks were at home in the daylight; nighttime made them uneasy.

We might best picture Hades as a gloomy altered state of consciousness, a prolonged nightmare, or aimless out-of-body wandering. Hades was, without question, the locale for a type of life after death, but an unpleasant ''life'' of servitude to dark, inscrutable powers—powers moderns experience through the revelations of art, drugs, and psychosis.

This gloomy idea of death was destined to evolve. With the philosophy of Plato and the Mysteries of Eleusis, a more positive conception of the afterlife emerged among the ancient Greeks, although the fear of Hades still dominated the popular mind.

The Greek philosopher who did much to fight the fear of life after death was Epicurus (341-270 B.C.). Epicurus used the materialism of Democritus to argue the case for the soul's dissolution at death. Epicurus is instructive in the present discussion, because he was clearly motivated to disbelieve in a life after death. Seen as a benefactor of humankind, he espoused a philosophy that was one of the most popular in the ancient world. He was thought of as a healer and professed a therapeutic philosophy. What did he heal? According to Lucretius, Epicurus freed the human race from the fear of life after death—the "dread of Acheron [the river of death] . . . troubling as it does the life of man from its innermost depths." Materialism, and the denial of life after death in Epicurean philosophy, freed people from the anxiety that comes from having to face the "innermost depths" of human life. I take these "innermost depths" to be the dark side of the unconscious, thought by the ancients to be what may await us in the afterlife.

The case of Epicureanism sheds light on the motives behind the rise of classical materialism. Two things are evident in the rise of this worldview, though they seem contradictory. On one hand, ancient materialism was a weapon for avoiding contact with the dark side of the afterlife—which we can take to include Jung's Shadow. (Hades, of course, is the preeminent domain of shades and shadows.) On the other hand, ancient materialism was an attempt to found a new religion, one which venerated the eternal character of matter. The atoms of Democritus have the defining feature of the gods, deathlessness.

The religious nature of classical materialism is clear from the origins of Greek natural philosophy. Starting with Thales, the early Greek thinkers sought to discover the *arche*—the source, origin, or principle of all things. Whether the defining principle was postulated as water (Thales), air (Anaximenes), fire (Heraclitus), the boundless (Anaximander), or atoms (Democritus), the quest was in essence for the *arche* of immortal power once enjoyed by the gods. Greek natural philosophy—from which came modern physics—moved from concern with personal immortality to hopes of capturing the timeless principles of nature.

Thus the origins of scientific materialism were rooted in a quest for the sacred. The *arche* of the physicists was a sublimation of *theos*—the divine and godlike. Plato's Ideas mediate between the cosmic *arche* of physics and the *psyche* of animism. In modern times, Einstein has expressed this same reverence for the cosmic mystery— the sacred dimension of the world studied by science.

By and large, however, modern science is phobic about any lingering traces of the sacred, the uncanny, or the numinous. Natural science is anxious to eliminate anything that hints of the shadowy "inner depths" that so frightened Lucretius. It would be sacrilege to destroy the unity of science by validating alien forces like mind and soul, for one might then be exposed to a Lucretian fear of the inner depths.

To Sleep, Perchance to Dream?

Human fears are historically shaped. The idea of life after death underwent a positive transformation with the Christian belief in the resurrection. Yet while opening the Western imagination to death's higher possibilities, renewed belief in the afterlife also raised the specter of guilt, hell, and damnation. There are good reasons why educated people in Western culture associate belief in life after death with oppressive institutions and cruel practices.

Religion has retarded the evolution of Western science, as Andrew Dickson White's classic *A History of the Warfare of Science with Theology in Christendom* makes clear in detail. Eastern ideas of karma, caste, and reincarnation raise similar misgivings. To entertain belief in life after death is to open an unpleasant can of worms: hell, devils, witchcraft, witch-hunting, hags, incubi, demons, and much more that many regard as superstitious, irrational, or reactionary.

A universe in which life after death is a fact would be a universe filled with unknown and possibly frightening entities and forces. If there were reason to believe in an afterlife, reports of demonic possession, hauntings, and other eerie phenomena could no longer be dismissed out of hand. I suspect that a fear of uncanny supernatural forces is alive and well in the unconscious of many contemporary human beings. The study of dreams and the behavior of psychotics shows how close the "shades" of the unconscious are to our mental life. The idea of life after death might stir up all kinds of fears in us; hence the appeal of a materialist paradigm, which shields us from such fears.

The spell of the paradigm prevents many from even considering the possibility of life after death. People invest their inner security in scientific materialism. Hints of psychic anomaly might awaken the Lucretian dread of Acheron. Groups like the Committee for the Scientific Investigation of Claims of the Paranormal (the infamous CSICOP), one begins to wonder, may be as motivated to believe in materialism as any Bible thumper is motivated to believe in heaven or the millennium.

The Prospect of an Afterlife

Fear of judgment, guilt, and karmic retribution. If we had reason to believe in a life after death, many of us might fear God, hell, or judgment. The prospect of an afterlife awakens ideas of sin, guilt, pollution, defilement, punishment, purification, and other concepts many people view as unsavory and disturbing. Like some genial exponents of "new age" thought, scientific rationalists are anxious to rid the world of ideas like guilt and hell. Thus in the interest of peace of mind, it serves some people's purpose to disbelieve in the afterlife.

Plato says in the *Phaedo* that the wicked would welcome death if it were extinction, for then they wouldn't have to worry about the consequences of their deeds. Likewise, if there were no reincarnation, they would not have to worry about striving for self-perfection from life to life. After all, not many of us relish forever struggling with our weaknesses. Thus, moral and spiritual laziness are also good motives for disbelieving in an afterlife.

Fear of enlightenment. According to *The Tibetan Book of the Dead* (as well as the reports of those who have had near-death experiences), at the moment of death we meet a dazzling, awe inspiring light. In the Tibetan tradition, this light is said to be profoundly disorienting. In the case of the average human being the "clear light" of death is just one more confusing experience on the way to reincarnation. Most of us are not spiritually ready to recognize the nature of this light, nor to merge with it and thus attain liberation from the realms of conditioned existence.

Now suppose that reincarnation were a fact. In that case, we might unconsciously remember past experiences of this light. The most unprepared for enlightenment, for merging with the light, might recoil from such meetings, which remind them of past failures to achieve enlightenment. The spiritually unprepared might actually be motivated to disbelieve in life after death. Extinction would be preferable, just as dreamless sleep is preferable to nightmare.

Fear of helplessness in a strange environment. The idea of having to carry on in a place where one's usual status, cognitive skills, and material possessions are useless is unsettling. In an afterworld, we would also need totally different internal skills.

If Plato is right, we bring nothing with us to the next world but our *paidea*—our education. People uneasy about their spiritual education might fear life after death; overly rational types would be reluctant to find themselves in a place where they had to rely on nonrational skills. The more rule-bound the mentality, the less cordially disposed one might be to the prospect of afterdeath.

Pessimism and the fear of life after death. The philosopher C. D. Broad once said he would be more annoyed than surprised if he found himself conscious after death. Life after death isn't likely to be much better than life before death, said Broad. And it might be worse. Broad knew that belief in an afterlife is logically independent of belief in God. In other words, there might be an afterlife but no God. We might find ourselves after death in a godless world where evil is as powerful as ever. Hence, a pessimist might fear life after death more than total annihilation. Extinction has its virtues. We would at least not be conscious and therefore not aware of moral or physical pain.

Past Lives, Present Meanings

Many people today are talking about their past lives. The interest, in most cases, has nothing to do with trying to authenticate memories of past lives. Past life lovers do not pore over the learned tomes of Dr. Ian Stevenson. From what I have been able to observe, most aren't searching for a rational foundation for their belief.

Something else seems to be happening. The current interest in past lives is, I think, part of a growing *myth* of reincarnation, myth that means different things to different people. For many the search for past lives is a search for present meanings. In other words, the "past lives" people say they have lived may really represent fragments of themselves, the "subselves" they need to bring to awareness in order to become more whole. The search for evidence, the slow procedure of testing hypotheses, only impedes the myth-making process for such people.

For this kind of seeker, then, failure to consider evidence isn't due to fear of life after death but to taking life after death for granted. They regard the scientific exploration of life after death as inferior to the more urgent task of making sense of their lives. Talk of "proof" only paralyzes the mythic imagination. I am tempted to conclude that what many want is not the assurance of an afterlife but the assurance that their present lives are meaningful.

A New Survival Paradigm

I have examined some motives for disbelieving in life after death and have shown that even believers may be motivated not to examine the question too critically. Both points of view can be obstacles to getting at the truth about an afterlife.

I want to turn now to some constructive thoughts about survival research. I suggest that we look at the afterlife from an evolutionary perspective. The usual assumption is that we either survive or do not survive death. If we adopt an evolutionary perspective, we have to assume that life and human consciousness have emerged over time. It follows that the afterlife must also either have emerged in the past or be emerging presently. The view I would like to suggest is that the conditions of the afterlife may still be emerging.

One advantage of this view is that the ambiguity and incompleteness of survival evidence makes more sense; the incomplete evidence then reflects the incomplete evolution of afterlife mechanisms. Suppose, for instance, that not all of us survive, or that some people survive for a brief time, or survive in different, dissociated, fragmentary ways. Fragmentary forms of survival might be the cause of the uneven, fragmentary quality of survival evidence.

Are we, in fact, still evolving the "organs" of our immortality? We don't really know the evolutionary implications of such things as mediumistic transports, near-death visions, out-of-body travels, apparitions, poltergeists, miracles of saints and avatars, and so on. Such phenomena may be only the beginning of a groping evolutionary process. We know that scientific anomalies are often signals of major paradigm shifts. We should consider the possibility that psychic anomalies point to other, still unfinished, stages of human evolution.

Would-be builders of a new death paradigm could investigate an assortment of death related psychic anomalies, ranging from telekinetic displacement of physical objects at the moment of death to transcendental deathbed visions. Though there are quite a few puzzling things about death, most scientists sweep them under the rug. Mainline science, as we've noted, is seldom comfortable with the strangeness of death, and survival research is a neglected branch of study, even among parapsychologists. In my view, we need a new approach to the whole survival question.

To clarify this point further, consider three types of afterlife research. The new paradigm that I see emerging would combine all three approaches.

First is the *trace* model. Reincarnation memories, apparitions, out-of-body experiences, mediumistic claims, electronic voice phenomena, photographs of spirits, and so forth allow the living to capture a trace of a deceased human being. From such traces, people are led to believe that some individuals have survived the death of their bodies.

The trace model has problems. For instance, where does the trace come from? Is it from the deceased person, or is it, as some say, a psi-mediated phantom, engineered into existence by the subliminal mind? The trace model has often proven suggestive, but so far it remains inconclusive. However, the material seems to warrant further investigation. People who have had real encounters with ghostly entities respect their puzzling nature.

A second, more direct approach to survival research, is called *state-specific*. The near-death experience is a case in point. Say a person has a certain kind of extraordinary experience that leaves him or her with a dramatic sense of conviction, a noetic feeling of certitude. The result is that the person becomes *subjectively* convinced of the reality of an afterlife. Such experiences can change people utterly, often in interesting ways.

This model might be called "gnostic." Afterdeath gnosis might come through near-death as well as other transformative experiences, such as deep meditation, ecstatic lovemaking, UFO encounters, great dreams, psychoactive drugs, trance-dancing, collective apparitions, channelling, and so forth. (See Chapter 13 for further discussion of current patterns of transformative experience.) The result of such encounters is that a person feels sure he or she has contacted something otherworldly.

By itself the gnostic or state-specific model isn't sufficiently convincing. It needs to be supplemented by the trace model. To avoid delusion and psychic inflation, state-specific "knowledge" needs, if possible, to be confirmed by objective fact. But even this combination of approaches may prove insufficient. They stand to gain from being supplemented by a third approach to survival evidence I call the *resurrection* model.

According to this model, the ordinary living human body has a potential to evolve into a spiritual body. According to this hypothesis, human bodies have hidden potentials for transmutation. The Christian tradition thinks of this transmutation in religious terms. The resurrection model, which stresses the potential to mutate, is an evolutionary model of survival. Religion here foreshadows a possible natural development.

Is there any evidence for this model? For Christians the best "evidence" is the resurrection of Jesus. Jesus also predicted people would come after him and do greater works than he did. There would come in his place a Comforter—a Healing Spirit. And Jesus was right about the prodigies to come. To cite only one source, the annals of the Catholic Church contain impressive documentation of exotic marvels of human potential. These marvels or miracle data may be interpreted as support for the resurrection model. They tell us something about the possible evolution of the human species. Levitation, stigmata, healings, materialization, bodily incorruption, inedia (living without food), and other extraordinary phenomena have been documented.[4] It is possible to see them all as fragmentary evidence for the reality of our evolving spiritual bodies.

Why are these phenomena important for survival research? In the first place, if valid, they demonstrate the reality of agencies that operate independently of the known laws of physics. They point to the existence of a different physics, a physics of the creative spirit. From this point of view, the miracle data are evidence for partial and fleeting "resurrections," for remarkable elevations of human bodily function.

The survival paradigm I am proposing would make use of all three models: trace, state-specific, and resurrection. All three have something to offer, and each is needed to complement and complete the others.

The trace model has left researchers with a mass of puzzling facts, whose main effect is to startle people into a sense of extraordinary possibilities. The value of studying the elusive traces of deceased persons is to open people's minds to ideas that the dominant paradigm forbids.

But theory is not enough. As human beings, we need to feel our truths, as well as think them. The gnostic model of survival research is a route to subjective truth. (Some philosophers might deny there is such a thing as "subjective truth"; but this position assumes an impractically narrow definition of truth.)

I think we are fortunate if we have an experience that fills us with confidence about an afterlife. An out-of-body experience on the brink of death, an abduction by otherworldly beings, a visionary encounter with the Virgin Mary—such experiences, so often reported today, may be telling us something about the afterlife. In such experiences, the "afterlife world" envelops and at points intersects with this life. Certain types of extraordinary encounters might thus be windows into the "other world."

As people share their otherworld experiences, they will build a new consensus. The creation of this new consensus may have implications for evolution. For if a need coalesces into a group dynamic, if a new "morphogenetic field" of intentions solidifies, some of the habits or laws of nature may be broken or changed, thus making new forms of life possible. If a new consensus of state-specific believers agree that there is an afterlife, nature may respond and create a new form of life after life.

I said that the state-specific approach to survival offers only subjective truth. But there is another type of truth. *Verum et factum convertuntur* is Vico's formula for historical or evolutionary truth: what is true and what we make true are one and the same.[5] Adopting a Vichian model of truth makes it possible to look at the afterlife question in a new way. For the afterlife to *be true,* according to this model, we would have to *make it true.* This is a model of creative truth I have already mentioned and return to in the following pages.

At this point the resurrection model becomes significant. In this model, the concept of the "afterlife" or "next life" actually refers to certain extreme potentials latent in *present life.* The accent is not on immortality but on resurrection—on the transformation of the body. In this practical, experimental model, the afterlife becomes part of the evolutionary potential of this life, and the only way to know it is true is to make it true.

But how? One way is to transcend the limiting principles of bodily existence. Extraordinary saintly phenomena—levitation, inedia, hyperthermia, materialization, bilocation, and the like—transcend the limiting principles of bodily function and, in so doing, point to possible forms of function in future humanity.

According to the resurrection model of survival research, then, the embodied world will become the new field for "afterlife" studies. It is here on earth that humanity must search for the first signs of the afterlife. The most suggestive signs are the psychophysical anomalies called "miracles." When Joseph of Copertino levitates, or Padre Pio produces the stigmata, or Therese Neumann stops eating and drinking for long periods of time,[6] physical existence may be in the process of being transmuted into forms that increasingly resemble a spiritual afterlife. As Copertino's body is literally drawn upward toward heaven, it looks as if matter is gradually becoming transparent to the aspirations of spirit.

But these are spectacular examples. The resurrection model also applies to aspects of people's everyday lives. The concrete "resurrection" of the individual on earth would also be part of this experiment. Every life saved, liberated, or enhanced adds to the building of the new earth. In the transformation of earthly existence the afterlife would be *proven*—in the Italian sense of *provare*, experienced.

Let me state my view as bluntly as I can. The best way to prove life after death is to bring "heaven" down to earth. C. D. Broad had a point. People need assurance that the prospect of a future life is desirable. The only cure for Broad's pessimism is a taste of heaven on earth.

In this ecological age, this idea of life after death is the only one that is morally justifiable. The dream of paradise is really a dream of the earth. The first step toward creating heaven on earth is to heal the ecology of the planet. A healed earth would be a foretaste of paradise. (*Paradise*—a Persian word for "garden.") Once humans begin to transform the planet into a garden—into a place increasingly akin to paradise—we will be taking steps toward materializing the "afterlife" here and now. By restoring the beauty of the planet and liberating the splendor of earthly life, we will move toward overcoming the dualisms that have plagued humanity since the dawn of consciousness: the dualism of heaven and earth, eternity and time, divine and human.

What higher duty than to try to create paradise on earth? Humanity's diabolical genius for causing pain and ugliness on earth gives grounds for hope in the resurrection model. For we might marshal the same energies of destruction to fashion paradise on earth. But to create paradise on earth would call for a revolution in metaphysics. Our ideas of God, truth, value, work, power, and human relations will have to change radically.

Is there an afterlife? Let us make it so by creating paradise now.

7
Evolution, Survival, and the Imaginal Life

The world of imagination is the world of eternity. It is the divine bosom into which we shall all go after the death of the vegetative body.

William Blake

The average educated person today finds it difficult to accept the idea of an afterlife. One reason is the prevailing scientific materialism—the view that mental life and personality are so closely tied to the body as to make the idea of an afterlife impossible. But the metaphysical presumption that an afterlife is impossible ought not to sway us. The arguments that identify mind and brain are by no means conclusive, and there are enough facts to challenge most of our ideas on the mind-body relation.[1]

It has also been said that the wish for an afterlife is a kind of betrayal of our earthly duties. For example, Nietzsche makes his Zarathustra say:

> Remain faithful to the earth, and do not believe those who speak to you of otherworldly hopes! Poison-mixers are they, whether they know it or not. Despisers of life are they, decaying and poisoned themselves.

Is there really a contradiction between belief in a future life and full appreciation of our present life? It's true, of course, that belief in an afterlife has often been used to oppress people. For example, the doctrine of reincarnation has bolstered an unfair caste system, while the Church has exploited the fear of hell and purgatory.

To deal with this objection, it is necessary to distinguish between belief in an afterlife and the cultural form the belief takes. Individuals do not have to commit themselves to any religious form of the doctrine of a future life; belief in an afterlife can be perfectly compatible with passionate fidelity to the goods of this life. There are, in fact, reasons why I think contemporary people should be open to the survival hypothesis.

The Survival Hypothesis

Repression of the immortality instinct. To begin with, the modern view that death ends life is at odds with the instincts of nature. The philosopher Henri Bergson once wrote about the awareness of death and the power of the imagination:

> The certainty of death, arising at the same time as reflexion in a world of living creatures constructed to think only of living, runs counter to nature's intention. Nature, then, looks as if she is going to stumble over the obstacle which she has placed on her own path. But she recovers herself at once. To the idea of inevitable death she opposes the image of a continuation of life after death.[2]

Thus, according to Bergson, there is a biological need for images of continuity of life after death. Jung also argued that we need a myth of death that confirms humanity's instinct to live. One might almost speak of an instinct to believe in immortality. Spinoza was probably right when he said it was unwise to meditate on death. The healthy thing is to meditate on life, to imagine life after life. If it's healthy to wish to live well and long, why shouldn't it be healthy to wish to survive death? Scientific attempts to retard aging, even cryonics, are acceptable to the modern mind. Why should research on the afterlife be an unworthy or quixotic pursuit? Why, in general, should people repress the need to believe in immortality?

The need for images of transcendence. Judging by world mythology, people in all cultures produced images of other worlds and afterlives. Belief in such things is a universal psychic fact, part of the spiritual heritage of humankind. Neanderthals buried their dead and probably believed in a life after death. Cultures have spontaneously formed images of transcendent life: reincarnation, Platonic immortality, biblical resurrection. Relative to the mass of human experience, the modern acceptance of death as extinction seems anomalous.

The political fallout of repressing the immortality instinct. If biologically (Bergson) and psycho-mythically (Jung) people are disposed to believe in an afterlife, then a culture (such as the modern one) that represses this belief might suffer as a consequence. Writers like Miguel de Unamuno, Norman O. Brown, and Ernest Becker have argued that the inability to cope with death deforms humanity's capacity to live.

For Unamuno the specter of annihilation creates a terrible thirst to "singularize" oneself, to stand out at all costs and to count in the great scheme of things.[3] Becker sees in the denial of death the roots of a fanatical quest for power and, with Unamuno, a way to compensate for feelings of impotence in the face of death.[4] Brown ties repression of the idea of death to repression of the body, a procedure that deters people from full contact with life.[5] Afraid of death, they hold back from life. To free themselves from this crippling fear—to live their lives fully—people need a vision of a life beyond. Belief in a life beyond is therefore in the interests of life here and now.

A moral consideration. There is another reason moderns should be receptive to the afterlife hypothesis: it seems morally callous not to be. Looking at history, it is clear that great numbers of human lives are regularly thwarted, botched, ruined, and cruelly aborted. Hegel spoke of the victim—the most common type in the cast of characters in the drama of history. Very few lives are well spent, very few fully realized.

An afterlife that allows people to carry on in hopes of unraveling the tangle of life's ills ought to be a welcome prospect. To ignore, in the face of suggestive evidence, the possibility of continued life implies a readiness to tolerate without protest an enormous amount of unjustified suffering.[6] A worldview that tries to deal with the moral monstrosity of ordinary history seems more humane.

Another moral point is raised by Plato in the *Phaedo.* Disbelief in an afterlife frees people from fear of the consequences of their actions, and makes them more cynical and thoughtless than they already are. By contrast, belief in an afterlife might be an incentive for individuals to perfect themselves morally. For if we survive death, we will have to deal with the consequences of our actions.

The historic task of psychical research. Psychical research originally sought to enlist science to investigate one of the great mysteries of religion and philosophy: the nature of the soul. The nature of the soul (or Self) is a problem shared by all religions and philosophies. By applying rational skills to something that touches on the soul, humanity moves toward healing a deep fracture in its being.

Nor has the research been without results. A large quantity of data on survival has been amassed. Experts who study the evidence find it either tantalizingly suggestive, as did William James, Henry Sidgwick, C. D. Broad, and Alan Gauld, or convincing, as did Frederic Myers, James Hyslop, Mrs. Henry Sidgwick, and C. J. Ducasse.

There are, then, psychological, spiritual, political, moral, and scientific reasons why contemporary people should at least be receptive to evidence—even if it isn't conclusive—that supports the belief in an afterlife.

Survival and Evolution

The topic of this chapter is the possible connection between evolution and the survival of bodily death. If biologist Rupert Sheldrake is right that "the universe of the new cosmology is an evolving organism,"[7] if, in short, humanity inhabits an evolving universe, then postmortem survivability must, like all natural functions, be a product of evolution. This chapter looks, therefore, at the survival problem from an evolutionary perspective.

At first glance this approach may seem unpromising. After all, it was Darwin's theory of evolution that provoked the crisis of faith in the nineteenth century, driving the founders of psychical research to look into the strange and sometimes unsavory world of spiritualist phenomena in hopes of gaining an empirical foothold on the ancient soul riddle. Darwin's evolution clashed with the biblical view of creation, making the idea of an immortal soul implausible.

Two points can be raised about this. First, a theory that undercuts a literal interpretation of the Bible doesn't necessarily undercut the notion of survival. Belief in an afterlife is logically independent of belief in *any* religion. So, for example, it may be that there is no God, yet some human beings may survive bodily death. The converse is also possible. God may exist, but none of God's creatures may survive the dissolution of their bodies.

Second, non-Darwinian theories of evolution are possible, theories less remorselessly mechanistic, more compatible with ideas of survival. The fact is that at least two of the leading ideas of Darwin's

theory—gradualism and the role of randomness in natural selection—
are increasingly under attack.[8]

Afterdeath survival may be a byproduct of organic evolution, a fact
independent of religious belief. Scientific understanding of evolution
is far from complete; evolutionary biology is rife with puzzles, if not
mysteries and anomalies—not least among them the evidence for psi
and the facts suggestive of life after death.

Strictly speaking, evolution is *about* survival. The incredible variety
of living forms display an astonishing ingenuity for overcoming
obstacles to life. *Survival* is indeed an apt word. It derives from the
French *survivre,* which literally means "to live beyond." The essence
of living organisms is to "survive," that is, to "live beyond"
themselves. The simplest example is the replication of DNA, the du-
plication of the cell.

Biologists know of no limits to the forms life may take. This seems
especially so if life is thought of as a category of experience, not just
as a physicochemical mechanism. If life or the "basic stuff of the
world" is a category of "creative experience," as the process philosopher David Ray Griffin says, and if life is something essentially
self-transcending,[9] then the notion of creatures evolving beyond the
limits of bodily existence seems less implausible. I see nothing self-
contradictory in the notion that life has the capacity to develop forms
that somehow transcend ordinary bodily death. Henri Bergson
ruminated on the meaning of evolution in his *Creative Evolution:*

> All the living hold together, and all yield to the same tremendous
> push. The animal takes its stand on the plant, man bestrides animal-
> ity, and the whole of humanity, in space and time, is one immense
> army galloping beside and before and behind each of us in an over-
> whelming charge able to beat down every resistance and clear the
> most formidable obstacles, perhaps even death.

Alfred Russell Wallace, recognized with Darwin as the cofounder
of the modern theory of evolution, apparently had no difficulty in
reconciling evolution with the belief in life after death. Wallace, who
claims to have been "beaten by the facts," was an avowed spiritualist.
Although he obviously believed in the value of natural selection, he
also held that some puzzling phenomena of evolution might be explained by spiritual principles. Wallace was receptive to psi phenomena and to evidence for an afterlife, and he was aware of the limita-

tions of natural selection. As such he was a forerunner of the survival hypothesis viewed from an evolutionary perspective. Predictably, most modern scientists consider Wallace's interest in psi a blot on his reputation.

What Survives?

Nevertheless, there are difficulties to be considered. For example, from the biological perspective, particular organisms seem to play an inferior role to the needs of the species as a whole. Schopenhauer implied this when he wrote a famous essay on the metaphysics of the sexes, stressing the inevitable conflict between individual personality and the mechanism of sexual reproduction.[10] Romantic love, for Schopenhauer, was merely nature's trick for perpetuating the species. Similar ideas have been updated scientifically in the idea of "selfish genes."[11] Life, in short, seems to be a mechanism for replicating types, not individuals—species, not personalities.

Everything happens as if the fate of the individual were subordinate to the survival of the species, the collective entity. Viewed this way, survival is accomplished through the species itself. The survival of the individual, understood as the carrier of the "immortal" genes, would then be redundant: in other words, nature has already arranged for our "survival" by safeguarding the perpetuity of the species.

There are several ways to blunt the force of this objection. A critical step in this counter-argument would be to focus on the emergence of a rich inner life in some living form of nature. For the sake of argument, it is possible to stipulate that a critical mass of internal cohesiveness and autonomy is necessary for survival to occur. This critical mass would be a precondition for overcoming nature's bias against individuals. Now, however, the problem arises of determining the critical mass. What degree of complexity, cohesiveness, and autonomy is necessary before nature begins to ally itself with the transcendent needs of individuals?

Do apes, dogs, birds, rats, flies survive bodily death? There is little to say about this empirically, except that there is some evidence for animal apparitions and animal psi. Perhaps there are degrees and varieties of survival in the nonhuman kingdom as there may be in the human. Consider the following possibilites.

Survival may occur only among *some* human beings, as taught by the Chinese text *The Secret of the Golden Flower*.[12] Survival may also last for only a few seconds, or for centuries, or in a timeless way as Plato or Plotinus speculated.[13] Some people may survive unconsciously, perhaps in a form of dreamless sleep; some as vacuous Homeric-type eidola (images); some as C. D. Broad's "psi factors" or W. Whately Carington's "psychons"; some as memory systems revived through reincarnation or as localized fields such as William Roll theorizes;[14] some as solipsistic dreams; or some as societies of souls linked together by mutual fears or affections in a world of telepathic hallucinations such as H. H. Price envisioned.[15] If these possibilities apply to human afterlife, similar varieties in forms of survival may exist across the whole of living nature.

From this base a speculative question arises. At what point in the mental life of an organism does survival become interesting enough to be desirable? The passage quoted from Bergson's *Creative Evolution* suggests one line of speculation. Perhaps when consciousness is rich enough to foresee the inevitability of death, as it is with human beings, two things happen: First, the need to survive death is intensified, which may accelerate the development of forms of consciousness *capable* of surviving death.

Second, given a sufficiently rich consciousness, a system of memories, a clear self-identity, and a vivid imaginal life might all come into play. When consciousness became rich enough in this sense, human beings may have regarded survival as "desirable." Richness of consciousness then promoted social life, and social life created opportunities for further growth, greater learning, communal memories, and shared aspirations. All these, in my opinion, constitute circumstances that made the idea of an afterlife meaningful and worthwhile. They might also be the conditions required by nature to evolve the vehicle of an afterlife.

Another question comes up when survival is thought of in relation to evolution. Is our capacity for survival a fully accomplished fact or may it yet be something in the making? I have already pointed out the different senses, often fragmentary and incomplete, in which survival may take place.

Some Taoists think that only spiritually evolved people survive bodily death. Spiritualists say that some deceased souls—particularly the ones that haunt the living—aren't fully conscious of having "passed over." The Greek idea of Hades may symbolize the unfinished work of afterlife evolution; in Homer's world, dead souls are listless, shadowy remnants of what they once were. Only under special conditions, such as after blood libations or animal sacrifices, may a shade revive and recapture its former fullness of selfhood. Perhaps there are souls waiting in some Hades of half-realized potential for conditions to allow their full afterlife awakening.

So it is possible that living creatures survive in different ways, depending perhaps on the richness and integrity of their level of consciousness achieved at the time of death. Development may continue after death, a notion implied by the Catholic doctrine of purgatory. In purgatory, souls are purged of their sins in preparation for union with God; purgatory thus implies a process of growth and development.

Another Catholic practice is saying Mass for the dead. This implies that the community of souls is larger than the community of the living. If the living and the dead are part of the same community of souls, it follows that the fate of the dead may still be open to influence from the living. Thus, as humanity evolves toward the future, it may, in a sense, be changing the past. A living man may help his deceased father, and the future of the living may be shaped by forces yet unborn. The afterworld need not be a static thing but can be instead an evolving matrix. The possibilities are many, and the incomplete evidence for survival may reflect the incompleteness of the survival process itself.

The Imaginal Life

I want next to bring in the concept of imaginal life. From the amoeba to *Homo sapiens,* each new form of life evolves within some niche of the terrestrial world. But humans in their "afterlife" state are a form of life that may prosper beyond the terrestrial, indeed, beyond the physical environment. Evolution requires that this new form of life be situated in a world or environment within which it may unfold. I propose as a candidate for this ultra-terrestrial niche the imaginal world: a zone of being whose furniture is crafted on the lathe of the creative psyche.

By *imaginal environment* I mean the human internal environment, made up of image. I define *image* as a form of consciousness. Images are not exclusively visual; they occur in all sensory modes. Whatever I am conscious of is an image; even abstract concepts have their imaginal components, to the extent that they have form. This immediately experienced world of imagery may be the evolutionary niche of postmortem humanity.

Human beings are amphibious; they inhabit both physical and mental worlds.[16] In their amphibious lives, humans oscillate from immediate sensory experience to memory, reflection, dream, reverie, fantasy, or hallucination. As long as humans are embodied, they are more or less anchored in the world of sensory reality.

The question now arises whether humanity will ever be *totally* disencumbered from sensory reality and thus free to explore a purely imaginal sphere of being? To answer this question, it is necessary to look at the general function of psi in nature.

All organic capacities in living nature serve a function. The function of the eye is to detect light and orient the organism to a spatial environment. The function of the ear is to detect sound and also orient the organism to the environment. And so on for every organic capacity.

It is different with human psychic abilities. Psi, unlike normal organic capacities, is nonspecific in the way it relates to the environment. Psi doesn't function with respect to any one particular aspect of the environment—light, sound, or olfactory stimuli. Secondly, in most organisms, psi behaves as a nascent, marginal, sporadic, unreliable function. The possible exceptions are saints, yogis, shamans, mediums, and other rare types who seem to exercise their psi powers more copiously and more reliably.

Psi doesn't seem to help us interact with the physical environment in any obvious or routine way. On the other hand, I don't doubt that psi plays some role in everyday life; what I doubt is that psi helps us adapt to the physical environment in a *reliable* way. The sensorimotor apparatus has clearly evolved for that purpose. If then the "extra" sensorimotor apparatus is not there to help us adapt to the external environment, what is its function?

Frederic Myers has suggested that psi's function is not to serve us in the terrestrial environment; its real purpose is to adapt us to the afterlife environment:

> Man is in course of evolution; and the most pregnant hint which these nascent experiments have yet given him is that it may be in his power to hasten his own evolution in ways previously unknown. . . . The point from which we started was an analysis of the latent faculties of man. The point toward which our argument has car-

ried us is the existence of a spiritual environment in which those faculties operate.[17]

The purpose or function of psi—of what Myers calls the "latent faculties"—would be to enable us to inhabit a "spiritual" or what I'm calling an imaginal environment. In a well-known paper, Price described what he called the "imagy" world we humans might inhabit if we survived the death of our bodies. The imagy (or imaginal) afterlife-world would be a kind of dreamworld.

The interesting thing about the spiritual or imaginal environment is that human beings themselves help create and give it form. This may be a refinement of what normally occurs in nature. Richard Lewontin comments on the active role of the organism in creating its own environment:

> Organisms do not experience environments passively: they create and define the environments in which they live. Trees remake the soil in which they grow by dropping leaves and putting down roots. Grazing animals change the species composition of herbs on which they feed by cropping, by dropping manure and by physically disturbing the ground. . . . Finally, organisms themselves determine which external factors will be part of their niche by their own activities.[18]

Human beings "create and define the environments in which they live" through culture. They construct and inhabit worlds of sensory and memory images; they also construct and inhabit worlds of archetypal images, which circulate in the bloodstream of social and spiritual history. Indeed, they reshape and redefine both their external and internal environments in many ways.

The human world picture becomes its "niche," the place humanity inhabits, its inner habitat. Its cultural forms and images become the hunting grounds, the circumstances in which humans survive or perish, the places where they cultivate or contaminate the world.

Life in the inner habitat obeys its own laws. Jung spoke of the stages of life; there is, for example, a point in personal evolution when attention begins to turn from the plane of life and individuals enter upon a course of "involution" and "centroversion."[19] Traveling through the stages of life, there comes a time when people naturally turn inward and gravitate toward the imaginal plane. How far does this turning inward go?

Is evolution using the inner powers to create a new habitat, a new niche in the cosmic environment? Is a new "place" emerging for us human beings to carry on the adventures of evolution? This new niche need not be solely *post*mortem; in other words, we may already be "there," as we transform the world through the power of imagination. Before pursuing this idea further, it is necessary to say something about the expressive nature of mind and PK.

PK and Mind as Expressive

PK is an expressive function. Suppose I "intend" a pair of dice to turn up sevens and obtain more sevens than I would by chance. Perhaps the deviation from chance *expresses* my intention to produce die faces showing sevens. To illustrate the expressive nature of mind and PK, consider a spectrum of examples:

A student raises her hand in class to signal she has a question.

In a state of anger, a man's blood pressure rises.

Van Gogh paints *Starry Night*.

A pious hysteric spontaneously produces the wounds (stigmata) of Christ.

A child is the focus of poltergeist activity; chinaware inexplicably flies off the shelf and is shattered.

Joseph of Copertino levitates.

What all these forms of behavior have in common is their expressiveness. There are obvious differences, of course, between raising one's hand and levitating. The latter we ascribe to "PK," a mysterious power some people seem to have. The former is a plain case of voluntary movement.

Is PK involved in ordinary voluntary movements? Some researchers distinguish between "endosomatic" and "exosomatic" PK. In the former, people use their bodies to express their intentions through PK; in the latter they apply PK to external bodies. What reasons are there for assuming that the same principle is involved in both cases?

Consider the first example of body movement. Does anyone really understand how the girl raises her hand—how her thought results in body movement? I think not, for there is a gap that separates mental intention and body movement, and even neuroscientists don't know how it is crossed, just as no one knows how a player can influence the roll of the dice by PK. The girl raising her hand is so common, most people never stop to wonder how it's possible. But the gap between mind and body is as radical in ordinary voluntary movement as it is in the paranormal movement of objects.

The same gap comes into play in trying to explain blushing due to embarassment or a sudden rise in blood pressure due to an angry thought. In other words, *involuntary* changes belong to the same spectrum of expressive psychokinetic phenomena. If this theory is correct, each item on the list of examples I cited above is part of the same continuum.

In fact, on close examination, the overlap becomes apparent. For example, anger might cause a rise in blood pressure in many people; but in rare cases with poltergeist subjects, an angry impulse may exteriorize itself and destroy chinaware instead of increasing blood pressure on arterial walls. The same emotions in another person of artistic skills may help to produce a work of art, or lead a sociopath to commit criminal acts.

At the far end of the spectrum are reports of phenomena labeled paranormal or miraculous—stigmata, weeping icons, materializations, saintly (or diabolic) levitations.

From this perspective, the human world is pervaded by PK. PK, seen as a basic function of mind, covers the gamut of expressive human activities: art, science, technology—and, of course, religion. PK, the active, expressive side of psi, has an incarnational dimension, and may be the source of the human ability to transform physical existence.

Pictures of an Afterlife

From this perspective, the basic idea of an evolutionary afterlife paradigm is that we are evolving a new type of body. This body could function free from the ordinary restraints of physics. The empirical basis for this hypothetical body is the existence of ESP and PK. According to the model being sketched, ESP and PK are part of a process of evolution toward a form of life that transcends bodily death. The model has a forerunner in Western religious traditions.

In the Western tradition, the afterlife has been pictured in two ways—the Platonic picture of the immortality of the soul and the Christian picture of the resurrection of the body.[20] Evolution, acting through psi, seems to support both traditions. Evidence from ESP suggests that the soul can exist without the body—that is the Platonic picture. Evidence from PK shows that the soul can also transform the body—that is the Christian picture of the resurrection.

Alongside these two traditions is a third that blends the Platonic and Christian views of the afterlife body. The so-called astral, subtle, or etheric body of popular occult thought seems like a fusion of the Platonic soul body and the Christian resurrected body.[21] This type of body has form, extension, and sensuous properties, but it is no longer subject to the laws of ordinary physics.

In order to understand this new form of bodily existence—however it is termed—superphysical, astral, psychic, resurrected, subtle, etheric, or imaginal—it would help to think of specific examples the form might take.

Padre Pio's stigmatized body or Copertino's levitated body can be thought of as examples of paranormal psychophysics in action. These phenomena, if real—and I believe the evidence suggests they are— may be examples of the emerging form of bodily existence. As such they are concrete examples of a new form of embodiment which tends toward transcendence of physical death.

Previews of Imaginal Survival

According to this theory, life as humans live it now and the life to come—if such a life there be—are parts of a continuous process of development. If there is an afterlife, then, it must emerge out of this life.

Now, what sort of "after" life are humans heading toward? To understand possible human evolution in another world—the future of humanity—it is necessary, I submit, to explore the outer reaches of the psychic imagination—the subject of this book.

If mind survives death, imagination must be the key to the afterworld. A mental afterworld would be a world in which individuals would have to reckon with the powers of imagination. In such a world, images would be reality.

If we create the afterlife from our imagination, then the best way to investigate the "afterlife" is through the study of imagination. Kenneth Ring has argued that if there is an afterlife, its content would in some intimate way be drawn from the depths of the human imagination.[22] Similar ideas have been expressed by theosophist Jacob Boehme and mystic Meister Eckhart. Thus in order to explore the "next" world, the direction to go is *not horizontally in space and time, but vertically, inward—into the abyss of the imagination.*

Such a vertical exploration can begin with a consideration of experiences that bring out the imaginal world as clearly as possible. Such experiences can be thought of as previews of the evolving imaginal environment. What follows is a brief consideration of a few examples, a few reconnoiterings into humanity's possible future environment. Each involves intense imaginality.

Dreams. Dreams are a good place to begin. Dreams exemplify the purely imaginal, the archetypal mind-dependent world. Dreams are puzzling phenomena, and there is no consensus on what they are. Nor is it scientifically clear why we sleep. It is clear that dreams are a common vehicle for ESP and a medium for archetypal encounters. Dreams make up the purest imaginal environment we are acquainted with. Dreams may thus offer useful clues to our evolutionary destiny.

Hallucinations. These psychic presentations without sensory input are natural features of mental life. In addition to sleep, many conditions give rise to them. Dreams are hallucinations in the sense that they are psychic presentations without sensory input. Some hallucinations are pathological, as in schizophrenia or senile dementia. Others are caused by stress, starvation, sleep-deprivation, daydreaming, reverie, sensory isolation, sensory ambiguity, falling asleep (hypnogogic), and waking up (hypnopompic). (Drug-induced hallucinations are a special category, as noted below.)

Hallucinogenesis is a ubiquitous phenomenon. Instead of asking, Why do we hallucinate? researcher Ernest Hartmann has asked, What stops us from hallucinating constantly?[23] His answer is that ordinary sensory input and "reality-testing" inhibit hallucinogenesis. The natural state of the mind, when it is allowed to express itself from within, is to hallucinate, to generate images. The mind itself is thus naturally hallucinogenic.

For the most part people are absorbed in the business of everyday life; but the moment attention wavers, as in drowsiness, states of perceptual ambiguity, sickness, or meditation, people often drift into hallucinogenic worlds. This drift toward hallucination is a normal feature of mental life in sleep and dreams.

Attention is normally hypnotized, fascinated by, and fixated upon the physical "plane of life."[24] The moment attention is deflected from the plane of life, the latent image-producing mechanism comes into play. People dream, see visions, try to give imaginary objects shape and form in the arts. If the curious data are examined closely, they might reveal a natural progression, culminating in complete escape from the plane of life, in that projection into pure imagination called death.

At death, when sensory inhibition stops completely, the spontaneous hallucinogenic capacity of mind can be expected to switch into high gear. The psyche finds itself in a totally mind-dependent world. Death, in this perspective, signifies the complete release of the imaginal powers.

Intoxication, the fourth drive. Psychoactive plants are another route to heightened imaginal life. In a recent book, Ronald Siegel argues that intoxication is a fourth drive (in addition to hunger, thirst, and sex).[25] Although not innate, the fourth drive operates across species and, when acquired, may dominate the three primary drives. Siegel wonders if intoxication has an evolutionary meaning. The one thing he is sure of is that the drive to intoxication is "unstoppable." Consequently, he deplores as absurd all talk of the "war on drugs." His recommendation is not to legalize an old drug technology but to develop a new and effective one.

The idea of a fourth drive is intriguing. Siegel is saying that all living things are driven to explore the imaginal environment. As it turns out, nature is full of plant toxins with all manner of mind-altering aftereffects. Many kinds of living creatures, as Siegel documents, have discovered in these toxins what can only be called psychic alteration properties. Could it be that evolution has stumbled upon plant toxins as a way of exploring imaginal worlds?

How psychoactive substances act on mind and brain is puzzling. Aldous Huxley once theorized that they block the brain from performing its normal job as a filter of consciousness. He held that the function of the brain is to insulate us from being overwhelmed by reality, and that these sacred toxins open the floodgates to the sea of what he called Mind at Large.[26] Mind at Large may be viewed as synonymous with the total imaginal sphere.

From this perspective, intoxication is one of nature's ways of accelerating imaginal evolution. This idea might help society to look at the drug crisis in a different light—as an evolutionary problem of consciousness. Perhaps intoxication, even with all its dangers, may be one way nature is trying to break through to the "next" world.

Mystical and visionary experience. Mystical and visionary experiences enhance the imaginal and may also anticipate future environments. Transpersonal experiences are often intertwined with paranormal elements. People who have such experiences normally claim they know (not just believe in) real, objective—indeed, super-real, superobjective—states of being.

The mystic experience seems to have a core of transcendent sameness; despite cultural variables, something fundamental appears to lie at its base. The great mystics, who stress detachment from the plane of life, touch the deep structures of the imaginal sphere. Could mystics be the avant-garde in the evolution of the race?

Culture and history: the incarnation of the imaginal. How do culture and history figure into all this? As Vico pointed out, it is clear that culture and history are works—"inventions" Vico would say—of the imagination.[27] We are surrounded by works of the imagination. Mythology trades in imaginal worlds, coded in words and paint and stone. Music, dance, architecture, and poetry are all imaginal expressions in their respective media.

The bond between art and the evolving imaginal environment is clear in one of the great ideals of modern art, autonomy. Modern art was obsessed with autonomy. In plain language, artists have always wanted to create a new nature, an alternate reality. According to art historian Lionello Venturi, the "enchantment" of Giorgione's art lies in its appeal "to all those who find concealed in their innermost nature the romantic desire for what is unseen, unknown, and out of range of human possibilities."[28] Giorgione, thus, was a seer, a visionary of things beyond ordinary human possibilities. But the artist is also a technician who uses tangible material to remodel nature in the image of an imagined supernature.

Painters like Mondrian, Malevich, and Kandinsky were deeply interested in the metaphysics of modern art. Kandinsky wrote in 1938, "This art [that is, non-objective art] creates alongside the real world a new world that has nothing to do *externally* with reality. It is subordinate *internally* to cosmic laws."[29] In short, a work of art is a law unto itself yet it remains in harmony with the *cosmos,* a Greek word meaning "ornament."

The link between art, dream, and hallucination is clear in Surrealism, whose manifestos spoke of materializing the imagination and concretizing the world of dreams. Surrealist artists consciously sought practical ways to push back the boundaries of the real—to become *sur-real.* Thus, in his *Conquest of the Irrational,* Salvador Dali proudly declares: "My sole pictorial ambition is to materialize by the most imperialistic rage of precision the images of concrete irrationality."[30]

Modern art wants to create objects with the coherence of what Aristotle called "substance." In a definite sense modern art aspires to the godlike. Immanuel Kant was a daring thinker on art. Kant was timid and orderly in his everyday life, a man who lived his life like a piece of clockwork, ever obedient to the laws of Newton's mechanistic universe. Perhaps for this reason, this sane and rational man paid tribute to the power of the imagination. In the *Critique of Judgment* Kant wrote, "The imagination (as a productive faculty of cognition) is very powerful in creating another nature, as it were, out of the material that actual nature gives it."[31]

What does Kant mean by a productive faculty of cognition? Perhaps he means the power of the mind to produce, to synthesize new realities. And what is the material nature gives the mind for this task? Clearly, the raw stuff of experience that can be structured, according to practical imagination. Kant goes on to reveal some secrets about how the genius of creative imagination works. The secret, he says, is to be purposeless—art must become an activity for its own sake, like Aristotle's divine mind thinking about thinking. For Kant the implacable Protestant, art is the playful but harmonious exercise of human faculties, a dance of spirit performed with full psychic skills and energies.

Art is thus a longing for the imaginal power to suspend oneself above or alongside nature; art wants to build a *new nature*. Art, like religion, fuels humanity's imaginal evolution. Many philosophers have reflected on the transformative power of art. For example, Herbert Marcuse,[32] and before him, Friedrich Schiller[33] saw in artistic modes of thought a new form of consciousness, a herald of the next transformation of human society.

Like art, technology speeds the evolution of material existence; it also speeds imaginal evolution. The ubiquity of the machine is a fact of contemporary life. Machines are literally physical extensions of our minds. In a way, machines are vehicles for out-of-body experiences. Or, more obviously, machines are extensions of human bodies. Astrophysicists become the machine probing the atmosphere of Jupiter, as oceanographers become the machine exploring the bottom of the sea. Human beings build machines to extend consciousness.

I have come to see the machine as a type of entity midway between the natural body and the imaginal body. My car, for example, incarnates my enlarged capacity for physical movement. And so it goes with all machines. We become them, and they become us. For instance, television can be thought of as a kind of mechanical clairvoyance; the telephone as an example of mechanical clairaudience; film and photography as kinds of mechanical retrocognition. An excellent example of the marriage of technology and imagination is the technology of computer-generated travels in "virtual reality." The ability to create, simulate, and sensorily explore possible worlds may, from the present perspective, be one of the most important developments in the twenty-first century.

Mythology, indeed, all the the arts, are products of imagination. So are languages, rituals, institutions, wars, treaties, governments, and traffic jams. All are products, direct or indirect, deliberate or accidental, of the human imagination. From ideas of truth and justice that have shaped world history to our clothing and silverware, history is a fabric of forms forged by the individual and collective imagination.

Immortality and the Future of the Body

What does all this have to do with immortality and the future of the body? The great pictures of our future body, Platonic, Christian, astral, have been shown to have a psychic dimension. Platonic immortality is based on ESP; Christian resurrection on PK. ESP demonstrates that the soul can function apart from the body; PK shows it can transform the body.

Is evolution taking two routes toward the same goal? It wouldn't be the first time that a function was discovered in the course of evolution using different materials and beginning from different starting points. Flight, for example, evolved four different times—in insects, pterosaurs, birds, and bats. And if human aviation is included, five times.

Resurrection from an evolutionary perspective. Consider the "resurrection" body as a working evolutionary hypothesis. Let it signify the full range of the developmental possibilities of the human body. At the limit of this development may be a capacity to "overcome" death itself. The outer edge of evolutionary development would be a body capable of self-regeneration. In this context, the term "resurrection" would refer to an organism's capacity to resuscitate and regenerate itself.

This state of affairs would constitute a case of what Michael Murphy calls "evolutionary transcendence." In Murphy's terms, "metanormal" gifts are signs of evolutionary transcendence; he cites life itself and the appearance of Homo sapiens as examples of such transcendence.

Murphy offers a threefold analysis of stages of human development. They range from animal-hominid to psychosocial and what Murphy calls the "metanormal." Correspondingly, there are three stages of natural history: one of specialized organs of bodily movement such as wings, legs, or flippers; one of enhanced agility, grace, and stamina acquired from psychosocial discipline; and the latest stage involving hyperdeveloped or metanormal agility, such as *lung-gom-pa,* or Tibetan trance walking, and even levitation. Finally, at the fringes of the possible, humans may develop abilities such as traveling clairvoyance, and from there, Murphy speculates, may learn to ascend into "extraphysical worlds in dreams and trance."

A direction is discernible here toward greater degrees and new grades of embodied freedom. It is as if there were a force in human beings that keeps overcoming obstacles to movement; it is as if the living bodies of nature, in the course of evolution, are being guided by an impulse to increase the elasticity, speed, and expansiveness of a body meant to move in the free space of pure imagination.

Murphy, who was one of the founders of Esalen, points to the ultimate development of metanormal embodiment:

> As we develop metanormal cognition, love, and delight, conceivably, our bodily structures would develop to support and express them. I find support for this proposal in the considerable lore of various religious traditions which indicate that many bodily changes mediate increased yogic or contemplative capacity. And this principle might hold after death, if our surviving consciousness involves some sort of subtle body, "soul-sheath," or *linga sarira,* as various Western and Eastern religious traditions maintain.[34]

In a consonant vein, Colin Brookes-Smith wrote in 1973 of the development of paranormal organs:

> The evidence suggests that if a volitional impulse demands action or seeks information beyond the range of limbs or senses, then an appropriate tenuous-matter structure is temporarily exteriorized which not only performs mechanical tasks but also acts as a sensory organ. Almost certainly such a paranormal organ only crudely

parallels our five normal senses already produced by long evolutionary processes but it might nevertheless amount to a wider and more generalized awareness far beyond what we at present conceive as possible.[35]

The well-documented "ectoplasmic" hands of Eusapia Palladino[36] may serve as examples of Brookes-Smith's "paranormal organs." They may be prefigurings of an evolutionary "omega" body.

In Murphy's *Future of the Body* is a great deal of data that backs the present survival model. The extraordinary behaviors of mystics, saints, shamans, athletes, yogis, lovers, and other adepts considerably enlarge our conception of the possibilities of embodied life. Murphy has produced a brilliant taxonomy of the higher developmental possibilities of the human body, amassing, sifting, and organizing evidence from numerous sources.

Levitation, for example, is an extreme departure from the ordinary habits of nature. If human beings can levitate, other possibilities, Murphy notes, may emerge as part of a larger pattern of potential transformation. Particular manifestations of paranormal ability are likely to be related, to be parts of a system, signals of an overall intentionality. So the power to levitate may be one explicit feature of a deeper and wider "implicate order" of transformation. In my view, this implicate order may point to the emerging human body. According to this theory, the omega-point of evolutionary meandering will be a universe of godlike creative imagination.

The more one studies these super-manifestations of psi, the less one feels constrained by the orthodox idea of death. The pattern of coordinated potentials seems, in fact, to prefigure the evolution of a new kind of organism—an organism with extraordinary potentials.

"Resurrection" as PK in Action

The resurrection model of survival is practical, concrete, personal, "creation-centered." In the poet Schiller's sense, it is a model of "esthetic" education. And it is similar to the model of the God-Idea: cocreative and democratic. We human beings are all invited to participate in the adventure of transformation, of "living beyond" ourselves.

In the model of survival by PK, the images hatched in human souls are agents of transformation in everyday life. This covers a wide range of possibilities. At one end of the spectrum are the miracles of the saints and swamis, who play extravagant games with the forces of nature. These are the fantastic extremes—the dramatic pointers to the possibility of a supernature.

But immediate human needs are more humble. The possibilities of PK in daily life—the small miracles of transformation—are infinite. Small but significant gestures of love and healing, words and deeds that speak to the life of the soul: these are possible for us all. The great miracles are mere reminders—tiny thoughts painted on a giant canvas.

For me the secret to the mechanism of survival by PK lies in the only experiment that counts—the experiment of life itself. By exploring the fringes of psychic evolution, one discovers human "survival," the venture into the "beyond." The method is as simple as it is obvious: experience the fuller, higher ranges of human becoming. One will find, I venture, that survival by PK means moving toward greater animation.

As humanity moves toward greater animation—toward "resurrection" of life on earth—interest in life *after* death will wane. Once humankind knows the fullness of actual life and tastes eternity by learning to see, as Blake said, "heaven in a wild flower," the fear of death will fade and trouble us no more.

IV
Blueprint for Psychic Evolution

Man is something to be surpassed. What have you done to surpass man?

Nietzsche

The new evolutionary cosmology invites us to see our native religious beliefs in a new perspective. The questions of God and immortality acquire new dimensions of meaning once seen in the perspective of time and becoming. God is drawn into the orbit of evolving humanity; immortality becomes a question of earthly transformation.

Part Four looks at patterns of data that equip us with more detailed images of what may be involved in this earthly transformation. These patterns of data may be blueprints for possible human evolution.

If we think of spiritual life as futuristic, it is possible to view the cult of the guardian angel as an experiment in future science. The guardian angel is an image of human potential that links us to hidden resources of higher development. Chapter 8 looks at how it may be possible to draw on these resources.

Chapter 9 looks at another ancient experiment in future science. During the Hellenistic era, many people engaged in "experiments" of psychic and spiritual regeneration. Known collectively as the Mysteries, countless people were drawn to these august rites, which, judging by testimonials, often resulted in profound inner changes. In particular, this chapter explores the secret of the Eleusinian Mysteries, the greatest of the ancient rites of deification.

Next, human beings who seem like forerunners of the future are considered—models of a form of life not yet fully realized at large.

Jesus of Nazareth and Paul of Tarsus have already been discussed from this point of view. However, in investigating extraordinary claims about people from ancient times, we today are hampered by a lack of reliable eyewitness testimony. In such cases we can only apply the coherence test of truth. If modern science says that telepathy or paranormal healing occur, we may assign degrees of plausibility to comparable reports of telepathy and paranormal healing in the ancient world. We can only speculate on possibilities based on modern information.

Chapters 10 and 11 look at two twentieth-century spiritual leaders who have many eyewitnesses: Sai Baba and Padre Pio. They have been photographed, filmed, and observed repeatedly for long periods of time, often by critical, or even hostile witnesses. I have chosen them as contemporary examples of some of the higher possibilities of human development. There were of course many other options, evolved spiritual beings such as Ramakrishna, Mother Teresa, Krishnamurti, Thomas Merton, or Meher Baba. I chose Padre Pio and Sai Baba as examples of extraordinary development for several reasons. First, I wanted to compare an Easterner and a Westerner. In addition, both men have worldwide followings and had public careers spanning at least half a century. Both are reputed to have extraordinary abilities which, if even partially true, say something about our evolutionary potential. The reports on these men—if accepted—compare well with those concerning the spiritual masters of antiquity.

I do not claim this testimony is infallible, but there is enough to make tentative comparisons worthwhile. In these delicate matters, where exaggeration, misobservation, and fraud are possible, readers will have to judge for themselves.

In any case, Padre Pio and Sai Baba challenge the ordinary idea of what a human being can do. The two men came from different traditions—Padre Pio, a Capuchin monk from southern Italy; Sai Baba, a swami from Puttaparti, India. Both came from poor, undistinguished families and backgrounds and found their vocations at an early age. Both were friends of the people, serving them practically as well as spiritually.

In each story, the obscure place of origin becomes a center of spiritual attraction: a shrine, a focus for pilgrimage, a source for change and renewal. Millions feel the shock waves of a powerful spiritual energy. Padre Pio and Sai Baba have struck deep chords of response in people of all ages, sexes, and cultures. In the eyes of their admirers, they embody models of spiritual greatness.

Finally I look at another set of data with transformative potential— experiences of contact with otherworldly, ultradimensional, or extraterrestrial beings. In these cases the acceleration of human evolution is not based on intention nor on extraordinary people but on spontaneous experiences occurring to ordinary people. Chapter 12 focuses on the growing phenomenon of Goddess appearances, also known as Marian visions, and Chapter 13 on extraterrestrials.

8

The Cult of the Guardian Angel

He will give his angels charge of you, to guard you in all your ways.
Psalm 91

Belief in guardian angels is very old. Guardian angels were first pictured as spirits of the dead, similar to the Japanese *kami,* the Roman *manes,* or the Germanic *valkyries.* Zoroastrian tradition, which influenced the Bible, refers to *fravashis*: benevolent, protective spirits, whose services required ritual offerings. Mysterious servants and ministers of God turn up frequently in the Old and New Testaments. Angels, however, aren't just relics from bygone ages; they are enjoying a comeback. Consider one example.

The Catholic Tradition

Biblical origins. Although the belief in guardian angels is strong in Catholic tradition, it lacks solid biblical credentials. It is not dogma that everyone has a guardian angel; but, as St. Jerome once said, the idea is "in the mind of the Church."

Several passages in the Old and New Testaments and the apocryphal story of Raphael and Tobias are the basis for believing that such beings exist. The belief runs deep that overseeing intelligences haunt the invisible corridors of the universe. The cult of guardian angels is an outgrowth of thousands of years of mythology. Some seed images include the following.

In Exodus Yahweh declares to Moses: "I myself will send an angel before you to guard you as you go and to bring you to the place that I have prepared. Give him reverence and listen to all that he says" (23:20). Here the angel's job is to protect the tribe, "If you listen carefully to his voice and do all that I say, I shall be enemy to your enemies.''

Psalm 91 is a panegyric to God's protective power: ''I rescue all who cling to me, I protect whoever knows my name, I answer everyone who invokes me, I am with them when they are in trouble.'' A few lines above state: ''He [Yahweh] will give his angels charge of you, to guard you in all your ways.'' In this psalm, the angels and God seem hard to distinguish; later there is a separation, a hierarchy forms, and the angel becomes a personification of God's help.

In the Book of Tobit, the archangel Raphael guides the young hero Tobias on a dangerous journey and reveals magic formulas that protect him from the demon Asmodeus; Tobit uses the formulas to restore his father's sight. Angels are also agents of healing.

In Matthew is found the source of the belief that each person has a guardian angel from birth: ''See that you never despise any of these little ones, for I tell you that their angels in heaven are continually in the presence of my Father in heaven'' (18:10). Guardian angels exist in the presence of the Most High. The angel is thus an intermediary, a ''messenger,'' who brings good tidings from the Godhead. The guardian angel is an image that links us to divine power.

Saint Paul's letter to the Hebrews calls angels ''spirits whose work is service sent to help those who will be the heirs of salvation'' (1:14). In the context of this passage, Paul is anxious to distinguish between Christ and the angels and warns against the dangers of a cult of angels. It is easy, I think, to see what he fears. An angel might easily turn into a gnostic tool for personal spiritual adventure, thus emancipating the individual from the Church, even from Christ as the sole and supreme link to divine power.

From the standpoint of the early Church, the peril of angels was the peril of gnosticism, which was perceived as the peril of spiritual anarchy. People today who are open to the new polytheism of higher consciousness see these matters in a different light. Angels are welcome as yet another tool for dialogue with the Transcendent.

The contemporary Opus Sanctorum Angelorum. The Church sanctions many attitudes, practices, and movements that it doesn't necessarily raise to the rank of dogma. One of these is the cult of the guardian angel.

In the Judeo-Christian monotheistic world, the cult of the guardian angel looks like an attempt to overcome the remoteness of God. In more than one way Catholic Christianity struggles to overcome that remoteness. Christ, the incarnation of the Transcendent, is an obvious example. But the effort doesn't stop there. The impulse is to close further the gap between human and divine.

This impulse leads to the cult of angels, and as well the cult of saints and the cult of Mary. Each of these practices strives to hew a more intimate path to the feet of divine reality. Like the mono-poly-theism of Hinduism, Catholic Christianity, in spite of its official line, offers a multitude of paths to exploring the Divine.

Several lively movements within the Church are devoted to the angels. One is called the *Opus Sanctorum Angelorum* (The Work of the Holy Angels). This movement (*Opus,* for short) was sanctioned by Pope Paul VI in 1968. Earlier, in 1950, Pope Pius XII urged renewed devotion to the angels, especially, he said, in the trying times to come. Tradition relates the advent of angels to the Second Coming, and Pius was suggesting that the winds of apocalypse were blowing.

Another source of inspiration for the *Opus* are reports of angelic appearances in the twentieth century. Padre Pio, the mystic known for his stigmata, seems to have been on close terms with what he called his "celestial companion." An angel appeared in 1916 in Fatima to three shepherd children, a herald to their 1917 visions of the Virgin. (Mary, like the guardian angel, plays an increasing role in the spiritual consciousness of popular Christianity.)

The goal of the *Opus Angelorum* is the work of conscious "collaboration among the angels and men, for the greater glory of God, the salvation of humanity and the regeneration of all creation."[1] The *Opus* is a movement dedicated to the marriage of humanity with the angelic order. Guided by priests enrolled in the *Opus,* there are three degrees or stages in the rite of divine conjugation.

The promise. First, candidates make a promise to their guardian angel. All those who love their angels and want to be guided by them are entitled to make the Promise. Candidates kneel in the presence of a priest and promise to love God's "holy companions" and respond to their commands when heard through the voice of conscience.

The consecration to the guardian angel. After a year of preparation, candidates take part in a ceremony during which they hold a lighted candle in the presence of the Blessed Sacrament. After speaking

the ceremonial consecration, candidates write it in their own hand-
writing. The following is part of the statement:

> Holy Guardian Angel, who [has] been given to me from the begin-
> ning of my life as my Guardian and Companion. I, poor sinner,
> desire to consecrate myself to you. . . . I promise to acknowledge
> you always as my holy Guardian and to promote the veneration
> of the holy angels as help which is given to us in a very special
> way in these days of spiritual combat for the Kingdom of God.

Candidates ask to become *like* the angels in perfect love and will.
The consecration is a rite of assimilation to the angel.

The *Opus* is a work for "these days of spiritual combat"—an allusion to the possibility that we are nearing Endtime. To consecrate
oneself to one's guardian angel is to certify one's task as spiritual
warrior.

As a boy, I often heard these solemn words spoken by the priest
at Mass, part of a prayer to Saint Michael: "Be our protection against
the wickedness and snares of the devil . . . and do thou, O prince
of the heavenly hosts, by the power of God, thrust into hell Satan
and all evil spirits who wander through the world seeking the ruin
of souls." A spiritual warrior knows that the world is full of snares
and pitfalls. Satan is a magnificent homage to the Shadow, a reminder
that life is a spiritual struggle.

The Consecration also includes this plea: "I beg you, holy angel
of God, obtain for me a love so strong that I may be inflamed by
it." The task of cooperating with angels is thus the dual one of becoming sacred warriors *and* divine lovers.

The older tradition of the Church Fathers mirrors this balance; each
person is said to have a good angel and a bad one. Origen wrote,
"All men are moved by two angels, an evil one who inclines them
to evil and a good one who inclines them to good. . . . If there are
good thoughts in our hearts, there is no doubt that the angel of the
Lord is speaking to us. But if evil things come into our heart the angel
of the evil one is speaking to us."[2]

The consecration to all angels. In the last stage of the *Opus* the
candidate is consecrated to the whole realm of angels. According to
the Church Father Athenogoras, "the Demiurge and Creator of the
world, God, through the medium of his word, has apportioned and
ordained the angels to occupy the elements, the heavens, the world,
and whatever is in the world." Since angels sweep through all ranges

of being, from the human to the cosmic, the ultimate goal of the Work of the Angels is to live in communion with all things.

Now, while this grand cosmic goal may be the climax of the human spiritual adventure, the core of the angel doctrine is more practical. All human beings, saints and sinners, Christians and pagans, enjoy the services of guardian angels. The concept, in short, is archetypal—it applies to the psyche universally. The guardian angel is portrayed as existing "face to face" with God. Thus there is in every human being an unconscious inlet to the highest creative source. As I read it, the doctrine of the guardian angel implies recognition of this psychic fact.

More specifically, the *Opus* teaches that the guardian angel can "ward off danger to body and soul; prevent Satan's suggestion of evil thoughts; remove occasions of sin; enlighten and instruct; offer our prayers for us; correct us if we sin; help us in the agony of death; conduct us to God or purgatory at death." This is a remarkable list of functions. To mobilize them, we need "to venerate and pray to our Guardian Angel; reverence his presence; have confidence in his care; feel gratitude; follow his admonitions; show tender devotion to him."[3] The benefits human beings might reap from angels depend on our ability to summon deep feelings and draw on psychic energies.

An Imaginal Model

According to Catholic tradition, angels are conscious beings, possessing great intellectual and voluntary power, unimpeded by the restrictions of physical nature.

It would be hard to make a case for the literal existence of such beings. The theologian or rational fundamentalist may feel the need to do so. However, in my opinion, any overly rational attempt to demonstrate the precise existence of angels is likely to weaken their psychic and spiritual utility. With angels, one suspects, to analyze is to destroy. A Cartesian analysis of angels might be fatal.

A different approach is to regard angels as psychic images. One great alternative to Descartes in modern philosophy is Vico, the philosopher of imagination. Vico's anti-Cartesian battle cry was *verum factum ipsum*—the true is what we make true. From a Vichian perspective, then, angels can be viewed as matters of the practical imagination.

From this perspective, angels may not exist as some literal-minded theologians say they do, but they do exist. Whatever they are in themselves, I suggest that angels exist as far as human beings imaginally cocreate them. I stress the word "cocreate." Something "out there" interacts with something "in here." Like Jung, Vico believed in universal images common to whole peoples, even to humanity as a whole. The guardian angel is such an image, and its concrete "truth" depends on how we make it true, on what we "do" with it. We make angels "true" by endowing them with psychic life. But how?

What exists are imagings of angels. The existence and ministry of angels thus depends upon the depth and duration of their imaginal life in human souls. When angels are understood in this way, it becomes clear why the Church—an ancient organization devoted to fabricating powerful imaginal constructs—holds certain views that we, from our modern perspective, may consider a little strange and offensive.

What looks strange and offensive, however, may serve a psychic function. The absurd rules and offensive dogmas may be necessary to sustain the imaginal life of the angels. "I believe because it is absurd," said Tertullian. Tertullian was concerned with the imaginal health of the psyche, not with the exercise of reason. For the soul's sake, it is sometimes necessary to break with the system of worldly reason. To some, belief, faith, or trust may seem signs of infantilism; to others, they are the atmosphere in which the creative imagination can breathe freely.

Angels are true to the extent that we make them true. That is the point I want to underline—a point not quite in harmony with traditional religion *or* with modern science. Tradition, however, instinctively understands the relationship between faith and imagination. This same instinctive understanding is, I think, available to us all.

What does it mean, for example, to say I "believe" I can swim thirty laps? It means I can "imagine" myself swimming thirty laps. The same applies to the higher objects of faith. To say, for example, that I believe in God or in my guardian angel is to say that I entertain a set of images of what is possible. "I believe in God" might mean "I imagine a powerful benevolent being who loves and cares about my highest good."

Even if the images are abstract—God as the Light of Being, or the Source of Unconditional Love—an image is still placed before the inner eye. "Blind," unhesitating faith in some thing or idea may thus be seen as an attempt to hold a "clear" unwavering image of that thing or idea. The clearer and more unwavering the image, the greater its creative power. "Blindness" of faith thus may translate into clarity of imagination.

In the consecration to the guardian angel, an aspirant promises obedience and loyalty to Mary, to all the saints, and to all the teachings of Mother Church. To the nonbeliever—and also to many believers— this may seem stifling and authoritarian.

However, the *Opus* is not about intellectual exploration or civil rights. It is an experiment in cocreating angels. In other words, to get results, certain psychological conditions, internal and social, are needed. In Vico's view, the laws of the creative imagination are "barbaric"; they aren't based on the critical and liberal sensibilities of the "age of men." The most creative phase of a civilization, Vico says, comes at the dawn of a cycle, the "age of gods," the stage of psychic evolution in which imagination is dominant. The current revival of interest and belief in angels, then, may be a return to the creative barbarism of the dawn stage of a civilization. Angels may be a symptom that we are at the end of an old era and at the beginning of a new one.

The Parapsychological Component

I have suggested that the guardian angel is a psychoimaginal construct that can be endowed with life when we treat it with unswerving belief, love, loyalty, devotion, prayer, and gratitude. We bind ourselves to the angel by a promise, a vow. Our relation to the angel is a kind of marriage or cocreative process.

The dogmas and practices of the Church, from a psychological viewpoint, are meant to intensify the psychic reality of angels and other imaginal entities. When we give such entities a psychic life of their own, we forge a link to our higher selves, and to the archetypal and paranormal forces of the unconscious. Everything takes place as if we actually believe in the independent existence of the guardian angel. This state of belief is important, for it eases our surrender to the dynamics of higher consciousness.

The guardian angel is presumed to guard, assist, direct, and enlighten us in various concrete ways. The Bible is full of stories that show the practical and often apparently miraculous abilities of angels. Devotees of the *Opus* make similar claims.

Likewise, modern mystics like Padre Pio inspire extraordinary stories of the ministry of angels. A remarkable book *Send Me Your Guardian Angel* by Father Alessio Parente, a close confederate of Padre Pio, contains a collection of stories about guardian angels.[4] Some of the stories tell of spiritual help; others have a distinctly paranormal component. Consider a few examples of the latter.

Padre Pio often told people that when they were in distress they should send him their guardian angels (thus the title of Parente's book). In one case, a man who was about to be an unwilling participant in a robbery with a group of shady companions "sent" his guardian angel to the Padre for help. A police car appeared out of nowhere and foiled the scheme, according to Parente.

The skeptic would probably dismiss this as mere coincidence. Others might see invoking the guardian angel as a way of increasing the probability of helpful coincidences. Many tales of angelic aid suggest this kind of invoked meaningful coincidence.

Other stories—if true as reported in Parente's book—clearly involve the paranormal. For example, a woman reported that while driving her car, she was about to strike a large object on the road. At this moment, she called on her guardian angel. The car, she alleged, inexplicably jumped over the obstacle. In stories with testimony less easily discounted, Padre Pio's guardian angel helped him to translate Greek—a language he didn't know. (See Chapter 10.) Parapsychologists call this ability to understand and speak a foreign language "xenoglossy," a rare paranormal phenomenon. Ian Stevenson has analyzed some contemporary cases.[5]

Can parapsychology help us understand the psychic power of the guardian angel?

I assume the extraordinary claims about guardian angels refer to *something* real and significant. Any idea that leaves such a clear residue of belief must be grounded in some kind of reality. This, of course, does not rule out the possibility of delusion, though the widespread reports over centuries tend to discount delusion as the only explanation. I believe that if we take seriously all that we know about the soul—its archetypal and parapsychological dimensions—the guardian angel is an idea we might find newly meaningful. It might in fact turn out to be an idea for a future psychic science.

What follows is meant to suggest how this might be so. My aim is not to argue for any particular claim of "angel"-mediated miracle, but to show in general how such claims might be empirically based on paranormal psychodynamics.

The creative power of belief. One of the well-confirmed findings of modern parapsychology is that belief and expectation in the paranormal increase the occurrence of paranormal effects. This idea has already been stressed in the discussion of the God-Idea. The guardian angel is supposed to have virtually unlimited powers over space, time, and matter—powers to heal and to bring individuals into harmony with the Supreme Principle. Believing in such a being might therefore be a way of activating a person's own paranormal potentials.

This correlation helps to explain the rules of devotion to the guardian angel as taught to believers in the *Opus*. The more they devote themselves with love and loyalty to the guardian angel, and believe in its powers, the more this belief is likely to activate their latent powers. Anything that destroyed the delicate balance of belief would destroy the angel's capacity to do the job.

The guardian angel is truly a venture in cooperation. Human beings have to give something to the angels, if they expect the angels to give in return. Disbelievers reject such a venture; they refuse to give unless they have tangible proof that they will get something back. In effect, they lock themselves out of the experiment.

The spontaneity of angels. As spirit blows where it will, so do angels ride the winds of spontaneity. One of the best predictors of psychic ability is this same spontaneity. Researchers have found from many types of studies that the less rigid one's mindset, the more likely it is that a paranormal force or idea will break into experience.[6] The more "unworldly" the mind, the more detached from habitual patterns of response, the greater the openness to promptings from a higher reality source. The fewer the mechanical restraints—the more spontaneous the mode of being in the world—the more likely it is that extraordinary things will occur. Angels thus represent the pure spontaneity of human soul powers.

Angels and release of effort. Researchers say that any wrong effort, any anxious self-doubting of the ego trying to "make it" happen, inhibits paranormal occurrences. Belief in a guardian angel helps people release themselves from the wrong kind of ego-involved effort. The guardian angel may be an image of our own psychic potential, but if we hope to realize that potential, we have to turn the controls over to something beyond us, something not restricted by fear and self-doubt. By placing all in the hands of a guardian angel, we release ourselves from inner obstacles that block cooperation with our latent powers.

This methodology tallies with the great spiritual traditions. From the Lord's Prayer (*Thy* will be done) to the Taoist idea of *wu wei* (action through nonaction), the consensus among spiritual masters is that to come into full ownership of our being we have to abandon ourselves to Divine Providence. We human beings cannot serve two masters; at some point we must let go of the personal will. Belief in the guardian angel is one way of freeing the power of the transpersonal will.

Personifying angels. At a certain stage of the *Opus Sanctorum Angelorum,* devotees are invited to name their own guardian angel. This step is critical to the work of cocreating angels. Naming is a way of personifying and thus shaping a channel to the inner potentials symbolized by the guardian angel. In the Bible only four angels are named: Michael, Gabriel, Raphael, and Uriel. The vast legions of angels said to crowd every nook and cranny of being remain unnamed. This is a curious hint of the angel's unfinished nature. By naming an angel, a person adds to the *opus* of bringing the angels to full psychic life. In essence, of course, when we name an angel, we also name and personify our latent soul powers.

The group dynamic for cocreating angels. When devotees name an angel, do they bring something new into being? Once again I believe that the work of Kenneth Batcheldor on paranormal group dynamics sheds light on the genesis of angels. Batcheldor's work has shown that ordinary people, by learning a special psychological skill, can levitate objects and produce other supernormal physical phenomena. The research suggests that the type of phenomena produced are based on *what the group expects and believes possible.*

"Philip," mentioned in Chapter 3, was an invented personage whose story was also made up and then experimentally "believed in." Though only an imaginal entity, Philip took on a life of his own—producing localized sounds in different physical substances, levitating objects, and responding intelligently to questions in line with his fictional personality. The experiments were carried out in full daylight, at times before a television camera, and were observed by impartial witnesses. The group has not yet succeeded in creating an apparition of "Philip," but enough has been "conjured up" to validate the Tibetan idea of *tulpas* and the theosophical idea of thought-forms.

Batcheldor's work has yielded enough empirical evidence to prove that it is possible for a group of people, who invent a myth (a story in images) and practice a special group dynamic (believing, expecting, and behaving spontaneously), to create an independent psychic entity with the ability to "do" things considered "paranormal."

This research has implications for the theory of angels. It also has implications for other "supernatural" or imaginal entities, including God. In my view, believers in gods and angels may use unconsciously the same psychological techniques that Batcheldor and his followers used consciously and formally. They create a story, personify a psychic entity, and give themselves over to passionate belief in this story and entity. Batcheldor's researchers obtained results.[7] Why shouldn't believers in guardian angels get similar results?

The Return of the Angels

The belief in angels as a way to the Higher Self, a bridge between our everyday minds and the greater Mind at Large has persisted to modern times. In fact, the assorted psychic entities currently popular may be functionally very similar to the archetypal form of the guardian angel.

The idea of angels—images of mediation, beings that act as links between human beings and a higher reality—may be detected in several areas of contemporary experience. In Chapters 12 and 13, I discuss these experiences in some detail. The cult of believers in UFO contact is an "angel" related phenomenon. The light-beings of the near-death experience also resemble guardian angels. Apparitions of Mary are increasing today, and one of Mary's cognomens is "Queen of Angels." Mary herself is called the Angel of Peace, and her appearances are often preceded by visions of angels.

The modern psyche is suffering from what Vico called the "malicious" decay of rationalism—intelligence turned against the needs of civil society. The return of the angels is, in my view, a sign of the return of "barbarian" times. Barbarian for Vico was a term referring to the primal imagination. In these new barbarian times, the gods and goddesses, demons and fairies, griffins and guardian angels who have been ousted by scientific rationalism are returning with a vengeance.

9

The Eleusinian Mysteries

The evocation of a beatific vision at Eleusis was an annual venture, repeated over a period of a thousand years. Under conditions which were kept strictly secret, after preparation, which proved their worth for many centuries, . . . the venture succeeded time and time again. This success was in the nature of a psychic reality.

Carl Kerenyi

In many ways the ancient Graeco-Roman world mirrors our own. From the time of Alexander the Great to the third century of the Christian era, the Mediterranean world was in a state of spiritual ferment. The state religions of Greece and Rome had ceased to captivate the hearts and minds of people. The great city-states were in decline, and in their place arose an empire that made possible trade, travel, and a common language, Greek. Ideas spread easily across cultures.

People were breaking away from old beliefs and loyalties. It was an age of marginal men and women—it was, as E. R. Dodds has shown, an age of anxiety.[1] Anxiety increased, as it always does, when individuals split from family, tribe, state. The more keenly people felt their individuality, the more keenly they felt anxiety. As Freud pointed out, the ego is "the seat of anxiety." The growth of consciousness is a psychically costly affair. The classical world was in decline, and the Mediterranean basin had become a conduit for a host of Eastern influences. The curtain of history was about to rise on a new act.

During this first ancient wave of culture shock, people from all classes of society, torn from their ancestral moorings, were hungry for spiritual sustenance. The power of the old spiritual forms was on the wane, and many were searching for new ways to feel at home in the universe.

These turbulent times, known as the Hellenistic era, are marked by several qualities. The first is a rare tolerance for the variety of spiritual paths. Graeco-Roman tolerance gave rise to "syncretism," the combination of different forms of belief. A democracy of spiritual paths was the rule of the day. All paths to spiritual progress were possible; seekers sensed a hidden identity of gods, rites, and beliefs; they borrowed from one another, gave to one another, and in the private realm of inner life were willing to live and let live.

To some, the idea of syncretism may have bad connotations, implying a mishmash of ideas lacking cohesion and a vital center. Still, the syncretic spirit may be in some ways a prelude to breakthrough and creativity. The Graeco-Roman epoch showed a healthy trend toward synthesis and personal experiment. Christianity itself succeeded because of the careful exercise of the catholic and syncretic impulses of its predecessors.

As the Roman Empire declined, the appeal of the mystery religions grew. As external life became decentralized, people turned inward to find their center. For many the Mysteries were the answer to the need for psychological renovation. The appeal of the Mysteries went back to legendary Orphism. From the Orphics branched the Mysteries of Dionysus, Cybele, Mithraism, Isis, and other schools.

Orphism, like all the mystery religions, gave expression to the urge to transcend ordinary human existence. Each mystery religion consisted of a myth and a rite, a vision and a practice, a set of thoughts and behaviors, directed toward *palingenesis*—regeneration, or spiritual rebirth. The Mysteries had three parts: a cathartic prelude, a secret initiation, and a culminating vision.[2] Each was an experiment exploring the frontiers of the soul.

An experiment in psychic transformation—such were the Mysteries of Eleusis. These Mysteries were the most popular form of esoteric Greek religion, lasting for two thousand years, and claiming as initiates Plato, Sophocles, Aeschylus, Cicero, and many others. The historical evidence agrees that the Eleusinian Mysteries were effective. They changed peoples lives, values, and outlooks.

What really happened during these ancient ritual experiments remains shrouded in secrecy. No one quite knows how to account for their remarkable effectiveness—their ability to elevate celebrants to higher states of consciousness. Like Paul's conversion, the Eleusinian Mysteries are a puzzle to students of mental evolution; however, they deserve attention, for, I believe, they point to important potentials latent in us all.

The Mystery of the Eleusinian Mysteries

For close to two thousand years, Greek-speaking people from all over the Mediterranean world participated annually in a mystery rite at Eleusis. The climax of the rites was a visionary experience (*epopteia*) in the innermost sanctuary (*telesterion*).

The mystery is *what* was seen at these festivals and *how* it produced such extraordinary and lasting effects. To this day no one knows. George Mylonas, who has spent much of his life studying the subject, writes: "A thick, impenetrable veil indeed still covers securely the rites of Demeter and protects them from the curious eyes of modern students. . . . [T]he ancient world has kept its secret well and the Mysteries of Eleusis remain unrevealed."[3]

Gathering information on the Mysteries is hampered by two facts. One is deliberate secrecy. What happened in the *telesterion* was to be kept secret on pain of death. So serious was this threat that revelation of the secrets created some notable scandals and led to executions in Greek antiquity. The Mysteries were secret in two senses. They were *aporheton*, "not to be uttered," thus forbidden. They were also secret in a deeper sense, implied by a different word: *arheton*, "beyond utterance," ineffable. The second thing that hampers research is the problem of hostile witnesses. Some of the data are suspect, because they came from early Christian converts who were reluctant to be fair in their accounts of competing faiths. Witnesses like Clement of Alexandria stressed the worst side of the older rites.

What Is Known about Eleusis

In spite of the secrecy and the difficulty of finding reliable data, scholars do know some facts about the Eleusinian mysteries. For instance, in 364 A.D. the Mysteries of Eleusis, along with other nocturnal rites, were prohibited by edict under the Catholic Emperor Valentinian. The date of the Mysteries' origins, however, is more obscure. Eleusis itself is located about twelve miles from Athens; traces of a temple "Megaron B" have been excavated there by archaeologists dating back to the early Mycenean period, 1500 B.C. Prior to the construction of the temple, initiation may have taken place by dance. Thus it is probable that the Mysteries lasted for two thousand years.

In their remote origins the Mysteries were a closely-knit affair associated with two priestly families, the Eumolpidae and the Keryx: "those who sang beautifully" and "the heralds." Over the centuries the Mysteries developed into a panhellenic festival. Participants had to know Greek. Murderers, people mixed up in shady occult affairs, and others deemed impure were barred.

The Homeric Hymn to Demeter

The Mysteries reenact the myth of the goddesses Demeter and Kore. The Homeric hymn to Demeter[4] dates to about 800 B.C. It tells the story of a mother's separation from her daughter. Demeter, the august queen of the seasons and giver of gifts of the earth, had a daughter, "trim-ankled Kore," or Persephone. The Maid, as she was called, was playing with the daughters of Ocean in the fields of Nyasa. As they were gathering flowers, the Maid reached out with both hands to touch a marvelous, radiant narcissus; suddenly the earth opened up and the Lord of the Underworld—known as Hades—sprang up on his immortal horses and ravished Kore, kidnapping her and carrying her down to his underworld kingdom. The Maid cried out bitterly as she was taken, but only the goddess Hecate and Helios, Lord of the Sun, heard her and knew her fate.

Demeter too heard the wails of her abducted daughter; in grief she wandered for nine days over the earth with flaming torches in her hands, fasting from ambrosia and nectar and refusing to bathe. At dawn on the tenth day she met Hecate and Helios and learned what had befallen her daughter. Angry and unconsoled, she wandered on until she came to the house of Celeus, the Lord of fragrant Eleusis. There she sat near the Maiden Well, grieving in the mortal form of an old woman, bereft of Aphrodite's gifts.

At length she was greeted by the daughters of Celeus and his wife Metaneira, and given the task of nursing Demophoon, the child of Metaneira's old age. Demeter nursed the child with the intent of transforming him into an immortal, feeding him ambrosia by day and putting him to sleep in the sacred fire by night. Metaneira, ignorant of the purpose of this process, once spied upon Demeter's proceedings with her child.

Angered by the untimely exposure, Demeter took Demophoon from the sacred fire and threw him to the ground. She cast off her old woman's form and revealed her divine splendor to the awestruck Metaneira. Now the child would have to suffer the common lot of mortals.

In her rage Demeter called upon the people of Eleusis to build a temple to worship her. Terrified by her awful splendor, the people built the temple, to which the Goddess retired to nurse her wrath over the wrongs done to her daughter Kore. As she mourned, she caused a barrenness to come on the earth, in which even the seeds planted by men stopped bearing fruit. Famine threatened the race of mortals. The gods on Olympus feared that the human race would vanish and that they might lose their accustomed gifts and sacrifices. So the Olympians strove to placate Demeter, who had become a menace to the cosmic order.

Hermes, messenger from loud-thundering Zeus, implored Hades to give up his wife, Kore. In response to this plea, the Lord of the Many Dead released Kore but first tricked her into eating a pomegranate seed. Henceforth she would have to spend one-third of the year in the underworld with him, returning to earth in the spring in unison with the bloom of flowers. So Kore was restored from the gloom and darkness of the Kingdom of the Dead and reunited with her Goddess Mother. And earth was alive again with the bloom of fruits, flowers, and grains. Then Demeter taught her secret rites and showed her mysteries to Eumolpos, Triptolemos, and others of the house of Celeus of Eleusis.

Testimonials to the Eleusinian Transformation

The Homeric Hymn to Demeter describes the initiate's beatitude: "Happy [*olbios*] is he among men upon earth who has seen these mysteries; but he who is uninitiate and who has no part in them never has lot of like good things once he is dead, down in the darkness and gloom."

The Mysteries thus conferred supernatural euphoria. Initiates saw something tremendous. Those who saw experienced a radical change in their idea of death. What they saw convinced them that good things were possible after death—an amazing novelty for Greeks weaned on Homer.

The ancient families that led the rites knew how to produce the desired effect. After the Eleusinian experience, initiates felt their lot in the underworld would improve; they believed they would have a share of better things. The spiritual technicians of Eleusis produced these effects repeatedly, for close to two thousand years. How were they able to jolt large crowds of people annually into an altered experience of reality?

A fragment from the poet Pindar reads: "Blessed is he who, after beholding this, enters upon the way beneath the earth: he knows the end of life and its beginning given by Zeus."[5]

It is hard to say what these enigmatic words mean. Beholding the Mysteries enabled one to know the end (*teleutan*). The word "end" might refer to the purpose, the goal, or the ultimate design of life. In beholding this, the initiate also saw the beginning (*archan*): the source, principle, or archetype of life. The Eleusinian seer stepped outside the cycle of time, it would seem, passing beyond the relativity of beginnings and endings and seeing into the oneness beneath the ripples of change called life and death.

It would be wrong to think of this process as escapist and otherworldly. The boon the Mysteries conferred was for this life as well as for the next. The *Anthologia Palatina,* a poem of Krinagoras of Lesbos, declares that if you have seen the long sacred nights of Demeter, your *thymos,* "soul or spirit," will be *akedia,* "carefree among the living" and *elaphroteron,* "lighter," when you join the multitude of the dead (XI 42.3-6). *Elaphros* means "light in weight," the opposite of *barus,* "heavy." It can also mean "nimble," and in the *Bacchae* of Euripides, *elaphros* has the sense of "giddiness" or "light-headed madness" (851). After the Eleusinian experience, in other words, the soul feels lighter about the prospect of death.

In Sophocles' tragedy *Triptolemos* is another reference to the beatitude achieved at Eleusis: "Thrice blest are those among men who, after beholding these rites, go down to Hades. Only for them is there life; all the rest will suffer an evil lot."[6] Thus a soul must be prepared for the "lightness" of death. This notion leads to reflection on the concept of "enlightenment." Michael Psellos, a Byzantine scholar acquainted with records still available dealing with the Mysteries, described the culminating state of seeing as an *ellampsis,* a "flaring up," and as *autopsia,* literally, "seeing with one's own eyes." *Autopsia* is a term used for divine apparitions, believed to be induced by magical ceremonies.

This "seeing with one's own eyes" gave everyday existence a new brilliance. This gift of vision was the *euangelos,* the good news of pagan antiquity, and like the Christian gospels that lit up the overcast psyche of decadent antiquity, it infused existence with a new joy, while at the same time helping people to look forward to future existence with hope. In the words of a notable pagan initiate, the Roman Cicero: "We have been given a reason," he writes in his treatise *On the Laws,* "not only to live in joy but to die with better hope."

Three centuries before Cicero, the Attic orator and rival of Plato, Isocrates, wrote a panegyric on Athens in which he described the two gifts of Demeter: the civilizing influence of agriculture and the Eleusinian Mysteries. Of the latter he wrote: "Those who take part in them possess better hopes in regard to the end of life and in regard to the whole aion" (IV.28).

The word *aion* may refer to the individual lifespan of a person or to the duration of the world. But the main point of Isocrates' remark, as Carl Kerenyi says, is that, "Participation in the Mysteries offered a guarantee of life without fear of death, of confidence in the face of death. This is why the poets looked upon the initiates as so superior to other mortals." Kerenyi states that "Greek existence," the Greek way of life, its peculiar creative capacities and unique modes of self-affirmation, was uniquely tied to the Mysteries held at Eleusis.[7]

After the edict of Valentinian, which prohibited the mysteries in 364 A.D., the pagan Greek historian, Zosimos, wrote this of Praetextatus, a distinguished Roman initiate:

> But after Praetextatus, who held the office of proconsul in Greece, declared that this law would make the life of the Greeks unlivable, if they were prevented from properly observing the most sacred Mysteries, which hold the whole human race together, he permitted the entire rite to be performed in the manner inherited from the ancestors as if the verdict were not valid.[8]

The Mysteries kept the whole human race together; life would be unlivable for the Greeks if they were deprived of their source of spiritual refreshment.

The Being of Light

The Eleusinian experience had several key effects. It (a) produced a state of bliss and beatitude; (b) did away with the fear of death, encouraging a positive attitude toward life beyond the grave; and (c) cast a new and radiant perspective on life itself.

I believe that near-death research can help explain the power of those ancient rites. NDEs also induce a state of transcendent euphoria and reduce the fear of death—indeed, they radically change one's idea of death—and they bring about overall changes in values and outlook. In a word, the NDE is a remarkable spur to the transformation of human consciousness.

Did the ancient Mysteries induce a ritual encounter with what is today called the "Being of Light"? The modern near-death experience and the Eleusinian visionary experience show striking similarities. For one thing, both awaken an extraordinary consciousness of death and rebirth.[9]

Language, Altered States, and Purification

The Eleusinian initiate underwent a powerful experience. Archaeological evidence rules out the likelihood that the secret of Eleusis consisted of any dramatic spectacle or ritual pantomime; there simply wasn't enough room. The Telesterion was filled with columns which prevented large audiences from focusing attention on one prominent scene.

Nor would the display of ritual objects account for the state of beatitude and the shift in attitude toward death said to occur in the celebrants. Another explanation of the Mysteries can be disposed of easily, the idea that they imparted some secret doctrine. It is implausible that learning a new doctrine could cause the radical changes of consciousness associated with the Mysteries. On this we have the testimony of Aristotle: "The initiates did not learn anything but had an experience and were put into a state."

How was the initiate "put into a state"? What were the experimental procedures for inducing the transformative state of consciousness? There were at least three: the fast, techniques of ritual purification, such as bathing in the river Ilyssos, and the drinking of the *kykeon*. It is now pretty much known that the *kykeon* or drinking potion used at Eleusis was a powerful mind-expanding substance. (For a fascinating account, see G. Wasson, A. Hoffman, and C. Ruck, *The Road to Eleusis,* 1978.) All three of these procedures were designed to purify and amplify the initiate's state of consciousness.

On reaching the Telesterion, the initiate, having fasted and drunk the psychedelic potion, was in a highly suggestible state. The ritualistic precautions taken are understandable in light of this deliberately induced suggestible state. Since psychoactive plants amplify consciousness, a person taking them would be very foolish not to take advantage of the opportunity to "purify" beforehand. The details of the rite were thus designed to eliminate any "noise" that might otherwise mask experiencing the "target."

In view of the dangerous sensitivity to associations characteristic of altered states, silence and secrecy in the ritual induction also make eminent sense. The Greek word for ritual silence was *euphemia,* "auspicious speech." One did not utter anything with ill-omened associations; for such utterances, in an amplified consciousness, might very well swell to gigantic proportions and overwhelm the speaker in the process.

Euphemia presupposed another primitive, magical doctrine that affirms the creative power of language: *nomina sunt numina,* "names are sacred power." In the initiate's deeply altered and suggestible consciousness, words could take on awesome powers. This sensitivity to the power of language may explain why Apollonius of Tyana was barred from the Mysteries. Apparently he practiced witchcraft, which meant using sacred spells and formulas. In the altered environment of Eleusis, such spells and formulas might have interfered with the job of the Hierophant.

Concerning the need for ritual purity at the Mysteries, L. R. Farnell remarks on a curious rule at Athens: if a person laid a suppliant bough on the altar of the Eleusinion of Athens during the season of the Mysteries, he or she could be fined or put to death. Farnell, in *The Evolution of Religion,* remarks: "The laying of a suppliant-bough indicated a grievance and was a legally quarrelsome act, and therefore a violation of the purity of the solemn season" (88).

The initiate was preparing to undergo a volatile ritual of consciousness expansion. To lay the suppliant bough on the altar might suggest a train of thought which, amplified to great dimensions, might sabotage the visionary experience. Participating in a mystery was an elaborate psychological and social event. Thus even the smallest details had to be perfect to assure the success of the great experiment in the Telesterion.

The Setting of the Mysteries

The Greeks celebrated their Mysteries by torchlight, under a dark night sky. Kenneth Batcheldor, the modern researcher into the mysteries of paranormal group dynamics, stresses the need for darkness to obtain desired levitation effects. The dark, I suppose, is a simple aid to regressing to the unconscious.

Darkness is also needed to overcome "ownership inhibition," the sense or feeling of being personally responsible for producing strange and anomalous effects. In darkness, where boundaries aren't visible, participants find it easier to melt and expand into each other. It is also less clear who is responsible for what is happening. Inhibition is therefore reduced, and the powers of the unconscious are set free.

Darkness liberates the imagination, creating an atmosphere of sensory ambiguity, an indeterminate, free-floating, internal panorama. With external restraints lifted from the initiate's mental processes, archetypal flights of consciousness can be stirred up much more easily. Perceptual ambiguity was heightened by the *Dadouchos,* the leading torchbearer, and the dance of the female torchbearers must have contributed to the collective mood.

On the nineteenth day of Boedromion (September), the Mysteries officially began. That day was named *agyrmos,* which meant the "gathering"; henceforth the rule of secrecy was upheld. On the morning of the gathering, a procession formed and departed from the sacred gate of Athens. The initiates—the troop of *mystai*—could be identified by their white garments. In this part of the Mysteries, the celebrants mimed the sorrow and wanderings of the Goddess, her experience of death and separation, her anguish, and the bane of infertility she brought.

After Demeter lost her daughter—who symbolized the immortal aspect of herself—she entered into time, transformed into an old woman. Earth itself sank into the throes of death. Crops failed, flowers faded, winter seemed endless. The fallen Goddess had become a wayfarer searching for the lost part of her divine self.

The job of the *mystai* at this point was to reproduce solemnly the movements representing the sorrows and searchings of the Goddess. They put their hearts into her sorrow, which was similar to Mary's pietà, the sorrow of giving birth. The celebrants were one with the human sufferings of the Goddess; only by beginning in sorrow could they share in the bright epiphany of her revival.

Not far from this saga of gloom lurked the prancing, life-affirming spirit of Dionysos. He could be identified by many signs, the abundance of myrtle in the hair and on the arms of the *mystai,* the ivy and the vine, the emblems of Dionysos. The wise and oracular Heraclitus once said that Dionysos and Hades (god of the underworld) were one and the same. And so it seemed, for in Eleusis, as the initiates approached the gates of the sanctuary, they heard the crowds cry out "Iachhos!"—another name for Dionysos.

On the road to Eleusis, the celebrants had to cross a bridge over a river, now dry with the sands of time. At this point the so-called *gephrismoi,* or "bridge jests," took place. In one version a *hetaira,* a courtesan or "special friend," performed the obscene gestures that made the Goddess laugh; in another, the jester was played by a man disguised as a woman. The Greeks linked a comic inversion of reality with cults of fertility.

Before entering the Telesterion, the final place, the goal, (the word *Eleusis* itself means "the place of happy arrival") the *mystai* utter the password: "I have fasted, I have drunk the *kykeon.*"

Time passes. It is night now, after the long march and the long fast. Now the magic potion begins to work its magic. The priestesses dance around the Sacred Well, commemorating the stations of the Goddess, the places she visited upon her arrival at Eleusis. The *Dadouchos* (torchbearers), *Mystagogos* (leaders or celebrants), priestesses, Hierophant, the *Hierokerkes* (Mystery heralds) lead the throng of excited celebrants.

On votive tablets is a faded image, a "boy from the hearth," a noble boy chosen by lot and initiated at the cost of the state. Kerenyi explains the significance of the boy of the hearth, whose mythological ancestor was Demophoon: "[I]t was he who now precisely enacted the prescribed sacred actions in behalf of the entire festive community, so moving the goddess to grant the great vision of which the mystai were to partake in the Telesterion" (82).

Demophoon is the soul of the Mysteries: the mortal transformed into an immortal. The myth points to resurrection from the dead: the human being, symbolized by Demophoon, shall *see* the realm of the immortals. But what concretely did that mean for the Greeks? Scholars now think that the culmination of the entire elaborate investment of time and money was to see a vision of the Kore—the "ineffable maiden." In Kerenyi's view this was the secret of the Mysteries. He holds that the hierophants annually produced a collective visionary experience of the resurrection of the Goddess. This supernatural revelation would account for the euphoric, hope-inducing effect of the Mysteries.

Imagine being there with the man or woman about to be initiated. Inside the Telesterion the Hierophant strikes a loud funeral gong, called the *echeion*, an instrument that imitated the sound of thunder. It was used in the Greek theatre because it was thought to echo the sound of the underworld. Such special effects were designed to heighten the sense of being in the underworld, or, in current understanding, in the midst of unconscious presences.

The Vision

Plutarch's writings have helped modern scholars enter the innermost sanctuary of Eleusis, by which I also mean the sanctuary of the worshipper's mind. At first the procession presses forward turbulently, anxious to unveil the secret of the temple within.

"But he who is already within it," writes Plutarch, "and has beheld a great light, as when the *anaktoron* opens, changes his behaviour and falls silent and wonders." The *anaktoron* was an inner rectangular chamber within the Telesterion. Beside it was the throne of the Hierophant. Here was the focus, the center of visionary action.

Suddenly there is a great light, a blaze of fire within the *anaktoron*—the temple or dwelling of the gods. The sudden burst of flickering flame arrests the attention of the celebrants who fall into silent rapture. The Hierophant now rings the loud nerve-shattering funeral gong and cries out: "The Mistress has given birth to a holy boy, Brimo has given birth to Brimo, that is, the Strong One to the Strong One."[10] Brimo is the name, probably of Thracian origin, for Demeter, Kore-Persephone, and Hecate, in their aspect as goddesses of the underworld. The details of the images are obscure, but the main idea was extraordinary: the Goddess of death has given birth!

The Hierophant—"he who makes the sacred visible"—using his trained melodious voice, evokes a vision of the Goddess. The initiates have been carefully primed for this moment. By now the combined effect of a nine-day fast, a powerful psychoactive substance, the expectations aroused by a shared myth, the purification-induced sharp receptivity, and the cunningly devised perceptual ambiguity of flickering light against a backdrop of darkness—all this, plus the funeral gong and the Hierophant's evocation, trigger the experience of "having seen." The happy initiates become *epoptai*—"seers."

I do not suppose that a full-blown vision of the Goddess was produced in every candidate. Not every subject in this great "experiment" is likely to have enjoyed full success. The response must have varied. Plato's *Phaedrus* gives a clue to the variety of responses. There was a time, proclaims the myth in Plato's dialogue on love and language, when sad bedevilled humans were:

> permitted as initiates to the sight of perfect and simple and still and happy apparitions, which we saw in the pure light, being ourselves pure and not entombed in this which we carry around with us and call the body, in which we are imprisoned like an oyster in its shell (250c).

Thus, according to Plato, the highest state of consciousness, prior to the fall into bodily existence, is likened to the state of initiates into the Mysteries. Three things characterize this exalted state. First, there are visions, or apparitions, which are "happy" and which make one happy. Second, the apparitions are said to be *atreme,* "still and perfect." Plato seems to be referring to the ambiguous appearances probably produced by the visual white noise of the Mysteries. He implies that there is yet a more "still and perfect" way of producing the visionary effect. And third, Plato seems to be saying that an out-of-body experience was part of the Eleusinian experiment.

It seems from all this that the climax of the Eleusinian rites was leaving the body and entering a light of bliss. The practice of Platonic philosophy, it is implied, will provide such an experience in a more secure and reliable way. That Plato should have this view is consistent with his famous definition of philosophy as the practice of death and dying.

Plato's teaching is a refinement of the Orphic idea of *soma sema*— that "the body is a tomb." The Orphic image of the body as a tomb is similar to the image used by C. G. Jung to describe his near-death experience. In 1944 Jung had a heart attack after having broken his foot, and for some time hovered on the borderline between life and death. The details of his experience are extremely interesting:

In reality, a good three weeks were still to pass before I could truly make up my mind to live again. I could not eat because all my food repelled me. . . . Disappointed, I thought: 'Now I must return to the "box system" again.' For it seemed to me as if behind the horizon of the cosmos a three-dimensional world had been artificially built up, in which each person sat by himself in a little box. . . . Life and the whole world struck me as a prison. . . . I felt violent resistance to my doctor because he had brought me back to life.[11]

The image that emerges from Jung's near-death experience is classically Orphic-Platonic. Ordinary life is a box, a prison, says Jung—a tomb, a form of death, said the ancients.

Ordinary life is death. This declaration completely reverses the ordinary way we perceive the world. Is it possible that our ordinary perception of reality is so radically flawed, so totally inverted and perverted? Does an altogether higher, fuller, more luminous mode of being envelop us?

Did the ancient Greeks have an experimental method for inducing life-transforming states of consciousness? Two texts from antiquity support the view that the Eleusinian Mysteries were techniques for inducing the archetypal near-death experience.

(1) The first occurs in a passage from Themistios' essay *On the Soul,* preserved in Stobaios and Plutarch. The author compares the climax of the Mysteries to what happens to the soul at the moment of death. He is very explicit about the connection:

The soul at the point of death has the same experience as those who are being initiated into great mysteries. . . . At first one wanders and wearily hurries to and fro, and journeys with suspicion through the dark as one uninitiated. Then come all the terrors before the final initiation, shuddering, trembling, sweating, amazement. Then one is struck with a marvelous light, one is received into pure regions and meadows, with voices and dances and the majesty of holy sounds and shapes. Among these he who has fulfilled initiation wanders free, and released and bearing his crown joins in the divine communion, and consorts with pure and holy men, beholding those who live here uninitiated, an uncleansed horde, trodden under foot and huddled together in mud and fog, abiding in their miseries through fear of death and mistrust of the blessings there.[12]

Several points here resemble the archetypal NDE. First, the journey through the dark, which corresponds to the dark tunnel of NDE fame. Then the terrors before the final initiation—"shuddering, trembling, sweating, amazement"—so similar to what happens with psychoactive potions. The shuddering, trembling, and so forth seem like ritual counterparts to the shock, accident, cardiac arrest, or other cause of spontaneous NDEs.

The "marvelous light" one is struck with is a constant in reports of transcendent experiences. Then come the "pure regions and meadows" and supernatural landscapes, often reported in near-death encounters. As for communion with "holy men," they are like those religious figures and light beings sighted by near-death visionaries.

According to Themistios, the uninitiated, trapped in the mud and fog of the old Hades yet abide "in their miseries through fear of death and mistrust of the blessings there." This means that those who have not been initiated remain fearful and mistrustful of death.

(2) The second text is from *The Transformations of Lucius (The Golden Ass)* by the Latin author Apuleius. *The Transformations* is a religious novel about a man turned by magic into an ass. The Goddess Isis intervenes and changes him back into a man. The story tells how Lucius is delivered from "blind" Fortune and "the daily terror of death." In gratitude Lucius becomes a priest of Isis, whose Mysteries were similar to those at Eleusis. The experience Lucius describes sounds very much like a near-death experience.

> I have no doubt, curious reader, that you are eager to know what happened when I entered. If I were allowed to tell you, and you were allowed to be told, you would soon hear everything. . . . However, not wishing to leave you in a state of tortured suspense, I will record as much as I may lawfully record for the uninitiated. I approached the very gates of death and set one foot on Prosperine's threshold, yet was permitted to return. At midnight I saw the sun shining as if it were noon; I entered the presence of the gods of the underworld and the gods of the upper-world, stood near and worshipped them. Well, now you have heard what happened, but I fear you are none the wiser. (279-80)

A Spiritual Science?

I recall a conversation I had with parapsychologist J. B. Rhine, just before his death. Rhine, so far as I know, was the first to speak of the "parapsychology of religion"—a pioneer in the effort to bring together modern science and ancient wisdom. I asked him what he thought of the near-death experience. An experimenter to the last, he suggested there might be ways of bringing people—he hesitated, and then said animals—gradually closer to bodily death, without, of course, any risk of harm. Researchers might experimentally induce the near-death experience, he suggested, and then study it.

It was a bold suggestion, and one that the ancient Greeks apparently anticipated. The Eleusinian soul-scientists specialized in producing experiences that clearly resemble events now being studied by near-death researchers. The same phenomenology seems to be involved and the same aftereffects. If Kerenyi is right, this psychic experiment was the secret inspiration behind the creative wonders of Greek civilization.

This hypothesis raises an interesting question. What would happen to *our* civilization if we could learn to enter and recapture the psychic background, the imaginal universe of the ancient Greeks? The inner life of the Greeks produced a revolution of new paradigms for all aspects of humankind's encounter with the universe. Is this what we need today if we hope to get out of the bind we are in, as a technical civilization out of touch with its soul?

In conclusion, I want to suggest that the annual "experiment" of Eleusis, the mainstay of Greek spiritual life for two thousand years, may be rightly described as an ancient foray into future science. This science of the future may have relevance for our modern dilemma. The Eleusinian experiments produced a state of consciousness modern science is just now beginning to explore. In essence, the Eleusinian Mysteries brought a whole civilization to the frontiers of the soul.

10
Padre Pio

All human concepts, no matter where they come from, are both good and bad; one should know how to take and assimilate the good, offer it to God, and eliminate what is bad.

Padre Pio

During World War II the Americans had an airbase in Bari, about seventy-five miles from San Giovanni Rotondo, a village in Southern Italy that houses a Capuchin friary. According to U. S. Intelligence, the Germans had a munitions facility in the hills nearby. An officer was assigned the job of bombing it. As the planes neared San Giovanni, the officer saw in the sky before him the figure of a monk waving him back. Dumbfounded by this spectacle, he ordered the planes to turn back. When the war ended, he went to the friary and met the monk he thought he saw in the sky.[1] His name was Padre Pio (1887-1968).

Stories like the flyer's are legion. In the case of Padre Pio, the work of sorting out fact from fiction is still underway. Padre Pio's Cause—his case for canonization—is before the Church. Part of his Cause is supported by evidence of miracles. Many remarkable claims about Padre Pio are well documented; many are based on hearsay, part of the folklore growing around the monk. Padre Pio had a gift for catapulting people into living worlds of mythic imagination.

In Padre Pio's world, creatures of myth and fantasy come to life: madonnas, guardian angels, shapeshifting demons, bilocations, magical cures, time travel, and a good deal more. Whatever the literal truth of particular claims, the contents of Padre Pio's story are at odds with the routine picture of the possible. Around the padre, the incredible somehow became credible; the impossible, actual.

And yet, however remarkable, Padre Pio was a human being, a

creature of our own species. I assume therefore that his "miraculous" powers are latent in us all.

Who Was Padre Pio?

Before a survey of some of Padre Pio's phenomena, here is a quick glance at his life. Padre Pio was born on May 25, 1887, in the town of Pietrelcina near Naples. His family was poor, and Grazio Forgione (Pio's father) worked in America to earn enough for his son's education. Few regions in Italy observed as many saint's days as Pietrelcina, not to mention feasts, processions, novenas, and high masses. Pietrelcina venerated the *Madonna della Libera* (the Madonna of Liberation), said to have freed the countryside from invading Byzantines in the seventh century.

The same madonna stopped the plague on December 2, 1882, according to legend. In the same region is a bubbling spring, miraculously started by Saint Nicholas in the fourth century. Belief in miracles in these parts is further fortified by the periodic liquefaction of Saint Gennaro's blood in the Cathedral of Naples, a phenomenon that baffles scientists to this day.

Believers in southern Italy share a polytheistic approach to the Transcendent. Besides the saints, the Virgin Mary, and the relics, people make respectable use of witchcraft—*la vecchia*, "the old thing." Pio's mother, Beppa, once took Pio (Franci then) to a *strega* (witch) who lived nearby, to treat his bad stomach. Beppa carried a pair of miniature scissors to ward off the evil eye. In Beppa's and Franci's world, magic and religion were hard to separate. It was a world marked by intense imaginality. Young Franci grew up with an agile sense of the possibilities of the unseen. For him, as for most of his contemporaries, it was not a desperate problem to gain some hint of the Transcendent; everywhere sidedoors to sacred power were open.

On January 1, 1903, Pio, age sixteen, had a vision of himself fighting an evil being in the form of an enormous terrifying giant; in this vision, he found his vocation as spiritual warrior. On August 10, 1910, he was ordained a priest. In 1910 he first experienced the "transverberation" or invisible stigmata—which became visible on September 20, 1918. (He retained these mysterious wounds for fifty years until his death.)

Pio's early years were full of odd illnesses, diabolic attacks, and ecstatic visions. The attacks usually preceded the visions. Dancing back and forth between light and dark was part of what Pio and other mystics call the "game of love." The dark side always haunted Padre Pio.

From 1916 to 1918 Pio served in the military, which made him ill and prompted him to disappear. The military listed him as a deserter and finally found him in the hills of San Giovanni, busy at his true vocation of spiritual warrior. Once his fame as a stigmatist spread, however, his troubles really began. After centuries of experience, the Church does not jump every time a wonder is announced. So the Holy Office sent various physicians to determine the cause of Pio's stigmata.

"Better a mouse between two cats," the monk groused, "than Padre Pio between two doctors."

To be sure, the excitement caused by the young stigmatic disturbed the Holy Office. The Catholic Church has survived for two millennia, and it is wary of enthusiasm that threatens authority. To prevent a cult from forming around Pio, the Holy Office took measures. The effect on Padre Pio was unpleasant. In defense of the Church, one can say it was testing Pio's humility, the strength of his vow of obedience. Pio passed all tests with flying colors. On balance, it seems hard to justify the way the Church treated Padre Pio. True, the man ardently wished to suffer for Jesus; unfortunately, too many were eager to gratify his wish.

On October 14, 1920, rumors spread that the Padre was going to be transferred from San Giovanni. The townsfolk would have none of this; they rioted, and fourteen souls were dispatched to the next world. A young man called Donato entered the church and pulled a gun on the Padre, shouting "Dead or alive, you're staying with us." After this, the Holy Office scrapped its plan to relocate Pio. (Pio, by the way, forgave a penitent Donato.)

Rumors of Pio's transfer persisted, however, and from 1920 to 1933 the people of San Giovanni Rotondo engaged in small-scale guerrilla warfare against the Vatican. Every attempt to move the monk was met with protest, threats of violence. Finally, the Vatican tried a different tactic and issued decrees restricting Pio's activities as a priest. In effect, the Vatican placed him under house arrest. On June 2, 1922, the Holy Office gave the order "to keep Padre Pio under observation." All "singularity and noise" were to be avoided. He was ordered to quit hearing confessions, not to display or discuss his stigmata, and to celebrate Mass at irregular hours—completely alone. (This edict was enforced for two years, from 1931 to 1933.)

In 1922 Padre Pio was forbidden by the Holy Office to write anything, including letters to his superiors. Fortunately, three volumes of his early letters still exist. In 1924, the Holy Office decreed that there was nothing supernatural about the priest's stigmata; the implication was that there was nothing remarkable about Padre Pio, thus discrediting his charisms and everything about him that was exceptional. In 1925, the Holy Office forced Padre Pio to "cease all communications, even by letter" with his beloved spiritual director, Padre Benedetto. The two men, faithful sons of the Church, never again spoke or wrote to one another.

The final phase of indignities began in 1960 and continued without let up till Pio's death. This "second persecution" has been documented by Ennemond Boniface. According to Boniface, the root of the persecution of Padre Pio was rationalistic skepticism. The persecution was "an enterprise of systematic destruction of the supernatural." Strange to say, the Church persecuted Pio *for* his miraculous deeds.

One of Padre Pio's achievements was to inspire the building of a great hospital at San Giovanni, one of the poorest regions of Italy, called the House for the Relief of Suffering. Released by the Pope from his vow of poverty, Pio, in a purely technical sense, became responsible for the hospital's finances. Immediately he was charged with mismanagement; fueled by an anticlerical press, rumors spread that the padre was making personal use of funds.

Rumors also flew that the seventy-five-year-old monk was trysting with local women. In hopes of entrapping Padre Pio and verifying this gossip, the Capuchins bugged his confessional, his cell, and other places where he spoke with people. Nothing incriminating was ever found.

Then there were the so-called *pie donne*—the "pious ladies." These were Padre Pio's "groupies," mostly local women who adored him. The sex rumors stemmed from their ranks. When the ladies were not slandering him, they fought among themselves to be near him, especially at Mass. They chained and locked up the front pews for themselves. They followed Pio around with scissors, and tried to snip off bits of his vestments.

Padre Pio remained calm in the midst of all this. He enjoyed the friendship of his Franciscan brothers, the daily camaraderie, eating and talking together. Padre Pio was a noted storyteller and practical joker. His attitude toward his own phenomena was interesting. He never ascribed any abilities to himself. For him, the source clearly lay beyond. He once said he was as amazed by his stigmata as everyone else, and he ironically referred to his own bilocations as "hallucinations." He challenged people who went on about his prodigies by saying: "How do you know? Did you see it?"

Occasionally, his humor turned black, as when a rich, older lady from the North gushed, "Tell me something nice; today is my birthday." The padre whispered in her ear, "Death is near."

The external pattern of his everday life was regular, except for an occasional jaunt to town to vote. He served mass, heard confessions, directed charitable enterprises. (He started a global network of prayer groups, for instance.) And he received people who came to visit him from all over the world. The curious, the hostile, the pious, the hopeful, the needy, the fascinated—they all came. Few left without being touched, often deeply. Some, like the writer Graham Greene, held back from Pio for fear of falling under his spell.

People from everywhere came steadily, and those who couldn't come wrote. The Holy Office burned a barn full of letters to Padre Pio. I suppose this grasping for grace could irritate even a saint, yet the monk received rich and poor, famous and unknown, with the same detached spirit. In 1902, the Russian Prince Karl Klugheit, a student of the occult, visited the Padre and was converted to the Catholic priesthood. He described Pio's personality as "submerged in the divine."

Padre Pio felt deeply. He laughed and cried easily. He cried when his mother died and got angry when his sister forsook her religious vows. A frequent visitor to the higher realms of consciousness, during ecstasy he chatted freely with Jesus, Mary, and his guardian angel. In the last three years of his life, he nearly succumbed to the "dark night of the soul"—that period in the life of the mystic when the light is withdrawn and the soul is left to be purged in the penetrating heat of spiritual pain. Yet in his dark moments he could ask, "What if all this is a prodigious illusion?"

Padre Pio's Mass

One aspect of Padre Pio's life merits special notice, the Masses he celebrated. They were legendary. At first Pio said Mass very early in the morning. Soon after midnight the young priest would rise, fretting and chomping at the bit, like a racehorse fidgety at the starting gate. "Without the Mass," he once remarked, "the sun would cease to rise."

During Mass he lost his senses, stood motionless, communing wordlessly with an invisible world. The peasants complained he took too long; they needed to go to work in the fields. His fellow priests learned to command him—telepathically—to come to his senses and get on with the rite.

Jung has written on the Roman Mass, which he called "a still-living mystery, the origins of which go back to early Christian times."[2] As with the Mysteries of Eleusis, the Mass is a rite of transformation. The Mass relives the life, death, and resurrection of Christ. At the Consecration, the priest effects a mystical Transubstantiation of bread and wine into the Lord's body and blood. The Mass, then, makes God present in space and time, allowing communicants to taste the divine presence. For Jung the Mass was a "rite of the individuation process."

With Padre Pio the ancient mystery rite came to life. An eyewitness observed: "The members of his body are numb to all external influences. For example, an extremely bright electric light, the flashing of a camera taking a picture of him in ecstasy at Mass, which under ordinary circumstances would have blinded him, could be done over and over without awakening him or leaving his sight impaired."[3]

According to Pio's own testimony, at Mass he was present with Jesus during the ordeal of Calvary. Pio became one with Jesus, reliving the divine drama. He heard the "yells, blasphemies, noises, threats," suffered the crown of thorns and the flagellation. After Mass, they wiped blood from Pio's head; his undergarments too were stained, soaked with blood. I have seen some of these blood-dyed cloths, now in glass frames; they make strange relics.

The monks asked Pio for all the details.[4]

"Do they hammer in the nails on you as well?"

"And how!"

"Are the stings of the crown of thorns and the wounds of the scourging *real* during the Mass?"

"What do you mean by this? The effect is the same all right."

The padre may not have been literally present at Calvary; but neither was he pretending, playacting, or verbalizing some abstract fancy. His experiences require a new category, a new way to classify a mode of being. The Mass, as performed by Padre Pio, was a surreal event, occurring in an imaginal (not the same as imaginary) world.

In this world, God became manifest for Padre Pio; human was temporarily transformed into divine. As Jung said, the Mass is a still-living mystery. The Mysteries were experiments in regeneration; they were, as shown in the last chapter, experiences of deification.

One of the monks asked Pio: "I am right then in saying that Jesus crucified walks in the midst of us?"

"Yes," Pio replied.

Pio, the monks said, was a "monstrance"—a physical manifestation of divine reality.

During Mass, Pio's wounds seemed to open and bleed more than usual. Some saw a crown of thorns on his brow. Some wept at the sight of the sacrifice. And Padre Pio himself wept.

"It is all one mercy, one embrace," he said.

The monks had the impudence to ask, "Where does Jesus kiss you?"

"All over," he replied.

"When Jesus comes does he visit only the soul?"

"All, the entire being," repeated Pio.

What is the essence of this hyperreal experience? What is really going on inside Pio? The climax of the Mass is the moment of Holy Communion. "It is a fusion," he said, "in the way two candles are blended together, not to be distinguishable any more."

Padre Pio became Christ—temporarily incarnating the archetype of the Christ—living the crucifixion and the resurrection. The rite is rooted in stark realism. Without suffering there can be no transformation; without shadow, no light. Without the butcher, the crown of thorns—all the instruments of torture—no renewal or transformation. The ego is crucified, the self regenerated.

The Recreation of Nature

"Tell me why you suffer so much during the consecration?" asked a confrere.

"Because right then a new and admirable destruction and creation takes place."

A new destruction and creation! How are people of the twenty-first century supposed to understand this? This book has tried to translate the phenomena of the great religions into ideas of evolutionary cosmology. In this view, the laws of nature are seen as habits, reflections of average behavior, not as dictators of absolute law.

Pio's phenomena support the idea that nature is an open field of possibilities, not a closed book written by a seventeenth or nineteenth-century scientist. Pio's life shows that nature is a field of possibilities. The examples of Padre Pio's extraordinary phenomena that follow attempt to describe a pattern, an integral movement of life, not a potpourri of marvels.

Writer John McCaffery states: "The full extent of Padre Pio's authentic miracles will never be known. They span half a century and cover all parts of the world. Most of them are destined to remain unrecorded."[5] Miracles ascribed to the monk are still reported, years after his death. In every issue of the monthly *Voce di Padre Pio,* such reports abound, many being more testimonies of faith than documented miracles.

Nature seemed to behave oddly around the padre. What follows is a look at three categories of reported phenomena that reveal a pattern. The first highlights Pio's extraordinary ability to enter the inner life of himself, other people, and nature. The second group of examples documents Pio's uncanny abilities to move about, free from the constraints of time and space. The third shows him to possess a disconcerting ability to modify physical reality.

Battles with Demons

I have argued that the direction of human evolution seems to be toward a richer internal environment. Padre Pio seemed to have special access to internal environments. From childhood he traveled in visionary worlds. At five, frightened by demoniacal visages, he cried so much that his father once lost his temper and threw him to the ground. Pio explained, "My mother would turn off the light, and a lot of monsters would come up close to me, and I would cry."

"It was the devil who was tormenting me," he also said. Terrifying visions continued throughout his life—inseparable from his visions of Jesus and the Madonna. The raptures, the ecstasies often lasted for hours. Accounts of them are found in his letters and in observations made by his spiritual directors, such as Father Agostino, who sometimes eavesdropped on the padre's conversations with invisible beings. These included Jesus, Mary, Francis of Assisi, and his guardian angel.

Pio's inner environment was also infested with hostile entities. Sometimes these dark forces appeared to him before his higher visions. Shape-shifting diabolic apparitions appeared as huge black cats, as naked women dancing lasciviously, as an invisible entity that spat in his face and tortured him with deafening noises, and as an executioner who whipped him.

According to his confreres, "Padre Pio was very alert to unexpected movements and sounds. He said that the devil appeared to him in all shapes. He had fear even of a mouse, because the devil would start out as a mouse and turn into a claw and go for his eyes."[6] The attacks Pio feared were physical. Some in Pietrelcina say one can still see claw marks and splattered inkspots made by demons. Once the iron bars of the padre's cell were found twisted out of shape after a night he spent wrestling with demons. The monks never saw anything but many heard the diabolic din. They often found the padre unconscious on the floor beside his bed, covered with welts and bruises.

A well-witnessed event took place in July, 1964. A possessed woman was dragged to San Giovanni. When she saw Pio, she growled in a deep voice, "Pio, we will see you tonight." That night the friars thought the house had been struck by an earthquake. The Superior rushed to Pio's room and found him on the floor bleeding from the head. Oddly, there was a pillow under his head. Pio said the Madonna had put it there. In the morning, the possessed woman (while being exorcised by another priest) shrieked, "Last night I was up to see the old man. I hate him so much because he is a fountain of faith. I would have done more, except the lady in white stopped me."

This story taxes my credulity as much as it must the reader's; nevertheless, John Schug, from whose book on Padre Pio this account is taken, bases his retelling on eyewitnesses not disposed to sensationalism. Pio's face was so disfigured by the event he was unable to appear in public for five days. On another occasion, he was found with the bones in his arms and legs broken. "I cannot describe to you how those wretched creatures were beating me!" he wrote in 1918. "Several times I thought I was near death. Saturday it seemed as if they really wanted to finish me." (Padre Pio da Pietrelcina, Epistolario, III, Convento Santa Maria, San Giovanni Rotondo, 1977, 311). Sometimes his tormentors came disguised as his spiritual director, Father Agostino, or as a saint or guardian angel.

Diabolic attacks lasted throughout Pio's long life. The psychologically sophisticated reader will doubt these reports of demonic assault. Wilhelm Reich believed such experiences were the result of repressed "orgone" energy turning against oneself. Or perhaps Padre Pio's demons were poltergeists. I am not sure how smoothly these explanations fit.

As for Reich, Pio suffered his "demons" to the end—he died at eighty-one. In 1967 Padre Pio (then eighty) called Father Alessio to his side during the night and said, "My son, stay here because they do not leave me in peace even for a moment." The padre was sweating profusely; when Father Alessio asked later on what happened, Pio replied, "If you had seen what I saw, you would be dead." Is it likely that such an old man was still consumed by energies similar to repressed sexual desire? As for poltergeists, most cases involve adolescent children. Pio is not a typical poltergeist "focus."

Pio's Guardian Angel

If Padre Pio battled with sinister forces, he also received supernormal favors. For example, Padre Pio's guardian angel was multitalented. Apparently he could translate French and Greek, languages Pio didn't know.

In 1912, Agostino, by way of experiment, wrote letters to Pio in French and Greek. When Pio received them, he was at Pietrelcina for medical reasons, under care of a parish priest, don Salvatore Pannullo. Pannullo wrote on August 25, 1919, "I, the undersigned, testify under oath, that when Padre Pio received this letter (a letter in Greek and in the Greek alphabet), he explained its contents to me literally. When I asked him how he could read and explain it, as he did not know even the Greek alphabet, he replied: 'My Guardian Angel explained it all to me.'"

The options on this are clear: either Pio and Pannullo contrived an act of pure deception, or the story is true. I leave it to the reader to decide if such a conspiracy is consistent with the facts.

"Guardian Angel" aside, assume the translation occurred by telepathy. It would be telepathy of a rare type; for the telepathic transmission of skills such as the use of a language is unknown in experimental parapsychology. Pio is also said to have heard confessions in languages he didn't know.

Guardian angels are well-rounded in their education. The next story shows they know something about automobile mechanics. In 1959, a woman was driving with her husband from Rome to San Severo. (The couple prefers to remain anonymous.) En route their car broke down. For two hours cars sped by without stopping. Toward nightfall, the woman grew anxious and prayed to Padre Pio.

Within ten minutes a black car pulled up and an elegant young man dressed in blue stepped out. He lifted the hood and said, "Look, you lost all the water from the radiator, and it's burnt out. Take your can and fill it up with water. Near here, there is a farmhouse, which has a well; take the water from there."

The husband took the can from the car trunk and did as the young man said. The man then took a black box from his car, produced a roll of adhesive tape, and sealed the radiator. He had beautiful hands with agile tapered fingers. The dog, who normally barked at strangers, sat in the car's back seat, strangely calm. The husband returned with the water and filled the radiator.

"You can return home safely; anyhow, you are quite near," said the mysterious helper, who then got in his car and drove off. The couple watched the car pull away and looked for the licence plate. There was none! Instead they saw a white strip marked with hieroglyphics. The car moved away slowly on Via Aurelia where it suddenly vanished.

Arriving home in a "dreamy state," the couple reflected on further oddities. The young man somehow knew there was an empty can in the trunk, also, that they lived "quite near." Later they tried to find the well and farmhouse but despite diligent efforts were unable to do so. They could find no farmhouse in the area where their car had broken down.[7]

Pio as Mindreader

Like Saint John Vianney, the famous Curé of Ars, Padre Pio showed powers of mindreading in the confessional. Hearing confessions was a most important activity in Pio's long ministry. Hour after hour, day after day, for over fifty years, Pio listened to people's sins and secrets.

John Schug gives an account of Federico Abresch's confession to Pio. According to Abresch, a Lutheran convert, Pio recalled actions and thoughts he had long forgotten. "He enumerated with precision and clarity all of my faults, even mentioning the number of times I had missed Mass.'' Pio also reminded Abresch of something he had forgotten years ago when he got married. Abresch had neglected to go to confession. Through Pio's remarks, Abresch was able to reconstruct his past. Pio seemed to know Abresch's unconscious mental history better than even Abresch himself.

Abresch regarded this as proof that Pio had an ability greater than mere human ''thought-transference.'' The fact that Pio could ''read'' the unconscious of another person seemed evidence of God's action, something totally beyond human potential. But, in my view, Abresch is mistaken in this opinion. Evidence from mediumship and experimental parapsychology shows that telepathic ''leakage'' from another person's unconscious mind does in fact occur.

Not only in the confessional did Pio read minds but also in more casual circumstances. ''Again, to take my own experience,'' writes John McCaffery, ''he would poke fun at me by telling me what I was thinking of the previous evening, or what my program was for the coming week, or what I had been discussing with the Father Guardian in his cell. He seemed to know everything.''

Pio's mindreading took odd forms. Once Padre Alessio was with Padre Pio while he was saying the rosary. Pio suddenly shouted, ''What do you want? What do you want? Come closer . . . come here.'' After a while the priest recited the formula for absolution. There was no one else in the room—no one, at any rate, visible.

John Schug also tells the story of a man who walked into church planning to murder his wife. ''Murderer!'' Padre Pio roared in the church. The man skulked away and returned the next day, penitent.

Pio not only ''read'' but changed or ''converted'' minds. The Gospels, as noted in Chapter 4, portray Jesus as a man who took immediate mental hold of his disciples. Pio, too, had this ability. For example, unemployed Laurino Costa sent Padre Pio a telegram asking for prayer to help him find a job. The padre sent a telegram back: ''Come to San Giovanni Rotondo at once.'' The young man arrived penniless and was standing with a crowd of men in the sacristy. Padre Pio, who never met Laurino, shouted at him, ''Laurino, come here. I see you have arrived.''

Bewildered, the youth approached. ''Laurino, you will feed my sick.'' (A cook was needed in the new hospital.)

"But Padre," Laurino protested, "I've never cooked an egg in my life."

The Padre insisted, "Go and feed my sick. I'll always be near you." Laurino went to the hospital and rang the doorbell. The Mother Superior answered, "You must be the experienced cook we've been waiting for." Within three hours Laurino was at work.

Laurino admitted to Schug, "To this day (fourteen years later) I still don't know what happened. All day long I found myself calmly working and telling others what to do, as though I were carrying out a routine I had been used to."

Mastery of Time and Space

Reports of Pio bilocating everywhere from the American Midwest to China and Africa are numerous. The idea of "bilocation" contradicts the belief that a human being is a physical object that occupies one region of space at a time. The idea that Jack, say, can be at Forty-second Street and Fifth Avenue in New York and simultaneously at Main and Third in Sheboygan, Wisconsin, is obviously absurd. Nevertheless, the annals of saints, psychics, and yogis contain many such bilocation stories, some well documented.

Padre Pio bilocated by means of his voice, his presence, and his aroma; he turned up in people's dreams, and sometimes his double appeared, fully materialized. Mary Pyle, one-time secretary to Maria Montessori, spent the last forty-five years of her life in San Giovanni Rotondo. She wrote the following in her diary:

> One day I went into the sacristy and said to Padre Pio: "Father, I believe my mother is in Florence today." His immediate answer, given with certainty was: "No, she is in Umbria." Surprised I said, "No, Father, I do not believe she was supposed to go to Umbria." But he insisted, looking far into space. "She's been in Umbria." A few days later I received a letter from my mother who told me: "Thank Padre Pio for the visit he paid me while I was sick in bed in Perugia (which is in Umbria). I did not see him with my eyes, nor did I hear him with my ears, but I felt his presence near my bed."[8]

Padre Pio apparently knew in advance that he would be able to bilocate at a particular place. For example, the Vicar General of Uruguay, Monsignor Damiani, a frequent visitor at San Giovanni, once told Pio he wanted to die in San Giovanni and that he wanted

his dear friend Pio to assist him at his death. Pio said the Vicar was
going to die in Uruguay, and that he should not bother staying in San
Giovanni. He promised to assist the Vicar when his day of reckoning
came, wherever he was. In 1941, the Vicar died in Uruguay. Cardinal Barbieri was in the
house where Damiani resided on the night he died. Someone knocked
on Barbieri's half-open door. Barbieri noticed a monk in Capuchin
robes pass; then he got up and went to Damiani's room. The Vicar
had died of a heart attack. A note on his dresser read, "Padre Pio
was here."[9]

Other bilocation stories revolved around healings. For example,
on June 12, 1952, Lucia Bellodi, stricken with pernicious diabetes,
was on her deathbed when she sat up and began to wave her hands.
She cried out that Padre Pio had appeared to her, told her she was
cured and that she should go to his monastery. By June 16th she had
regained her speech and stopped having to drink twenty-five quarts
of water a day. When she visited the Padre, he smiled and said, "I've
been waiting for you."

Perhaps the best authenticated type of Pio's bilocation was via his
characteristic odor, which some compared to the perfume of flowers
or the smell of oriental tobaccos. Reports of mysterious smells surrounding mediums and holy people are widespread. The odor of sanctity is also linked with the phenomenon of bodily incorruption.[10] An
odor of ravishing sweetness filled the room where the body of Saint
Patrick was laid out. The dead body of Saint Clare also exuded a sweet
odor. Hundreds of examples could be given.

Padre Pio's "perfume" also traveled; people far away, sometimes
thousands of miles, smelled it. Bernard Ruffin tells of the fragrance
occurring to a Lutheran seminarian, Robert Hopcke, in Plainfield,
New Jersey, in 1978, ten years after Pio's death.[11] William Car-
rigan, normally skeptical, reported to Ruffin his perception of the
aroma at his desk at Foggia (about twenty miles from the monastery),
"I had no trouble in identifying the aroma as that of Padre Pio. It
wasn't something you could confuse with any other odor."

Padre Alberto D'Apolito, Pio's comrade for many years, wrote in
1978, "The reality is that hundreds of thousands of individuals, even
unbelievers, have testified and continue to testify that they have suddenly and inexplicably perceived the perfume of Padre Pio." For example, Emilio Servadio, a leading Roman psychoanalyst and para-

psychologist, experienced Pio's celestial perfume during a visit to San Giovanni in 1937.

Precognition, if a fact of nature, baffles the normal view of time, cause, and effect. (How can anything that hasn't occurred influence people in any way?) Nevertheless, there are many reports of Pio's paranormal forays into the future.

For example, Pio seemed to know which Italian cities would be bombed during the war and which soldiers would return. Like holy men in other traditions, Pio also foretold the year of his death. He often had previsions of death. A young priest, Father Dionisio, on his way to Venice for studies, said goodbye to Pio. "Studies! Studies!" Pio muttered. "Think of death, instead, so that when it comes. . . ." His voice trailed off. "What a strange way to say goodbye," observed one of the brothers. Pio shrugged. In twenty days, Dionisio was dead.

In 1983 Pope John Paul II was almost assassinated; a Vatican official reported that Pio had told the Polish cardinal years before he'd be pope one day, adding that the Polish pope would be "brought down in blood soon."

In 1942 there was a moment when the Italian troops seemed victorious at Alamein. Pio was strolling with Dr. Sanguinetti and several others in the monastery garden when he told them, "We are going to lose the war." And he added, to the shock of those present, that it would be "a good thing." He then explained that to win the war would be to win for Nazism—which would be a calamity. Someone asked if that wouldn't be better than a Communist victory. "No," he said emphatically, adding, "On the contrary, the negative materialism of the Soviets will never succeed in satisfying the mysticism which is part of the Russian soul. Russia will return to religion and to God."[12] These remarks seem worth noting in light of the recent collapse of Communism.

Divine Shapeshifting

The great saints are artists who reshape human nature. How can the psychic power of the saints be understood? Do they perhaps embody a trend toward increasing openness to the goals of consciousness? With Padre Pio, it is as if a restless shapeshifting creative spirit wants to make matter more permeable to the divine will and imagination.

Eastern, occult, and Christian traditions tell of subtle, astral, pneumatic, light bodies. In general, the physical phenomena of mysticism show a trend toward increased lightness of bodily being. As said in Chapter 7, these phenomena suggest the hypothesis that we may be evolving into a body of light.

Incorruption, luminosity, inedia, the odor of sanctity, bodily elongation, levitation—all express different facets of this "enlightened" body. All seem aspects, phases, perspectives of a systemic transformation, symptoms of a new mode of existence, a new form of nature, struggling to emerge. Consider a few examples.

The stigmata. The stigmata illustrate the malleability of the human body to the power of spiritual imagination. Francis of Assisi was the first to reproduce the wounds of Christ in his own body, and since Francis hundreds of cases have been reported. The Church by and large takes a dim view of these often bizarre lesions, recognizing they may be symptoms of hysteria as much as signs of heroic sanctity.

But Padre Pio's stigmata were unique. Visible for over fifty years, the perfectly circular holes in his palms were never inflamed or infected; the blood was copious, bright red. Countless people report smelling Pio's perfume on his stigmatized blood. His wounds first appeared while he was praying before a crucifix; just before he died, they vanished without a trace of scar tissue.

According to Dr. Eugene Sweeny, a dermatologist from Columbia University whom I questioned about this, open wounds lasting fifty years that leave no scar tissue are "not natural." Dr. Sala, Padre Pio's personal physician in the last years of his life, said this about Pio's stigmata, "Such symptoms and behaviour . . . must be considered as outside of every type of a clinical nature. They have an 'extra-natural' character."[13]

Whatever our view of the stigmata, miraculous or pathological, they say something about the power of imagination. If imagination has power to cause such extraordinary changes in bodily function and structure, couldn't it also be mobilized for healing purposes? In my opinion, Padre Pio's stigmata have implications for healing. They also say something about our potential to harm ourselves.

Healing. Padre Pio's fame is also due to his reputation as a healer. Reports of extraordinary healings continue even after his death. Many of the healings ascribed to Padre Pio were probably from psychosomatic disorders. Intense faith, expectation, contact with an authoritative figure like the padre might well improve functional, psychogenic disorders.

Other stories imply a higher type of healing. For example, the account of Vera Calandra's dying child materializing a new bladder; Gemma di Giorgio's blind eyes being made to see; or Giovanni Savino's blown-out eye (due to a dynamite accident) being rematerialized.[14]

Materialization of a bodily organ is impressive. If such a thing is possible, it would have implications for the theory of evolution. It may be possible to influence physical change, and hence evolution, by psychic and spiritual power.

Materialization of a bodily organ was reported at Lourdes. Lourdes is the shrine in southern France where a mysterious apparition of a girl appeared to another girl, Bernadette of Soubirous. A spring seemed to gush from nowhere, and a shrine was founded; since then people come from all over the world for healings, physical and spiritual.

On the physical side, the authorities at Lourdes are scrupulous; they have set up an international Medical Bureau to study reports of healings. Their criteria for miraculous healing are strict, having been laid down by Prosper Lambertini, the scholarly Pope who studied the levitations of Copertino, and gave them his imprimatur.

Take the case of the Belgian peasant Pierre de Rudder, who was a cripple before his trip to Lourdes. A part of his right leg bone had been shattered and lost in an accident in 1868. His leg was so painful, Pierre could barely walk. When Pierre visited Lourdes, a new portion of bone materialized in the precise spot where he needed it.

The physician in charge, Dr. van Hoestenberghe, reported in 1868, "Pierre is undoubtedly cured. . . . Again, he has been cured completely, suddenly and instantaneously, without any period of convalescence. Not only have the bones been suddenly united, but a portion of bone would seem to have actually been created to take the place of those fragments I myself have seen come out of the wound." Pierre's leg bone is now on display in a Belgian museum.

Similar healings have been attributed to Padre Pio. Kelly Wilkinson was born in County Louth, Ireland, in 1976. Her heart had only one ventricle (instead of two), and she had an enlarged liver. The child wasn't expected to live, but she survived four years, sickly and fragile. Dr. Muriel Frazer, the consulting pediatrician, gave no hope to the child's parents. Mrs. Wilkinson prayed for intercession from the Virgin Mary and even brought Kelly to Lourdes. There was no change.

At the advice of a friend, the mother somewhat reluctantly brought her child to be blessed by a woman in Skerries who had a blood-stained mitten of Padre Pio's. (Many in Ireland are devoted to the Italian monk.) In the evening after the blessing, Mrs. Wilkinson prayed to Padre Pio to help her child. She and her husband had hardly finished their prayer when Kelly burst into their bedroom and announced that there was "an old man" in her room. Mrs. Wilkinson went into Kelly's room, where the child pointed toward the corner where she said the old man still was. Seeing nothing, the distraught mother put the child back to bed.

When she rose in the morning, the mother found a picture of Padre Pio that had been given to the Wilkinsons. Kelly exclaimed that the man in the picture was the man she had seen in her room the previous night. In Belfast the following day, the doctors examined Kelly. The cardiologist reported astonishing news:

> "Mrs. Wilkinson, I don't know how I'm going to explain this to you. . . . But I have in front of me Kelly's catheterization done at birth and it clearly shows she has a single ventricle, a congenital heart defect, and a grossly enlarged liver. And then I have here the catheterization done today. It shows absolutely no congenital heart defect. Kelly's heart today is perfectly normal. *The piece that wasn't there is now there.* And the liver is reduced in size."

From that day on Kelly has been a normal healthy child.[15]

Inedia. The ability to live without food or drink has been cited in many cases of Catholic hagiography. St. Lidwina (1443) is said to have eaten nothing for twenty-eight years. The venerable Domenica dal Paradiso (1553) abstained from food for twenty years; the Blessed Nicolas von Flue (1487), nineteen. More recently, Domenica Lazzari (1848) and Louise Lateau (1883) apparently abstained from food for twelve years, except for the consecrated Host received during Holy Communion.

Pio's is a case of partial inedia, but the facts are still remarkable. According to Dr. Pavone, a doctor from the hospital in San Giovanni, the priest ate once a day, consuming on average fifty to one hundred calories. The little he did eat was usually at the behest of superiors. What's more, Pio lost blood almost continuously. Moreover, despite a massive workload, he rested for only an hour or two each night.

Where did the padre get his energy? In the annals of the great saints are reports of supernormal vitality, often in people plagued by illnesses. Evidence for inedia and for supernormal vitality places the idea of a nonmechanistic *elan vital*—or life force—back on the map of speculative science.

Once Pio was sick with fever for four or five days and ate nothing. At the end of this period, his doctor weighed him, thinking he must have lost weight. Instead, Pio showed an increase of *nine pounds*. Dr. Pavone commented, "These things contradict human logic. They are against the natural law— . . . but they happened."[16] The padre joked that he would have to eat more if he wanted to lose weight. The American Father Joseph Pius Martin had the job of feeding Pio in the last years of his life, and confirmed all this to me when we met in 1979.

Are there conditions in which a human organism might no longer require food—or even drink—to live? In the normal way of things, a living system obtains its energy from other living systems, plants or animals. If inedia were a fact, it would suggest an alternate image of nutrition—the possibility of changing humanity's basic relation to nature. In the present scheme, human beings relate to nature as predator and consumer. Moreover, at present, we consume more than is necessary for our well-being and produce more waste than the environment can absorb. Based on cases like Pio and Lateau, we can imagine a new type of human being whose needs to consume are radically tempered. The biophysics of future humanity may empower us to nourish ourselves in new ways. "Man lives not by bread alone" may be true in ways science has yet to discover.

Animal Communication and Mastery of Elements

When I spoke with informants at San Giovanni, I was told of even stranger powers the padre had over physical nature. For instance, Pio is said to have been able to direct the behavior of animals. In one story, a woman who couldn't get up on time for Mass was sent a bird to awaken her and a troop of stray dogs to escort her to the church on time. Francis of Assisi tamed the wolf of Gubbio. Linnets and lambs, hares and songbirds obeyed the commands of Joseph of Copertino. Shamans the world over know the language of nonhumans.

The evolution of humanity may also include mastery of nonliving nature. The Gospels say that Jesus calmed a storm. Contemporary reports also speak of shamans commanding the elements. For instance,

John Neihardt observed Black Elk conjure rain from a cloudless after-
noon sky. It happened "during a season of drought, one of the worst
in the memory of the old men."[17]

Anthropologist David Barker was in Dharamsala, India, on March
10, 1973, when he observed a Tibetan, Gunsang Rinzing, stop a rainstorm to permit a festival of mourning. The lama built a large fire
and recited certain mantras with intense concentration for twenty
hours. Barker writes, "[T]he rain had diminished to a drizzle, and
by 10 o'clock it had become only a cold fog over a circle with a radius
of about 150 meters. Everywhere else in the area it continued to pour,
but the crowd of six thousand refugees was never rained on." Barker
observed that the atmosphere had an "airless" quality and says he
was disoriented for weeks after the experience.[18]

In light of all this, it is easier to entertain the story of a Roman
engineer, Pasquale Todini. Mr. Todini insists that Padre Pio once
shielded him from the elements. He had left the monastery in a rainstorm, caught without an umbrella, but Padre Pio told him not to
worry. Just go, he said. On his walk home the rain falling immediately
around him was reduced to a sprinkle.[19]

A Body in Transformation

Chapters 8 and 9 tried to show that certain ancient practices—the cult
of guardian angels and the rites at Eleusis—anticipated possible experiments in psychophysical evolution. This chapter looks at a person of the twentieth century, who appears to embody powers of a
higher type of human organism: the ability to enter the inner worlds
of other beings; the ability to escape the shackles of time and space;
and the ability to suspend the habits of physical nature.

One way to look at Padre Pio is as evidence that the human body
has yet untapped evolutionary potential. In line with what was said
in Chapter 7 about survival and the imaginal world, that is my con-
cluding point about the padre. Padre Pio's strange psychophysiology
suggests the potential to evolve an imaginal body—a spiritual or
psychoenergetic body, variously identified with the astral, the etheric,
and the resurrection body. Padre Pio's body may be seen as a body
graduating, evolving, mutating.

Padre Pio was a small man whose muscles ceased to develop in
early life. Yet Padre Pio's body, like those of many Christian saints,
was different. His body became a zone where the laws of nature began

to wobble and fluctuate, where her routines and everyday customs suddenly dissipated, lost their familiar structure, and took on the malleable shape of dreams.

Who was the artist shaping Padre Pio's dream body? One thing seems clear: Padre Pio's body was battered by mysterious forces. The first hint of this came in his illnesses; coughs, violent stomach disorders, raging fevers would appear and disappear, without normal rhyme or reason. Sometimes Padre Pio seemed to be burning up—on the verge of spontaneous combustion—consumed, transformed, perhaps by the serpentine energy the Hindus call kundalini. So high were his fevers, thermometers broke into pieces.

Instances of hyperthermia—being "overheated"—are often reported of the Catholic saints. It is as if the saint's body were being charged by a tremendous force that wants to reshape it. This increased porousness to the shaping force resulted in Pio's psychosomatic illnesses. In a letter dated July 19, 1915, Pio wrote, "My sufferings, although not essentially physical, but rather entirely spiritual, cause my body to participate in this suffering, even to a high degree and in an absolutely new and . . . unknown manner."

This total unification of body and spirit had both positive and negative implications. On the negative side, the spirit can make the body sick in strange ways. With Pio, however, the negative led to the positive. As always, crucifixion is essential for resurrection.

Padre Pio's letters detail his shamanic dismemberment—his crucifixion. On January 24, 1915, he wrote to his spiritual director, Padre Benedetto:

> Yes, my father, I am telling the truth. So great is the anguish that I suffer. . . . It seems to me that all my bones are breaking, and I feel myself—without seeing at all with the eyes of my body but seeing it well with the eyes of the spirit—being struck from time to time by a knife with a very sharp point that is almost on fire. It goes through my heart and sinks into my insides. Then he extracts the knife forcibly only to repeat the operation very soon.

Similar vivid pictures of dismemberment have been described by shamans from many cultures. The shaman, as Mircea Eliade describes him in his classic study, must be dismembered before reaching full status as master of worlds. It is a long—perhaps a neverending—ordeal.

The crucifixion of the ego is painful, but according to Pio, also blissful. The knife and the spear wound him but also create feelings of vivid sweetness. He stated that "this pain and this sweetness are completely spiritual," but also said, "it is also true that my body takes part in them even to a very high degree." He felt the vision in every cell of his body.

Pio called his initiation, his visitation from the "Father of Light," the "Divine Operation." For Pio, the Divine Operation began in 1910 in the form of an invisible wounding or dismembering, which became visible in the form of the stigmata in September, 1919. Pio's odd psychosomatic illnesses disappeared when the stigmata appeared. The spiritual energy from the Divine Operator had stablized itself in a form: the form of the rite of God becoming man—in the Christian myth, the crucifixion.

By surrendering to this operation, Pio fused with the divine energy, as he wrote in one of his letters, like "two candle flames" that have become "indistinguishable." In Pio's life, human communed with divine. People rise to God consciousness, and God incarnates in people. Theology calls this process transubstantiation; we might call it an evolutionary quantum leap.

Dr. Giuseppe Gusso is the medical director of Pio's brainchild, the hospital called the House for the Relief of Suffering, now an international center for the study of psychosomatic medicine. Dr. Gusso, writing about Padre Pio from the standpoint of a physician, states that "there are mysterious and unknown relations that exist between body and soul in the mystical state." This relation might be termed a psychophysics of God—or, as Dante put it, a "love that moves the stars."

If there is a love that moves the stars, then the same love might move and shape our bodies. Dr. Gusso continues: "These relations escape scientific investigation because they are outside biological laws. They could enter into a particular physiology of the supernatural organism, when it reaches its highest degree of development." If Dr. Gusso is right, at the highest degree of our development, we might enter into a physiology of the supernatural organism. Dr. Gusso's "supernatural organism" is consistent with the view this book has been exploring: that we humans are unfinished creatures, still evolving, still edging our way toward the frontiers of body and soul.

11
Sai Baba

I think, imagine, and it is there.
                                    Baba

Geographically and culturally, Sai Baba and Padre Pio come from different places—Baba's home is southern India. Yet Baba, like Pio, appears to have remarkable spiritual and paranormal powers. Sai Baba's miracles seem to compare with—if not to surpass—those of the Italian monk.

There are differences, however. For one thing, Padre Pio is dead and the Catholic Church is investigating his life as part of his Cause, or process of canonization. As I write, Sai Baba is very much alive. So far the Cause for Padre Pio has found nothing reprehensible or suggestive of fraudulence in his career, whether in his moral life or with respect to his supernormal powers. With Sai Baba, however, there are grounds for concern. One hears rumors and accusations of misconduct; for example, that the self-proclaimed avatar uses trickery to produce counterfeit "miracles."

But attacks on spiritual leaders are commonplace, especially while they are still living. Time alone generally reveals the truth in these murky matters. Controversy centered on Padre Pio all his life, though the people and most Church officials stuck by him. However, slander cost Jesus and Socrates their lives. Enemies accused early Christians of being pyromaniacs, sex fiends, and cannibals. So we have to be careful about rumors and charges of misconduct surrounding a man like Sai Baba.

Of course, spiritual leaders from all faiths do betray their callings from time to time. Matters are complicated by the testimony of uncritical believers, although debunkers and cynics muddy the waters with their biases, too. And there are other confounding factors. Take the issue of sex. It is unreasonable to expect highly evolved spiritual beings like Padre Pio and Sai Baba to have no sexual drives. They are probably more erotic than ordinary people. Suppose Sai Baba does have a clandestine sexual life. This might be inconsistent with his claims to be an avatar but not necessarily compromise reports of his psychic powers or even his spiritual insight. The shaman is typically someone with heightened sexuality *and* unusual psychic powers, and Sai Baba may be more a shaman than a traditional Indian renunciate.

Another confounding issue is trickery. Unfortunately, simple logic won't help here. Mediums, psychics, and shamans aren't either all true or all false, all genuine miracle workers or all cunning deceivers. Psychic phenomena tend to occur in dissociated states in which the ego loses control, and the "subselves" and "overselves" take over. (See Chapter 13.)

The shaman is often a trickster. He or she may not even know when tricks are being used, due to a tendency to dissociate. Great physical mediums like Eusapia Palladino cheated almost automatically, when they could; but they also produced extraordinary phenomena. Other times a gifted psychic may lose an ability and fake the desired effects. This, of course, is not supposed to happen to avatars, perfect beings here to guide human beings to enlightenment. Sai Baba may therefore not be an avatar, but he may yet be (or have been, since he could also fall from grace) a spiritually remarkable being. He is no doubt a highly complex man, a carrier of strange talents, which students of psychic evolution ought to study and try to evaluate.

An active public force for about fifty years, Sai Baba has a global following. Among his followers are people of high standing and good will. The quality of testimony to Baba's extraordinary feats is so great it would be unwise to dismiss it out of hand. In the present context, Baba makes an interesting comparison with Padre Pio, whom he matches in range of apparent extraordinary phenomena and spiritual influence.

A Strange Life

Sathya Sai Baba was born on November 23, 1926, in a village called Puttaparthi in southern India. As one American visitor wrote of this village, "Technologically, it is about ten minutes past the Stone Age."[1] It wouldn't be the first time a great spiritual being was born in lowly circumstances. Not of the priestly caste, Baba was the son of a poor farmer.

Southern India is conservative—almost archaic—in its religious outlook. In such backward locales, religion, magic, and superstition blend. This is worth noting; an environment of naive hyperbelief probably helps unleash raw psychospiritual power.

From ages five to fourteen, Sathya seems to have been a genial lad, playful and charming. He liked to joke, and he liked to pretend and imagine; he was what psychologists call "fantasy prone." His fantasy life often took a religious turn, and Baba liked to sing *bhajans*, "spiritual songs."

Sathya never liked the sight of pain or misery. Like Padre Pio, he was abnormally sensitive. As a child, Baba is said to have had a special magical bag from which he pulled pieces of candy and flowers and gave them away. He liked to make people feel happy. Asked about the bag, he said an angel gave him gifts. Other times he said it was a dead saint.

In 1940—the world was at war—Sathya announced he was God, an avatar, an incarnation of the Absolute. The circumstances of Baba's announcement were unusual, to say the least. At fourteen, Baba was bitten by a scorpion. As the story goes, he fell to the ground, his limbs stiffening, his mind dissociated. When he regained consciousness, he said he was Sai Baba—the saintly Sai Baba of Shirdi, a Muslim miracle worker who had been dead for eight years. The new Sai Baba invited people to worship him.

Many people who had known the mystic of Shirdi were convinced that young Sathya was indeed his reincarnation. He knew things, they said, only the deceased man could have known. When someone asked who he was, the young avatar tossed some jasmine flowers to the ground, which fell into a pattern that spelled out S-A-I B-A-B-A. Stories began to circulate that seemed to confirm the divinity of this farmer's son of Puttaparthi. Most interesting was Baba's reported ability to materialize objects. Sai Baba says he will live till 2020—a testable claim. He also says he will reincarnate once more as Prema Sai Baba. (*Prema* means love.)

Baba is not an original thinker but rather a twentieth-century spokesman for an ancient philosophy. To approach Indian thought, Westerners need to suspend several ideas about religion. For example, Indian religious thought is characterized by a tolerance of multiple views and ways of approaching Divine Reality.

Western religions stress the distance, the sheer otherness of the Divine. Christianity is the exception, claiming that once (but only once) God incarnated on earth. The Indian believes that incarnation keeps taking place, a part of the divine drama as it unfolds in time. Hence the Buddhist idea of the *boddhisattva* (a great being who incarnates in order to help others) and the Hindu idea of the *avatar*. Believers in Baba worship him as an avatar, as Christians worship Jesus as Christ.

Indian thought also affirms the experimental reality of *siddhis,* or "paranormal powers." The classic text here is the Yoga Sutras of Patanjali. Patanjali was one of the great transcendental psychologists, for whom the key to the siddhis was the practice of *samyama*. *Samyama* roughly means "intense concentration."[2] However, Sai Baba denies that his powers are siddhis—the product of any effort or austerity—but says that they are rather the plain tokens of his avatarhood.

The Alleged Powers

There is quite a bit of published and unpublished testimony dealing with the siddhis or paranormal powers of Sai Baba. Consider a striking example. Dr. Samuel Sandweiss, a psychoanalyst from California, wrote the following to his wife from Bangalore, India, on May 22, 1972:

> Dear Sharon,
>
> There is no doubt in my mind that Sai Baba is divine. I astound myself to say such a thing. What must I have experienced, a rational scientific man, to say such a thing? I believe I can't even communicate the experience. I know all this isn't hypnosis, mass delusion, hallucination, hysteria, an effect of culture shock or drug intoxication. It's too simple to say that I saw a materialization and then all of a sudden changed. I marvel at the experience, unable to relate it fully, joyful that I'm able to share it with so many who are also witnessing it.

This is a remarkable piece of testimony. Dr. Sandweiss "saw a materialization," which he insists was only part of the story. What did he actually observe? Two days earlier, on May 20, he wrote to his wife and family:

> Well, I clearly saw a miracle—a materialization. I have little doubt now that Baba has this power. Matter appeared out of thin air— right before my eyes. Baba rose about eight feet from me, turned in my direction, made a few circles in the air with his hand, and out came a very large religious necklace.

This manifestation struck a deep chord in the Western psychiatrist. Of primary importance to Dr. Sandweiss was "the mystery and magnificence of my experience of Sai Baba." And he adds, "He has taught me that the deepest, the most profound innate drive and yearning in us is not aggression or dominance or sexuality; it is merging— returning home to God."[3] Of course, a trained magician *could* easily have produced the same effect that Baba did that so impressed Dr. Sandweiss. The difference is that Baba's "magic" is apparently designed to alter an observer's spiritual outlook.

The Inner World

Sai Baba, like Padre Pio, apparently has the ability to pierce the mental barrier called privacy. Consider a story from the pen of Arnold Schulman, a Hollywood and Broadway scriptwriter. It's clear from Schulman's somewhat testy account[4] that this realistic, intelligent Westerner was no true believer. In fact, he ends his book on a skeptical note, reluctant to admit his wonder and bafflement.

Schulman had gone to India to observe and write about the famous swami. When Schulman arrived, the elusive swami left on a trip without him. Forced to wait for Baba to return, Schulman was swamped by stories of miracles. He was disgusted by India—people defecating in the open, disease and poverty everywhere.

Yet the first time Baba looked at Schulman was a powerful experience: "When their eyes met the writer felt as if the breath had been knocked out of him. His ears started ringing. He felt completely disoriented. When Baba looked away the ringing stopped."

At last Schulman was able to talk with Baba. Baba spoke in English and Telugu (the latter translated word for word). Baba explained that what he really wanted was Schulman himself, not a book by Schulman. The promise of a book was bait. "I want you. I want your faith. I want your love," said the swami. He then recited facts in Schulman's recent past, his trip to Japan, his study of yoga. Schulman wondered to himself if he had mentioned any of this to his guide Dr. Gokok, who might have told Baba.

The swami continued:

> Before you came to India you thought you might have to postpone the trip because a lump was discovered in your wife's breast, but two weeks later when she went back to the doctor the lump was gone, and you wondered if I did it, but the doctor said these things often happen so you decided I didn't do it. Well, I did it, I took the lump away, which is why I am telling you this now. You wondered before if you had told Gokok about studying Buddhism in Japan, but you know positively you did not mention your wife and that problem to Gokok or to anyone who knows me.

Schulman was speechless. Baba said several more things that seemed to show he knew Schulman's private thoughts. He pointed out that Schulman only half wanted to travel around with Baba because he was concerned about his physical comfort. He reminded Schulman of a dream he had of Baba; Baba claimed that the dream had been produced by him bilocating and appearing to Schulman in order to cheer him up. Schulman said he hadn't mentioned his dream to anybody.

Now an item clearly at odds with the theory that Baba deals in parlor tricks. Before parting, Baba materialized some sacred ash for Schulman. (This *could* have been sleight of hand.) Schulman was disappointed. He didn't want the ash, he thought to himself. Apparently reading Schulman's mind, Baba laughed and said in English: "Why didn't you tell me you didn't want *vibhuti*. All right, I will give you what you want." With a motion of his hand, he pulled from the air "a small color photograph on aluminum" of himself.

Before leaving Schulman had another chance to be alone with Baba. Called to his living quarters, Schulman found himself watching Baba sorting his mail. He wasn't opening any of it, just touching envelopes, pausing, thinking, putting some aside. Baba looked up and smiled at the American. He then rather amiably described his mission as one of love, saying that what he wanted from people was total trust and love. Schulman writes, "A kind of warmth and closeness he [the author writes about himself in the third person] had never known before was spreading through his consciousness and it frightened him.''

Schulman then asked point blank if Baba was God. ''First you have to understand yourself,'' replied Baba, ''and then you will understand me. I'm not a man, I'm not a woman. I'm not young, I'm not old. I'm all these.'' Baba then added somewhat ruefully that people are mistaken who believe it is all beautiful for the Lord to come to earth in human form. It's a trying responsibility. People expect too much, but there are limits to what a God-Man can do.

Finally, Baba ''pushed up his sleeve and rotated his open palm as he closed his fingers. When he opened them he was holding a gold ring with his picture painted on porcelain in the center, surrounded by sixteen stones which seemed to be diamonds. He put the ring on the writer's finger. It fit perfectly.'' Back home Schulman had the ring appraised; it was worth about $125.

The Mystery of Materialization

As with Padre Pio, there are countless reports of Sai Baba's mastery of time and space and countless reports of his healings. I could fill pages with them. All I can say here is that in scope and variety of phenomena, Baba is more than a good match for Pio. I want rather to stress something else.

Reports of materialization exist in Catholic hagiography and physical mediumship, many of which cannot be dismissed lightly. If true, the ability to produce physical objects out of nowhere would be an absolutely clear indication of a fundamental flaw in our current understanding of nature. The reports of Sai Baba's materializations are extensive and merit careful attention.

Consider a statement by Dr. S. Bhagavantam, physicist, scientific advisor to India's Defense Ministry, and past-president of the Indian Science Congress Association:

> How do I reconcile my background of science with what Sathya Sai Baba does? I have seen miracles performed by Baba perhaps in the thousands during the fifteen years that I have known him, materializations of an infinite variety of physical objects, healings of every description. I must confess that with the logic I know and the training I have, I cannot accept that Sai Baba is like you and me. He can transcend the laws of physics and chemistry. I have to therefore describe and declare that he is a phenomenon, that he is a transcendental being, that he is divine.[5]

What sort of man can cause people like Dr. Bhagavantam to make such an extravagant claim? The best way to answer this question is to look at reports of people who have had firsthand experience. Let me begin with Howard Murphet, a theosophist of open-minded and critical temper, and the author of two books on Sai Baba.[6] An *apport* is a type of materialization; a physical object is transported—"beamed"—from one place to another. The following seems like an apport. In the presence of several people, Baba asked Murphet in 1967 for the year of his birth and said he was going to "get" a coin for him from America minted in that same year. "He began to circle his down-turned hand in the air in front of us, making perhaps half a dozen small circles, saying the while: 'It's coming now . . . coming . . . here it is!'" Baba closed his hand, then dropped a heavy gold American ten-dollar coin into Murphet's hand, the year of Murphet's birth stamped beneath a profile head of the Statue of Liberty. Later, Murphet learned from an expert coin collecter that the coin Baba had produced was a rare and valuable one minted in San Francisco in 1906, the year of Howard Murphet's birth.

Was this a case of sleight of hand? If Baba knew in advance Murphet's birth year, and if he was able to obtain one of these rare coins from America, sleight of hand would be a possible explanation.

The following story, reported in Murphet's second book, if true, seems beyond the repertoire of any magician. It is the story of Joel and Diana Riordan. Joel, who was from Hollywood, was cynical about Baba, and went to India to expose the holy man as a conjurer. Joel explained to Murphet how he had planned to do this. The idea had come to him before leaving Hollywood, where he had said to a friend, "They say this character is God—so I'll ask him for something only God can make—a rainbow."

Joel and his wife arrived at Puttaparthi and walked up the hill behind the hospital for a breath of air. It was dehydratingly hot. At the hilltop they looked into the sky. Joel Riordan described what he and his wife saw to Murphet:

> Then in the western sky a bright rainbow appeared. I thought, how can you have a rainbow without a drop of moisture in the air? Something else struck me, too, as peculiar. Instead of being curved in the usual way, the rainbow stood straight up in the sky like a column. I felt a bit spooky about it. Had this character heard my words right across in America, and caused this phenomenon?[7]

When the two Americans came down the hill, they were summoned to Baba. The first words Baba said to Joel were, "Well, character, how did you like your rainbow?"

Joel was dumbfounded. It occurred to him that Baba may have merely read his mind, knew he used the word "character," then telepathically made him hallucinate the rainbow. At that moment Joel thought to himself that he would try another test and ask the swami for some fruit out of season—a fig. A few moments later, reports Riordan, Baba made a gesture and produced a fig out of nowhere, and silently handed it to him. Murphet interviewed Diana Riordan, who confirmed her husband's story.

Now consider a phenomenon observed by large numbers of people many times. On February 18, 1966, he celebrated the Festival of Siva-ratri (Night of Shiva). Every year since 1950 during this festival, Baba has been seen doing a very strange thing; in front of thousands of witnesses, he exhibits painful contortions in his stomach and chest and then ejects from his mouth one or more stone or metallic objects called a *lingam*. A lingam is a phallic symbol of the creative duality of Shiva and his consort Shakti.

Earlier on that day in 1966, Murphet observed Baba behaving listlessly, and a doctor later informed him that Baba was running a temperature of 104 degrees. Murphet asked witnesses if the swami could have hidden the lingams in his mouth before coming on the platform. Arguing against that possibility is the fact that Baba usually spoke and sang before producing the lingams, which would be very difficult to do without revealing the presence of one or more of these objects (from two to five inches long) in his mouth. One observer said that the previous year the lingam had been so large that when Baba pulled it out of his mouth, it caused his cheek to bleed. Also, on one occasion Baba spat out *nine* lingams—which would have been rather hard to conceal in his mouth.

Another interpretation is possible. Yogis are noted for their ability to control bodily processes, so it is conceivable that Baba swallows the lingams and then regurgitates them during the festival. This might explain the apparent pain he experiences, as well as the convulsions.

Here is what Murphet himself observed: "After about twenty minutes or so of watching Baba's mouth while he writhed and smiled and made attempts to sing, I was rewarded. I saw a flash of green light shoot from his mouth and with it an object which he caught in his hands.'' Shiva's lingam had arrived. Later Murphet was able to look at it closely. It was emerald, three inches high, with a five-inch-wide base.[8]

Several Western scientists, including Erlendur Haraldsson and Karlis Osis have been to India to study Sai Baba. Haraldsson, who researched deathbed visions in India with Osis, made ten trips to India and interviewed scientists, critics, disciples, and ex-disciples of the swami. The Icelandic parapsychologist restricts himself to reporting eyewitness testimony and leaves it to readers to draw their own conclusions.

Among the people Haraldsson interviewed, 75 percent said they observed a materialization.[9] The idea that any human being could, by means of a "divine wish" (*sankalpa*), cause a physical object to appear from nothing goes quite beyond our view of what is possible in nature. Sai Baba's miracles are of a kind we associate with fairy tales or mythology and seem too incredible to be true.

But the advantage is that the options for interpreting them are extremely limited. Either Sai Baba does materialize physical objects, or he is a consummate trickster. I do not see any plausible alternatives. In healings, for example, apparent effects may be explained by unknown or undetected normal mechanisms.

However, several points argue against sleight of hand as an explanation of Baba's "magic." The first is the sheer volume, duration, and variety of claims. It would appear that Baba has been producing objects for about half a century, virtually every day, and many times a day—"sometimes every minute,"[10] asserted one person, no doubt exaggerating.

Moreover, the variety of objects produced is stunning. Perhaps the substance Baba most frequently creates is *vibhuti*, "sacred ash." The way he does this varies. It comes "shooting from his mouth"; from his foot; from his forehead; from thin air (the most common procedure); from empty urns; and at a distance from the surface of his photos. Baba is also in the business of the paranormal manufacture of artworks and of precious materials such as gold, silver, ruby, and diamond. He apparently produces rings, coins, pendants, medallions, statues, necklaces, and rosaries and crucifixes for his Christian friends.

The swami is also a miraculous short-order cook, materializing various tasty treats from nowhere, such as different kinds of fruit (often out of season); sweets and drinks like nectar, *amrinth*, and *kova;* and curry, pancakes, and rice balls, often piping hot. And if we are to believe the accounts, Baba has the answer to the energy crisis, for he can make a car run on water. Other, miscellaneous objects have been unaccountably produced, such as a metal trident (used for a tonsillectomy) and even a telegram!

If Baba is a trickster, he has been successful for about fifty years in concealing thousands of different physical objects from innumerable people who have observed him and handled his clothing and personal effects. He wears a simple robe without secret sleeves, pockets, or cuffs. In performing his "magic," he often raises his sleeves—to placate doubting Thomases—and then seems to snatch a physical object from nowhere.

Another point argues against Baba as a master of sleight of hand. From where and how would he have obtained the thousands of pieces of jewelry and other objects he produces? (And remember, he gives away everything he produces.) Also, it seems quite clear that if he were a trickster, he would have needed assistants all these years. Indeed, we would have to assume that a very complicated conspiracy has been in place for half a century. As far as I know, no assistants have come forward or been exposed.

Haraldsson's book reviews Baba's critics, but no one has produced any evidence of deception. Although people have testified that Baba promised cures that weren't fulfilled, hostile witnesses still confirm many of the phenomena. In 1976, for instance, the *Times of India* published an editorial disputing Baba's miracles, which prompted a response of about one thousand letters, none of them "indicating fraud by Baba," according to Dr. Narasimhaiah, a skeptical nuclear physicist who was responsible for the anti-miracle crusade.

Consider the case of M. Krishna, a former close disciple of Baba who converted to Christianity. Here you might expect bias to discredit the miracles, but Mr. Krishna confirms them: "He frequently produced *vibhuti* by a wave of his hand, also talismans and sweets. For example, once when we were traveling, I asked Baba for an apple. He walked up to a nearby tamarind tree and picked from it an apple."[11] Apples, needless to say, don't grow on tamarind trees, which grow instead a leguminous fruit used for laxatives. Others describe the early years of Baba's strange ministry, in which there was a tree known as "the wish-fulfilling tree." Baba would ask people what fruit they wanted, in season or out. They might say pear, or apple, or orange. They would then climb a steep hill and find the fruits named growing on the tamarind tree.

Amarendra Kumar, another witness, tells other fantastic stories. Baba, asserts Kumar, would pluck at random a leaf from any plant and transform it into a delicious apple or fig. He also says he saw Baba take jeweled pendants or lockets from trees.[12] A related type of paranormal alchemy involved Dr. Y. J. Rao, head of the Geology Department at Osmania University, in Hyderabad. One day in Puttaparthi, Baba picked up a piece of granite from the ground and handed it to Dr. Rao, asking what it contained. The chemist described the mineral content of the granite. Baba asked, what else? Dr. Rao was stumped, so Baba took back the piece of granite, held it before the chemist's eyes, blew on it, and handed it back. It had turned into a statue of Lord Krishna playing a flute—a statue made of sugar candy! "Break off the foot and taste it," said Baba.[13]

However, the best argument against magic tricks is that Baba produces objects *on demand,* a feat no ordinary magician can emulate. Mr. Krishna tells how the swami often materialized a favorite sweet called *kova* for him on demand. An intimate disciple, he bathed and clothed the swami; his testimony therefore carries some weight, "None of us ever found anything suspicious as far as I know."

Another close and early disciple, Gopal Krishna asserts: "Whatever we would want he would give us; it was *not only on his initiative* [my emphasis]. Another person might ask for a ridli [rice ball], still another might want a piece of fruit that might not be available in India because it was out of season. He would give all this, and he did this a large number of times."[14] Again, I repeat: if these stories are true, they are inconsistent with the hypothesis of sleight of hand.

In 1972 Haraldsson and Karlis Osis were able to interview Sai Baba face-to-face. They explained they were scientists investigating psychic phenomena. Baba immediately obliged and, with a motion of his hand, took from nowhere a golden ring—a gift for Osis. The two scientists said they weren't interested in the impulsive display of miracles; they wanted the swami to perform controlled experiments. They discussed the merits of science versus religion, but Baba refused to submit to the routine of his Western visitors. The conversation drifted toward spiritual matters, and Baba remarked that "daily life and spiritual life should be 'grown together like a double *rudraksha.*'"

Haraldsson didn't know what a "rudraksha" was, and kept pestering

Baba for an explanation. Due to his spotty knowledge of English, the swami (even with the help of his translator) couldn't clarify what the word meant. But Haraldsson persisted until Baba, losing patience, produced an actual rudraksha—a kind of double acorn. To make matters more puzzling, a double rudraksha is a rare anomaly in nature.

Another consideration weighs against fraud. Sai Baba—like Padre Pio—has an overwhelming spiritual effect on people. Countless people describe being struck by a palpable presence, an alluring spirit of divine love. This, while not conclusive, weighs somewhat against the claim that Baba uses legerdemain to produce his effects.

One weakness in the case for Baba's miracles is the lack of evidence from controlled experiments. Haraldsson and Osis tried valiantly to persuade the swami to take part in experiments, but to no avail. Why did he refuse to participate? Had he done so, he would have made things harder for the skeptics.

Beside observations on materialization, Haraldsson records claims of other paranormal feats: healings, precognitions, possible bilocations, "mindreading," levitation or near-levitation, strange light phenomena, and Baba's reputed habit, especially in his younger wonder-working days, of disappearing from one place, only to reappear elsewhere *instantaneously.*

Students of psychic photography may find interesting the report that people who tried to photograph Baba without his consent often found that the film had vanished in their cameras or that the image came out blank. C. T. Chari tells of someone who tried to photograph Sai Baba: "[T]he Swami repeatedly predicted that his image would *not* appear on the developed plates. These predictions were fulfilled too often to be attributed to chance."[15] Similar reports exist of foiled attempts to photograph Padre Pio.

It is often stated that *siddhis* (paranormal powers) or charisms (powers in the Christian tradition) are a byproduct of spiritual training. From Haraldsson's study a different picture emerges—at least for Sai Baba.

In the first place, Sai Baba doesn't perform *sadhana* or "spiritual practice." As far as I can make out, his powers, if authentic, are a gift that cannot be attributed to any spiritual practice. According to Patanjali, *siddhis* arise from "birth, drugs, mantras, austerities, or samadhi [deep concentration]." It seems to me that Baba was born with his powers. When he was five, he became popular among his friends for producing candy from an empty bag.

Witnesses say that Baba did not start to evolve spiritually until the early 1950s. Before that time he was "really boyish—sometimes naughty, mischievous, most uncontrollable and very jolly-going." Until his mid-twenties, Sathya was more amusing than edifying. Another witness dates his spiritual awakening to the early 1960s. Until then, Baba didn't preach; "there was little or no talk on *seva* (service to others) or *prema* (love). But gradually he expressed more philosophy and more religion. Before 1960 there was mostly just friendly talk, joking, teasing."[16]

It appears then that Baba was born with extraordinary paranormal abilities, began to manifest them at an early age, and only gradually developed or manifested his spiritual personality. What are we to make of this? This pattern appears to clash with the view that spiritual development leads to paranormal abilities. Devotees of Sai Baba take his innate abilities as proof that he is an avatar. For example, Dr. Sandweiss has stated to me that he believes Sai Baba is a rare embodiment of "infinite consciousness." Dr. Sandweiss is convinced that Baba is omniscient and "in control" of the world scene. Dr. Sandweiss bases his view on twenty-two trips to India, during which he experienced the *prema* and the *shaktipat* of Baba—his "divine love" and "divine power."

Another way of looking at the data is more naturalistic. Some people might find it easier to think that Baba, however extraordinary, is not absolutely perfect. Let us suppose that Baba was born with an enormous dose of super-psi, a psychic imagination of extravagant intensity, a mysterious array of natural gifts: abilities to see the invisible and transform the visible. His first use of his powers was childlike, fun-loving; he created candy and flowers for his little peers. What could be more natural?

But Baba had been born into a rich spiritual tradition, a rich mythology of the spirit, a world of devas, goddesses, magic, and avatars. It was a mythology well-suited for a genial spirit with strange powers like Sathya. Growing up he sang the songs of his tradition, immersing himself in their spirit; his innate soul power now acquired a form, a direction, a self-consciousness. In this way the psychic evolved into the spiritual; Sathya became Sai Baba.

At first he was childlike and sweet, playful and teasing, singing the sacred tales and playing the sacred parts. A master of fantasy, he identified with all the deities of Indian tradition. In this way, a human being—and Baba is a human being—came to incarnate ideas and images of divinity in marvelous ways.

The Making of Miracles

Now and then Baba tosses out hints on how he manages his miracles. Osis and Haraldsson asked Baba how he materialized objects.

"Mental creation," Baba replied. "I think, imagine, and then it is there."

Baba, like Jesus, says we all have the power to do these things. Haraldsson quotes Baba as saying, "We are all like matches, only I am on fire." We all have the potential. It's simply a question of higher combustion.

Baba adds: "You should learn how to do this [make miracles] for yourself. It is possible. But even then you will not be able to explain it to others. You can only enjoy it."

"When he produces things, Baba explained, he does not have to think about the chemical composition. If he produces a sweet, he does not think about what is in it; he simply gets it."[17] This squares with one theory of how psi works—namely, it is the result of "goal-oriented" thinking. Modern parapsychology supports the magical idea of causality implied by Baba's miracles. Baba's phenomena, if valid, furnish spectacular evidence for *teleological causation*.

In spite of the evidence in his favor, a case can be argued against Sai Baba. A letter from Dale Beyerstein, from Vancouver, B.C., published in *Yoga Journal* (1991) states that books are available through the Indian Committee for the Scientific Investigation of Claims of the Paranormal (CSICOP) charging that Sai Baba is not celibate as he claims and that he is involved in "criminal wrongdoing" related to gold. I have not been able to obtain these books which are not readily available in America. Moreover, CSICOP is notorious for its bias against the paranormal. Besides, there is a well-known "insider's" account of positive duplicity on the part of leading CSICOP members.[18] So I would be cautious about claims made by this organization.

Beyerstein's letter also asserts there is a film of Sai Baba (*Christ in Kashmir*) by Richard Bock that shows Sai Baba "engaging in sleight of hand'' during the pause mode. I haven't been able to obtain Bock's film; but I have seen two other films produced by the same man, in which there are scenes of apparent paranormal manifestations. In one, for example, Baba appears to produce a very large necklace. I was unable to detect any sleight of hand in the pause mode. In my view, events viewed on film are not necessarily conclusive either way. I will say that two other alleged miracles I witnessed on film—the regurgitation of two lingams and the pouring of a huge amount of *vibhuti* from a supposedly empty urn—left me unconvinced, either way.

I myself interviewed a woman, Michelle L., who visited Sai Baba several times over five years. She accused him of several failings. According to Michelle, Baba mistreats and angrily abuses disciples, especially women, and in particular herself. She also said that Baba engages in homosexual practices. Michelle told me that while in India a young man personally victimized by Baba's sexual advances told her this story. Finally, Michelle asserted that Baba uses trickery to get his effects. For example, she said that tiny pellets of *vibhuti* are available anywhere for purchase in India. Baba holds these in his hands and pricks them with a fingernail at will, thus producing the appearance of *vibhuti*. She also alluded to a film in which the swami may be seen using sleight of hand.

As to Baba's rough treatment of disciples—this is fairly common among spiritual teachers. Padre Pio often behaved quite roughly toward people, which was part of a deliberate strategy. Whether this is the case with Baba is hard to say. The claims about Baba's sexual immorality cannot be dismissed lightly; but more evidence is needed. The same is true with the accusations of trickery. Michelle's negative claims do not outweigh the positive testimony I have assembled in this chapter. The question remains open.

Finally, Michelle's testimony is weakened by the fact that on returning from India, she admitted she had to be ''deprogrammed.'' She admits to having had several mystical experiences when in India which she now denounces as merely the product of her fantasies and expectations. She also admits to feeling bitter about having been ignored by Baba. On one occasion she was in the home of a Baba devotee and witnessed the inexplicable appearance of *vibhuti* on a photo of the Hindu swami. All these facts render her testimony against him inconsistent and possibly biased. So I withhold judgment on Baba's miracles. My discussion of the man is meant to be suggestive, not conclusive.

The Monk and the Swami

Many similaritries between Sai Baba and Padre Pio have already been noted. Each of these men as teachers want to lead people to the same goal, supreme love and supernatural joy. The monk and the swami are each in deep harmony with their traditions. Both men are able to light our fire—to strike the match of our divine potential. Padre Pio has been called an "extraordinary vivifier of dead souls." Sai Baba physically jolts people with *shaktipat*, as he did Arnold Schulman. Both can be gruff in their teaching. Padre Pio would shout and throw people out of the confessional. Sai Baba suddenly withdraws his affections or attention from disciples, making them feel uneasy, abandoned. Howard Murphet has described how Baba spiritually weans his disciples.[19]

However saintly or godlike, good humor and lightness of spirit mark their manner. Pio liked to tell jokes, and Baba once said to Dr. Sandweiss while they were driving in a car together, "I like to tease." Yet this playfulness is significant. Pio speaks of the game of love; Baba knows of *lila* and *maya,* the "divine play," the game of hide-and-seek with divinity.

The two men live a transpersonal life. They live in the collective, outside the sphere of their personal needs and desires. They excel in "self-donation," to borrow a word from Baron von Hugel, the great scholar of Christian mysticism. Thus, Pio says, "I belong to everyone. Everyone can say, 'Padre Pio is mine.'" And Murphet writes of Baba, "Once when I asked Swami if he would do something for me he answered 'Yes, of course. I'm your property. I have no rights.'"

Neither man does much sleeping or eating. Several writers say that Baba has never been seen asleep. All night he bobs about making little gestures with his hands; as if astrally traveling, responding to the needs and crises of devotees. This was apparently true also of Padre Pio; he always seemed on call, pausing to listen to invisible beings, asking them what they wanted, going away, and then returning.

Both men seem to display remarkable psychic powers. Moreover, the psychic powers fall into a pattern; they are expressions of an integral unfolding. Both men have unusual abilities to navigate the inner environment; both seem able to move freely across the normal barriers of time and space; and both are apparently able to shape and mold physical reality in remarkable ways. In the presence of Baba and Pio, nature seems more open to the workings of the divine imagination. Yet Sai Baba calls his miracles his "calling cards"; Padre Pio calls the celestial perfume he projected "sweets for the children."

What about differences? Baba's devotees think of him as God. This is not the way Christians think of Pio. Padre Pio was often troubled by an acute sense of unworthiness. He was a humble man. However, humility is not a prominent feature of Baba's mentality. Baba claims himself as the source of his miraculous power. Pio would emphatically deny such a claim.

Hinduism allows for multiple incarnations of the divine principle; Christianity allows for one incarnation. This may look like a big difference, but on closer inspection, it may not be. In the Christian tradition, the saints are the functional equivalents of Buddhist bodhisattvas and Hindu avatars. Saint, bodhisattva, and avatar—all are living tokens of a higher stage of evolution. Both traditions agree that superhuman development is a real possibility.

One difference I believe cannot be ignored—but it comes down to a difference between Hinduism and Christianity, not between the two men. It is true that Padre Pio can say, "All human concepts, no matter where they come from, are both good and bad; one should know how to take and assimilate the good, offer it to God, and eliminate what is bad." This is a powerful statement of spiritual universalism.

But Baba—or I should say Baba's tradition—goes much further, as, for instance, when he says, "The Lord can be addressed by any name that tastes sweet to your tongue, or pictured in any form that appeals to your sense of wonder and awe." He lists as equally acceptable possibilities Sakti, Jesus, Allah, the Formless, and the Master of all Forms.

Is there anything to say, based on the comparison of Pio and Baba, that points to the road to our higher developmental possibilities? The true point of convergence, it seems to me, is that both men lead lives centered on something beyond their personal selves. This, I think, is a clue to their supernormal abilities. In the lives of Padre Pio and Sai Baba, everything seems meant to work for the benefit of humanity as a whole. An orientation to exist beyond oneself is, I conjecture, what helps to liberate and develop the whole system of higher powers this book has addressed.

If the powers are used to serve the needs of human beings at large, not just individuals, the Source—however you think of it—unbolts the treasure trove and lets the gifts pour forth more freely and more lavishly.

Of course, ordinary, even selfish people have paranormal experiences. But their frequency, magnitude, and reliability are low, compared with saintly, species-oriented psi. Thus the psychic and the spiritual do converge, after all. Psi serves the spirit, as the part serves the whole. The indications, in my opinion, support the old view. All psychic powers are *in the long run* subject to the rule of the highest intentions.

I would state this rule as follows: the more selfish the intention, the more constrained our higher powers; the higher the intention— the more in harmony with the deepest needs and most lasting good of humanity—perhaps of earth itself—the more likely the higher powers are to be mobilized, released, and made available for our integral evolution.

12
The Marian Morphogenesis

What good is it to me if Mary gave birth to the son of God 1400
years ago and I do not also give birth to the son of God in my time
and in my culture? We are all meant to be mothers of God.

Meister Eckhart

Reports of visions of the Virgin Mary have been increasing since the
nineteenth century; the most spectacular and well-attested cases
occurred in the twentieth century—for instance, in Zeitun, Egypt,[1]
from 1968 to 1971, or the ongoing events in Medjugorje, Yugoslavia.
Sacredly luminous and awesome, these images of a female figure are
appearing in many places around the world, from Japan to Nicaragua,
from Lithuania to Lubbock, Texas. Gracing Catholic or Orthodox
Christian locales, they are usually thought to be Mary, the mother
of Jesus.

There are reports of private visions of a Mary-like figure that leave
little social aftermath, and no doubt many cases like these go unre-
ported. The visions that concern us are the ones with social consequences—visions that unleash powerful, transformative forces.

Though she was human and considered by many Christians as intermediary between humans and God, in our times we can revision
Mary as Goddess. But before we examine the question of psychic
evolution and the Goddess, we need a clear view of the phenomena.
What follows is an overview of the typical elements of the Marian
visionary experience based on a comparative study of them. This overview reveals seven stages or steps in what I call the Marian morphogenesis.

Annunciation
The typical Marian manifestation begins with an annunciation. Before
the Virgin arrives, her coming is signaled in various ways: in a flash

or beam of light; in the shape of cloud, globe, or bird of light; in the radiant shape of an angel. The signal may be auditory, as in a sudden strain of heavenly music that seems to come from nowhere. Or it may come through the smell of flowers, perfume, or incense. The appearance may be announced by an apparent materialization, as in 1531 when the Aztec Juan Diego found Castilian roses growing wild in Mexico on a barren wintry hill. This hill was the site of the old Aztec goddess Teontenantzin, which means "Mother of God."

The lapse of time between the signal and the appearance may vary from a few seconds to a few years.

Appearances

After the annunciation, the Goddess herself appears. The time of her epiphany has come. Typically, she is a female figure—young, beautiful, radiant. Lighted by the "white radiance of eternity," she appears in different colors—golden, silvery, bluish. "She was more brilliant than the sun, and radiated a light more clear and intense than a crystal glass filled with sparkling water, when the rays of the burning sun shine through it," wrote Lucia, one of the visionaries of Fatima in 1917. Supernormal light is typical of the Marian vision. In Guadalupe (1531), the stones, the ground, and the cacti lit up from within, as if they were made of gold or emeralds. In 1871 she appeared to a group of children at Pointmain surrounded by stars and candles. One witness said, "I see a tall Lady who wears a blue dress, with golden stars on the dress, and blue slippers and golden buckles."

Marian visionary experiences are overwhelming. Those who see them are enthralled, sometimes temporarily paralyzed and unable to speak. A Coptic Christian now living in Astoria, New York, had an awe-inspiring encounter with the Theotokos—the God-Bearer—at Zeitun in 1969. He went to the site of the visions at Saint Mary's Church in the busy suburb of teeming Cairo, in hopes of helping his wife, who was pregnant and had a heart condition. "It was as if we were alone—just she and I," he told me. He felt totally intimate with the "Lady Virgin," as though he was in a private room with her, sealed off from a quarter million screaming ecstatics that had descended on the church across the street from the all-night garage. A woman I once met who had recently returned from a pilgrimage to Medjugorje described herself as having entered a state of "perpetual bouyancy." Her face seemed suffused with an unearthly radiance.

In a critical book, firsthand investigators, Mariologist René Laurentin and physician Henri Joyeux, have documented the ecstatic state of the primary visionaries at Medjugorje, as well as supernormal healings and paranormal photic phenomena there.[2]

The Virgin appears in private to some and to small groups of privileged seers: three children at Fatima, six children at Medjugorje, four at Garabandal. Sometimes she appears in public; multitudes behold her or at least some of the strange aerial effects associated with her.

Not everyone present reports the same thing: the phenomenon is seen from different perspectives. The children at Fatima and Medjugorje were in full communication with the Goddess. They saw her, talked with her, experienced telepathic rapport with her. To an outside observer their responses seemed coordinated, as if one entity were present and had taken possession of their minds synchronously. Fascinated crowds that gather around the visionaries may report a different set of observations, such as unusual or spectacular light phenomena, like the "dance of the sun" reported at Fatima and currently at Medjugorje and San Damiano.

Not as well-known as it ought to be is the story of Zeitun, where the Goddess herself was seen by millions—and even photographed. She was seen walking, bowing, gesturing for thirty consecutive months. Every newspaper, religious or secular, reported the event. The highest officials of Church and government witnessed the appearances. A delegation of high officials from the Coptic Pope reported: "We then aimed at observing the Blessed Apparition with our own eyes in order to have the matter cleared up plainly and evidently. She appeared in her complete form moving on the domes, then bowing before the cross and at the end she blessed the multitude."[3]

Identification

In 1968 two Muslim mechanics thought they saw a woman on the dome of Saint Mary's Church in Zeitun, who they believed was about to commit suicide. They called up and begged her not to jump. A woman in the street, looking up when the men called out, cried, "Settena Mariam" (It's Mary), thus identifying the appearance as Mary. The Lady of Light never spoke and did not identify herself. But she responded to the devotion of the masses who saw her later.

The vision at Fatima, in response to questions about her identity, merely said, "I am from heaven." Only later was her identity as Mary revealed—or imposed.

Often in Marian visions witnesses are children or are uneducated. They may be baffled by the vision at first, but they are quick to assimilate it into local myth and tradition. The appearance is often identified by the visionaries. Sometimes an authority—a physician, priest, or body of judges—is called to the scene to either validate or invalidate the authenticity of the vision. Two steps are involved: first, a numinous form appears and second, it is identified as Mary.

Validation

Validation is critical. With validation the vision becomes a social force. However, there are obstacles to validation, either secular and rationalistic or religious and dogmatic. Perhaps the most dramatic and well-earned validation occurred at Fatima in 1917, where three young seers, Lucia, Jacinta, and Francisco, were abducted by authorities and threatened with being boiled in oil if they did not admit they were lying. The youngsters were not intimidated.

The children predicted months in advance that on October 13, 1917, a miracle of high strangeness would occur, and something clearly amazing *did* occur on that date.[4] A disc of light appeared in the sky before 70,000 witnesses. It dropped toward the earth in a falling-leaf, zigzag pattern, terrifying the multitude. Many fell to their knees, expecting the imminent end of the world. This occurrence, of course, helped to validate the vision.

Some Marian visions arouse animosity in Church authorities. For example, the bishops at Garabandal, San Damiano, and Bayside, New York, deny validity to alleged encounters with Mary. Political factors can be at work here. In San Damiano and Bayside, for example, the ladies claiming communications with the Virgin had the effrontery to scold high Church officials, and in one case accused the Pope of being in league with Satan!

Miracles, Signs, Wonders

Powerful forces at work in the Marian morphogenesis induce belief in "miracles" and in the reality of "signs and wonders." These visible and sometimes tangible evidences, real or imagined, are fuel for the Marian process. The miracles, signs, and wonders are the most powerful validators of Marian visions.

Extraordinary phenomena are reported: visionaries apart in space, yet responding simultaneously to a message (Medjugorje); levitation-like walks (Garabandal); immunity to fire (Bernadette at Lourdes); materialized hosts (Conchita at Garabandal); materialized flowers or images (Guadalupe); materialized tears (Akita, Japan); inexplicable springs and flows of water (Lourdes, Salette); precognitions, prophecies, ecstatic states—found in abundance among the seers.

In addition, the crowds that gather at the visionary sites experience strange things. At Fatima, Zeitun, and Medjugorje great crowds observed aerial effects, phantasmagoric lights, beams, rays; shape-shifting light forms; puzzling illusions of "dancing" suns; thermal effects (notably at Fatima where the countryside suddenly dried up after a torrential rainstorm); rosary beads changing colors (reported to me by several witnesses at Medjugorje).

Of great importance are reports of healings.[5] They may take place immediately (a Muslim's gangrenous finger was healed when he pointed to the "woman" on Saint Mary's dome) or occur after the visionary site has become a shrine or a cathedral. The most famous example is Lourdes where an international Medical Bureau was established to rule on alleged healing miracles. About sixty-five miraculous healings have been certified so far, according to the Bureau's strict criteria. Probably many of these healings are psychosomatic, but others are more remarkable, such as the reported materialization of organs or instantaneous cures of nearly hopeless cases.

Equally important for Marian visionary encounters is the *belief* that miraculous healings occur. Here the faith of the populace outstrips the scruples of critical science, and is reinforced by subsequent events.

As we know from parapsychology, belief increases the probability of psi events. Thus, as the "belief quotient" in miracles increases, the probability of "miracles" occurring also increases. The Marian morphogenesis creates an environment conducive to "miracles." Witnesses I have spoken with stress the miracle of love, the inner change experienced when they visit the visionary sites, even after the Marian epiphanies have long ceased taking place.

The Message

The signs and wonders reinforce the message—the cognitive, symbolic, and instructional content of the visions.

Cognitive. Perhaps the single most powerful idea that comes across from the Marian vision is an urgent warning. The world is on the verge of catastrophe; the Marian Goddess is here to warn us of this and to show the path of prevention. The only way to save the world is through spiritual renovation. This is a recurrent pattern in prophecy, and there is a long Catholic tradition of foretelling calamities of cosmic dimensions and terrible chastisements. Perhaps the most common doomsday image is of a rain of fiery death from heaven.[6] The main point of the message is to reinforce a spiritual outlook for society at large.

The warnings can be specific. Since the French and Russian revolutions, the direst warnings express a spirit that is antihumanist, antimodernist, above all, anti-Communist. Indeed, the war against godless communism—now apparently defunct—is cast in the imagery of a "Lady Clothed in the Sun" battling with the "Red Dragon."

Marian devotees have for many years made prayer the weapon to be used in the conversion of Russia—a technology quite different from America's during the Cold War. I have heard it said by devotees of Mary that it was the prayers of millions in the "Blue Army"— believers in the Fatima prophecies—that doused the fire in the mouth of the Red Dragon.

Marian visions can be thought of as aspects of the near-death experience of a culture. Anticlerical, anti-Christian forces did try to destroy the seers' spiritual culture—in France, 1830; in Portugal, 1917; in Egypt, 1968; in Yugoslavia, 1981; in Nicaragua, 1983. Perhaps spiritual communities have secret ways of responding to such crises. People on the threshold of death experience mysterious, uplifting visions. Perhaps a similar dynamic works in some spiritual communities.

Symbolic. The content of the messages is not just conservative, however. Prayer, penance, and spiritual practice are recommended, which seem conservative enough. Yet, at the same time, Marian encounters tend to deconstruct patriarchal Christianity, as there is something subversive about the popular adoration of Mary. In the Marian movement can be discerned a push toward the deification of Mary. One of her more provocative names is "Co-Redemptress." The popular imagination has transformed this insignificant figure in the New Testament into a Goddess for many of her devotees. As F.C.S. Northrop describes Mexico's attitude toward Mary, "She appears in the shrine of the basilica of Guadalupe alone and in her own right."[7]

In 1950 the Church declared the dogma of the Assumption, which states that Mary rose bodily to heaven. Like Menelaus who was teleported to the Elysian fields, Mary transcends death, thus escaping the common lot of mortals. In this Mary surpasses even Jesus who had to undergo crucifixion before resurrection.

A more subtle deconstruction takes place under the guise of ecumenism. For example, the apparition at Medjugorje stressed respect for other people's religious views. With equal emphasis, a universal message of peace came through at Zeitun in the late sixties. The message was conveyed, not in words, but in symbols. For example, the apparition held up an olive branch before the people, which symbolizes peace. (*Zeitun* means "olive" in Arabic.)

At Zeitun (and at Knock, Ireland) the Lady of Light did not speak at all. How different from the excessively particular and loquacious Mary said to have visited Bayside, Queens.[8] The silent gesture of the Zeitun madonna—like the Buddha holding up a flower—spoke to a place in the heart beyond ethnic differences. The Zeitun appearances pacified the crowds of pilgrims. Christians and Arabs, normally at odds over religion, forgot their old gripes and chanted together in public, something normally illegal and forbidden.

Below the surface message is a deeper meaning of Marian visions. It is possible that even some Christians miss the point, which is obscured by cultural and theological prejudice.

Consider, for example, the vision of Catherine of Labouré (Paris, 1830). Catherine saw a Goddess with a "serpent, green in color with yellow spots." Catherine's madonna is usually imaged standing in triumph over the serpent—what John of Patmos called "that old dragon, satan and the devil." Though in the Western world the serpent is the evil principle, in China, Sumer, Greece and other cultures the serpent is the principle of life.

Catherine's vision was shaped into a "miraculous medal." The image on the medal suggests conflict between the serpent and Mary, who is pictured standing on a globe and "crushing the serpent" under her heel.

But there is another way of looking at Catherine's tableau of the divine figure, world mandala, and serpent: the serpent might be symbolic of kundalini or serpent power of Hindu tantrism, the energy coiled at the base of the spine. Many hold that this is the psychoenergetic impetus of an individual's spiritual evolution. Catherine's serpent is green, a color said to symbolize healing, and gold, the color of consciousness. Catherine's serpent may therefore be seen as an image of healing consciousness.

It is possible to reinterpret Catherine of Labouré's vision and the famous Miraculous Medal—said to have been responsible for countless healings. Instead of "crushing the serpent" we may think of Mary as containing the serpent harmoniously within herself. That is why she is pictured resting on top of it, as a well crafted vessel rests upon and rides a great wave. This interpretation gives a clue to the secret meaning of the epidemic of Mary appearances—a meaning that runs deeper than the pious talk of repentence and self-denial. In this view, the appearances would signify the effort to unite with the energies of life. The vision would affirm the consciousness that comes from "raising the kundalini energy." Catherine's visionary serpent would then speak to the need in the West to reintegrate the feminine and the sexual into consciousness.

Instructional. In most, though not in all, of these visionary encounters, are found explicit commands and instructions. The seers are commanded to spread the word, to declare the sacred appearance to Church authorities and to the world at large. Or seers are told to tell the people to build sanctuaries and cathedrals, strike medals and medallions, engage in specific kinds of spiritual practice. This brings up the next element in the Marian morphogenesis.

Cult Formation

Once identified and validated, Marian visionary encounters can become the basis of a cult that cultivates ideas, dogmas, and practices of the Goddess. Such a cult can be said to incarnate a form of consciousness. There are different aspects to the process.

The naming of the Goddess. The history of the cult of Mary is littered with names of place (Our Lady of Pompeii, Our Lady of Lourdes, Our Lady of Fatima) or of function (Our Lady of the Miraculous Medal, Our Lady of Perpetual Succor, Our Lady of Tears, Our Lady of the Rosary). The names of the Goddess are as varied as the places and circumstances of her appearances.

Restoring sacred space. The Great Mother is concerned with the earth. In ancient times, she presided over agriculture, a first step in founding civilization. The new Goddess visions seem to have something to do with restoring a sense of the earth's sacredness. Repeatedly, for instance, we find that Marian visions lead to sacralizing specific locales of earth. Through the seers the people are instructed to build a shrine, usually on the spot of the appearance. A shrine that enshrines a sacred experience becomes the lodestone that attracts pilgrims, drawing a sacred circle on some portion of the earth. The Virgin-Mother-Goddess that is appearing all over the world today is making the earth sacred again.

Pilgrimage. Pilgrimage is basic to the Marian cult. It may be significant that pilgrimage sites are often remote mountain regions such as Fatima, Medjugorje, and Garabandal. Extraordinary individuals like Padre Pio and Sai Baba often come from the hinterland. Perhaps the rarefied mountain atmosphere disposes people to altered states of consciousness. Or perhaps there is less cultural noise to block the transcendent "signal." Or there may be geomagnetic or "ley" forces at work. In any case, people uproot themselves from their ordinary life habits to embark on a pilgrimage. And the pilgrimage can be a transformative experience.

Sacred artifacts. Building shrines, sanctuaries, and cathedrals often involves sacralizing nearby mountains, grottoes, springs, trees, and artifacts that become vehicles for spiritual activity. At San Damiano, Italy, there is today a pear tree said to blossom with pears out of season. At Lourdes a spring appeared that became the site of a great healing shrine.

A unique relic in Guadalupe, Mexico, consists of a tilma (scarf) painted with an image of the Virgin. The figure of a dark-skinned Indian girl is imprinted on a 400-year-old cactus cloth that should have decayed 360 years ago. This cloth and its image have some very puzzling features,[9] and form the basis for one of the oldest spiritual centers of the Christian Americas.

Spiritual technology. Catherine of Labouré's Miraculous Medal brings out another aspect of Marian cult formation, the development of spiritual technologies.

Rosary beads have been prominent in several Marian encounters, especially the one at Fatima. There the Lady urged praying the rosary. Indeed, Lucia, Francesco, and Jacinta, who often prayed the rosary, might well have eased into altered states of consciousness by the practice. As we know from parapsychology, altered states are psi-conducive. Not surprisingly, the Portuguese children were playing and praying the rosary when the weird cycle of events began.

The history of these inner technologies goes back to the time of the earliest Marian visions in Walsingham, England. In the thirteenth century, Saint Simon Stock, who died in 1265, had a vision of Mary holding the scapula of his order—a monastic shoulder band, later reduced to a small cloth worn around the neck. "This shall be a privilege unto thee and all Carmelites; he who dies in this habit shall be saved," declared the apparition. For centuries people have used such a curious piece of brown cloth, surrounding it with magical beliefs and expectations. The scapula, in fact, is part of a traditional *ars moriendi*—an art of dying. Marian visions, like the visions seen at the Eleusinian Mysteries, can lighten the gravity of dying.

Marian visions show the way toward greater lightness of being in other ways. Since 1981 the visions in Medjugorje have involved instructions on fasting on bread and water one day a week for spiritual transformation. The Medjugorje madonna declares that we can "suspend the laws of nature" by fasting. To fast is consciously to reduce the intake of material nutrients—an ancient technique for increasing spiritual power. We know practically nothing about the higher physics of fasting, but there is evidence that inediacs or near inediacs like Therese Neumann and Catherine of Genoa were able to tap into an enigmatic source of vital energy, perhaps the *prana* of yoga philosophy or Henri Bergson's *elan vital*. Fasting may be one method among many that enables us to draw upon this energy of transformation.

As noted, Marian visions give rise to cult formation. The cult is a way of turning vision into social reality. Indeed, the visionary experience seems to produce *more* Marian visions. Using spiritual technologies such as prayer, rosary, or fasting, one becomes increasingly receptive to paranormal encounters. The process draws on people's spiritual needs and energies and on cultures with receptive mythologies—Catholicism and Eastern Orthodox Christianity which venerate Mary—and it generates new forms and values of spiritual vitality. Hence the term Marian "morphogenesis."

A Multimedia Performance

The ingression of images of the Goddess into our public space is not just occurring in the shape of remarkable visionary experiences. The force of the archetypal feminine is manifesting today in many ways. A handful of examples follows.

Modern feminism is that part of the psychic and social evolution occurring on the planet today called by some the "Goddess arising," in which women proclaim their social, political, and economic rights in a world long dominated by the males of the species.

The Goddess archetype has a noble history among the freedom fighters of the world. The Statue of Liberty in the harbor of New York was a gift from France. It can be traced back to the Goddess of Reason, worshipped by French *philosophes* and revolutionaries; a memorial that brings us back to the Goddess of the European Enlightenment. She is still a powerful force today. It is worth noting that Poland, which led in the fight to overthrow Communist oppression in Eastern Europe, has for hundreds of years been devoted to Mary under her aspect of Black Madonna.

The power of the Goddess of the Enlightenment reaches to Asia. In May of 1989 the whole world watched Chinese students erect a statue of the Goddess of Democracy in Tianamen Square in protest against Communism. The angry old men smashed the Statue of Liberty to pieces. No matter, for the Goddess is on the move, and she is bound to keep returning to tempt the young at heart to revolt against oppression.

The Goddess has also become a topic of literary and scholarly investigation. An army of scholars and poets is on the march, deconstructing and revisioning Western theology.[10]

The Goddess, if she is truly returning, is not doing so only in the minds of scholars, theologians, and depth psychologists. We can expect to find her feisty, earthy spirit stirring the popular imagination. In fact, Goddess images are turning up in movies, music videos, and other pop media. In *Ghostbusters II*, for example, the Statue of Liberty comes to life—invoked to stop the ectoplasmic demon of New York City from going on the rampage. In the movie, we watch Our Lady of Liberty gliding across New York harbor, striding down the streets, holding up the torch of liberty, wearing a crown with seven spokes.

One wonders about the uncanny success of rock star Madonna (*sic!*), who fuses religious imagery with pixy eroticism. We see voluptuous Goddess images flashed daily among endless TV commercials, billboards, and magazine photography. And in a society of unscrupulous

men driven by the lust for profit, the ad people of Madison Avenue
know how to exploit the charms of Aphrodite, the Goddess of Love.

Thus, as part of a social movement, as a symbol of the pursuit of
liberty, or as a figure that haunts our dreams and controls our information industries, the Virgin is part of a secret sisterhood, larger and
stronger than we might think.

Views of the Marian Morphogenesis

In viewing the different data relating to the Blessed Virgin Mary as
a whole, a picture begins to emerge. A form, a type of being, a powerful image—there are many ways of putting it—is struggling to express itself, to become concrete and tangible. What are we to make
of this? At least three possibilities come to mind.

The first view is that Marian appearances are symptoms of a mass
religious neurosis. I think, however, more than this is involved. For
example, the appearances are often collectively observed, may contain prophetic information, and are related to phenomena of ancient
and prehistoric times. They sometimes have healing aftereffects and
even paranormal properties. We cannot be sure that Marian visions
are products of social pathology.

A second view is that the appearances are literally the mother of
Jesus and convey specific messages from heaven. Unfortunately, it
is hard to support the view that the apparitions are the historical mother
of Jesus. For one thing, nobody knows what Mary looked like, so
there can be no basis for identification.

The visions vary in appearances, and the variations reflect cultural
and ethnic particulars. For example, the image of the Virgin on the
Guadalupe tilma clearly resembles an Amerindian, not a Jewish girl.
The images often reflect artistic portrayals of Mary known to the visionaries. This is demonstrably the case with the apparitions of Zeitun.
In Nicaragua, Bernadino Martinez himself states that "she looked like
the statue of the Assumption" that was in the local church.[11] In
September, 1919, Polish soldiers resisting the Russian army saw in
the sky "Our Lady and her Child, just as they appeared in the belov-
ed painting at Czestochowa" (the image of the Black Madonna).[12]
I could give many more examples.

If the visions are neither neurotic illusions nor literal apparitions
of the mother of Jesus, there is yet a third hypothesis to consider:
Marian visions are expressions of the Goddess image, an archetypal

pattern of great antiquity and psychological power. There are general reasons for suspecting that this is so. The time seems ripe for Goddess epiphanies, with civilization and ecology both suffering from the excesses of male domination. The Goddess archetype often appears today in the mold of Mary; the cult of Mary gives a familiar psychic vehicle for the collective imagination to work through. The fact that the appearances resemble religious works of art suggests that the archetype is being expressed through the cultural forms at hand.

The archetypal approach avoids reductionism and also the absurdities of a literal interpretation without losing anything of importance. The spiritual side of the experience is valued and the unusual and distinctive features are fully acknowledged.

Imaginal life as a medium for evolution was discussed in Chapter 7. Marian phenomena afford data for understanding how imaginal evolution may be taking place.

Let me describe some stages in the development of this imaginal entity, the Goddess. It is interesting to watch what may be the genesis of a "divine" form, an emerging product of evolution.

A television report showed people rushing to a place in Queens, New York, who claimed to see a sign of the Virgin Mary. The camera revealed what was causing the commotion: a newly erected street lamp had thrown a curious shadow on a garage wall. You might see in it a veiled head suggesting the Blessed Virgin. It was fascinating to see how the shadow became the basis for projecting a form, just as we project forms onto a Rorschach card or an arabesque of tea leaves. Hundreds of people kept returning to the scene and remained in the grips of the seductive illusion—until the lamp was removed.

In September, 1984, a boy concerned about his mother's illness heard a voice in a grove of poplar trees in the village of Pulawy, Poland. The voice declared that his mother would recover, which she did. People came to the site of the audition and began to see a shape resembling the Virgin in the white bark of the trees.[13]

On July 26, 1987, hundreds of pilgrims at the Shrine of the Three Fountains in Rome reported that the sun turned blue-green and was bordered by white stars—traditional symbols of the Virgin. Others claimed to smell a "heavenly perfume" and saw the sun "dance." About the same time a group of Louisiana pilgrims were watching the sun dance in Medjugorje. Similar observations of the sun dancing (along with some odd photos of the alleged wonder) have been reported in Bayside, Queens, and in San Damiano, Italy. The "dance of the sun" was first reported in Fatima, 1917.

Again in Medjugorje, a travel agent from New Orleans, Jan Thomas, reported that he saw a wooden cross light up with a vision of the face of Jesus, as reported in *Newsweek*, July, 1987. Inchoate psychic phenomena often seem to crystallize and take living form around an archetypal image such as a cross or crucifix. Jung thought that archetypes stimulate psychic phenomena. A classic example is that of Saint Francis who was praying in front of a broken crucifix when he heard a voice command him to repair the Church.

There is a statue of the Virgin in a convent in Akita, Japan, said to become animated in the presence of Sister Agnes Sasagawa. The statue reportedly wept and spoke to the Sister three times in the 1980s.

Around 1985 thousands of people were visiting Marian shrines all over the Republic of Ireland, insisting that they saw statues move, strange lights in the sky, and other visions. The statue of the Virgin at Ballinspittle was the cause of a great deal of excitement. People from all parts of Ireland came to look at this statue, believers, half-believers, and skeptics; even the skeptics thought they saw the statue move. A collection of eyewitness accounts of the phenomenon has been assembled.[14] The statue was filmed and clearly did not move; but even hostile skeptics saw arms and lips of dead stone wave and smile. One writer noted "that deep in the psyche of this race are memories of the Great Mother Goddess Danu of pre-Celtic times."

The antics of the Goddess don't stop here. The phenomenon of weeping statues of the madonna is fairly widespread, the most spectacular instance occurring in Syracuse, Italy, 1954. In that case, liquid was observed by thousands to pour from the eyes of the statue, samples of which were examined by scientists and found to be chemically equivalent to human tears.[15]

This list of phenomena is not to review the evidence but to illustrate a continuum of types of reports, ranging from cases of obvious illusion to some with increasing degrees of "reality," and finally to cases suggestive of paranormal phenomena.

I want to offer an alternative way of looking at these kinds of phenomena: they might indicate the presence of a force seeking an outlet to objectify itself. The illusions reflect a zone of ambiguity where the boundaries between fact and fantasy begin to dissolve. This zone of ambiguity is a zone of creativity where the imaginal erupts into the physical and vision becomes actuality.

Skeptics who pounce on every obvious case of illusion or self-deception as proof that all is flim-flam have missed the point. They fail to see that the fictional elements often belong on a continuum with authentic paranormal manifestations. I maintain that the shadow mistaken for the Virgin on the Queens garage wall, the spectacular full-blown apparitions of Zeitun, and the massively witnessed aerial phenomena of Fatima all reflect pressures of the same archetypal energies struggling to manifest themselves.

I believe that the full range of evidence demonstrates the reality of a continuum of psychic phenomena, ranging from what is obviously subjective projection to paranormal experience with increasing degrees of physicality. The pressure to materialize the archetype follows the path of least resistance: children, peasants, the uneducated, people with belief systems that make them receptive to signals from the Marian "morphogenetic field"—if I may borrow an idea used by Rupert Sheldrake.

There is some evidence for the existence of such fields. Marian visions sometimes occur at sites of pre-Christian shrines to the Great Goddess. Consider a few examples. Cortez, with superb masculine daring and brutality, conquered Mexico in 1521. Ten years later, Juan Diego, a poor native and Christian convert, passed over a barren hill and saw a vision of a radiant young girl who said she was the "Virgin Mary, Mother of the True God." Before Cortez, this barren hill, Tepeyac, about 130 feet high, was consecrated to the Aztec Goddess, Teotenantzin—"Mother of God."

Christian Mary and Greek Kore seem cut from the same mold. Central to the Mystery Rites at Eleusis was the epiphany of Kore, the virgin daughter of Demeter, the great Mother Goddess.

A text of Epiphanios will illustrate. One night (January 5th or 6th) in ancient Alexandria, worshippers met at the temple of Kore and descended into an underground shrine where they danced and chanted around a wooden statue of the Goddess, naked and marked with the sign of the cross on her brow, her hands, and her knees. This seems a singular fusion—cross and naked virgin. Wrote Epiphanios: "The votaries say that today at this hour Kore—that is, the Virgin—gave birth to the Eternal (*Aion*)." Farnell comments:

It is at least probable that the prevalence of the cult and the name of "Kore," the Goddess who proffered salvation in the pre-Christian Hellenic world, afforded strong stimulus to the later growth and diffusion of Mariolatry, which is one of those phenomena in the history of the Church which cannot be adequately explained without looking beyond the limits of Christianity proper.[16]

The account of the statue of the naked cross-tattooed Virgin pinpoints the transition from pagan to Christian world.

The Goddess archetype is very old indeed. Prehistoric works of art—figurines of a fertility Goddess that date back forty thousand years—are proof of the primordial impulse to materialize images of this great power. So it is not surprising that at this stage of our evolution the Goddess should be appearing so frequently. Since the Reformation and the Scientific Revolution, the energies of the Goddess have been banished. Now, at the end of the twentieth century, she is returning.

A New Reality Principle

The Fatima phenomena were spectacular, so it is interesting to note that the Cova da Iria (where they took place) was also a place of ancient Goddess worship. Centuries ago in a place where the three children saw the "Lady from Heaven" in 1917, people worshipped Isis, the Goddess of many names. The Roman writer, Apuleius, describes an encounter with Isis. The Goddess said to him:

Behold, Lucius, I am come. Thy weeping and prayer hath moved me to succour thee. I am she that is the natural mother of all things, mistress and governess of all the elements, the initial progeny of worlds, chief of the powers divine, queen of all that are in Hell, the principle of them that dwell in Heaven, manifested alone and under one form of all the gods and goddesses.

This description of Isis anticipates Mary of the Middle Ages. It illustrates that the Goddess responds to feeling: "weeping and prayer" move Isis—not abstract principles. The medieval Virgin, too, typified a different reality-principle: love, not justice; faith, not knowledge; feelings, not deeds.

Many modern feminists have overlooked Marian visions. The reasons are not hard to find. The Virgin Mary is decried as an ally in the repression of women. The Church, they say, uses pious, pure, docile Mary as propaganda to subjugate women. Feminists say that talk of the feminine archetype as nurturing is inhibiting, insidiously curtailing the full range of their personhood. They reject a sanitized, etherealized, desexualized Mary as an enemy to natural woman. Feminists have therefore been more drawn to Earth religions than to Mariolatry.

There is some substance in these criticisms. But when a zealous feminist like Naomi Goldenberg calls Mary Christianity's "good girl,"[17] it shows a poor grasp of the historical function of the cult of Mary. Far from being Christianity's "good girl," the figure of Mary contains the seeds of a radical overthrow of Christian patriarchy.

Henry Adams published a book in 1905 on the architecture of Mont Saint-Michel and Chartres. Adams details the amazing psychic power that the cult of Mary exerted over medieval Europe. Huge chunks of the economy went into building her cathedrals. Adams admired Mary as an alternate reality-principle, as embodying "the whole rebellion against fate. . . . She was above law; she took feminine pleasure in turning hell into an ornament; she delighted in trampling on every social tradition in this world and the next."

The medieval cult of Mary revolted against the masculine idea of justice, thus, in effect, against the entire reality-principle that supports Western civilization. From this perspective, the Marian morphogenesis represents an unconscious reaction against two thousand years of repression.

What then is behind the present invasion of the Goddess idea? My conclusion is that Marian visions are increasing because psychic functions suppressed for centuries are erupting now, and they are urgently needed at this stage of our history. Marian visions are evidence of evolution groping to heal the soul of humanity.

13
Aliens, Allies, and Evolution

One day when the sky was serene and clear there was heard in it the sound of a trumpet, so shrill and mournful that it frightened and astonished the whole city. The Tuscan sages said that it portended a new race of men, and a renovation of the world . . . heaven had allotted to each [race] its time, which was limited by the circuit of the Great Year; and when one race came to a period, and another was rising, it was announced by some wonderful sign from either earth or heaven.

Plutarch

The statement quoted above from Plutarch on the Tuscan sages links "wonderful sign[s]" with the end of an epoch and the rise of a new race of humanity. C. G. Jung used similar words to talk about flying saucers in the 1950s, which he saw as signs of a new era, heralds of a changing of the gods. Since then new patterns of experience are being reported which strike people as powerfully as do Marian visions and flying saucers, experiences that shatter people's sense of reality. These experiences—as the ancient Tuscan sages said—give rise to ideas of a "new race of men" and "a renovation of the world."

This chapter contains a brief survey of several patterns of visionary encounter not yet discussed.[1] Ordinary people from all walks of life report visits by a variety of supernatural, extraterrestrial, or ultradimensional beings. For example, a man described to me voices he heard in his head that made him quit his job in the aerospace industry so he could go to school to become a forest ranger (an ecologically sounder vocation). A woman wrote about a mystical experience in which she sensed "the taste of evolution." Another man sent an account of a monster visitation in a large metropolis. Stories of alien contact are widespread in our culture.

At first glance, the types of phenomena described look very differ-

204

ent from religious visitations—and at one level they clearly are. Seeing a vision of the Virgin Mary is not the same as being abducted by a small gray-skinned, wall-eyed humanoid. At the same time, the more closely I look, the more I see intertwinings and crisscrossings among these reports. Of course it would be premature to say they are all related to a single source or mechanism. Nevertheless, I wish to suggest something like this as a working hypothesis. Is a common transcendent psi factor the root and ultimate cause of these apparently various phenomena?

Angel or Ideoplastic Psi Factor?

Angels, as discussed in Chapter 8, are a type of alien encounter. Consider a story in the Introduction to Gustaf Davidson's *A Dictionary of Angels*. After immersing himself in research for his book, Davidson suddenly found himself "bedeviled by angels." The shadowy forms he had been poring over in books and dusty archives suddenly and unaccountably came to life around him.

"I remember one occasion" he writes, "—it was winter and getting dark—returning home from a neighboring farm. I had cut across an unfamiliar field. Suddenly a nightmarish shape loomed up before me, barring my progress. After a paralyzing moment I managed to fight my way past the phantom. The next morning I could not be sure (no more than Jacob was, when he wrestled with his dark antagonist at Peniel) whether I had encountered a ghost, an angel, a demon, or God."

A remarkable experience, and an ambiguous one. What Davidson actually saw was merely a "nightmarish shape." A person who believes in ghosts might have sworn it was a ghost. Another—given suitable changes in viewpoint—might have seen it as an alien from outer space or a monster from another dimension. Davidson's description shows that, depending on one's conceptual furniture, beliefs, and expectations, one may read anything into such an experience—"a ghost, an angel, a demon, or God." Still, something, however nebulous, was there. Davidson's testimony supports the view that the form the transcendent factor takes is the *outcome of a cocreative process.*

Davidson concluded: "Without committing myself religiously I could conceive of the possibility of there being, in dimensions and worlds other than our own, powers and intelligences outside our present apprehension, and in this sense angels are not to be ruled out as a part of reality—always remembering that *we create what we believe.*'' This is close to the view of angels in Chapter 8 where I described a model in which belief, imagination, and expectation combine to release our psychokinetic potential in the creation of forms we call angels.

The Near-Death Journey

Thanks to modern resuscitation technology, many people are "raised" from apparent or clinical death. About 40 percent of those who come close to death have what is known as the "near-death experience." These people tell of leaving their bodies and entering a transcendent world of light, love, and bliss. In Chapter 3 the connection between near-death visions and the genesis of the God-Idea was discussed. Skeptics say that NDEs are the byproducts of traumatized brains, but the experiencers themselves insist they have seen other worlds. They claim an extraordinary encounter with reality, something immensely important and transformative.

Whether NDEs are hallucinations or true sorties into the beyond is an important question. In either case, they change people in ways that have implications for human development. Raymond Moody and Kenneth Ring have stressed this approach in their research: accept the reported experiences at face value; then study their aftereffects. Interesting physical, mental, and spiritual aftereffects have been observed. Ring, for example, has found a striking pattern of psychophysical changes he has suggested may relate to awakening kundalini, an evolutionary energy familiar in the East.[2]

The mental and spiritual aftereffects of NDEs are well known. David Lorimer, writer and founder of the British Scientific and Medical Network, wrote a book in which he argues that a new moral world order may be in the process of evolving from a matrix of mystical consciousness related to near-death experiences.[3] NDEs are introducing millions of people to higher worlds, transcendent beings, or soul-transforming light encounters. Could they be a pattern pointing toward some interesting possibilities for our psychophysical evolution?

Against those who classify NDEs as hallucinations, there are cases highlighted by cardiologist Michael Sabom in which resuscitated patients describe in detail what happened to them on the operating table.

Their descriptions are from a viewpoint above their bodies—at a time when to all appearances they lacked vital signs. Some patients made exact visual observations from locations far from their bodies. Even more startling are children's NDEs. Pediatrician Melvin Morse, in his book *Closer to the Light*, tells of a child who "died" and met—and later described—a deceased grandparent he had never met or known. Since the child acquired specific information during his near-death experience, the experience cannot be written off as wholly illusory.

Near-death experiencers believe they have been touched by something divine. This is the transformative core of the experience. Descriptions of the NDE shade off into the classic mystical experience, so that ordinary people seem to have stumbled upon a natural short-cut to the mystic goal. With increasing numbers claiming to have these experiences (the 1982 Gallup poll indicates millions[4]), spontaneous consciousness-expanding experiences are available widely. Here the potential of the alien to become an ally is large.

The Complex of UFO Encounters

The acronym "UFO" covers at least three categories of related experiences, each of which presents a facet of alien encounter. First, "unidentified" discs, lights, and crafts; second, experiences of "contact" with alien intelligences, usually depicted as benign Space Brothers; third, and more recently publicized, reports of alien abduction. Once again, as with the NDE, there are fugitive indications of objectivity (photos, bodily lesions, equipment malfunction), though at the same time much of UFO reality is shrouded in the mists of folklore and mythology.

The UFO experience is basic to our list of experiences with possible impact on psychic evolution. On almost any interpretation, the UFO experience has evolutionary implications. For example, if real extraterrestrials (ETs) are visiting us, our basic view of our place in the universe would change drastically. Or suppose instead that UFOs are psycho-terrestrials (PTs) from inner space. There would still be evolutionary implications. In Jung's classic study, disc-shaped flying saucers appearing in the skies are signs of closure in a great cycle of regenerative time. The disc, according to Jung, was like a mandala, a symbol of wholeness. The flying saucer phenomenon would then be signalling that our collective consciousness is decomposing and is in process of renovating and reconstituting itself.

Contact

The UFO complex includes more than sightings of flying discs and mysterious lights. Some people claim they have been contacted by aliens, usually via telepathy.

Leo Sprinkle, a psychologist from the University of Wyoming, has devoted years to listening to people who claim contact with extraterrestrials or ultradimensionals. In the literature, such people are known as "contactees." Dr. Sprinkle provides a forum—and a network—for people who have had what Whitley Strieber calls the "visitor experience."

"Contact" may be a rare or a regular occurrence. It may occur by visual signs, by locutions, or by telepathic impressions. The range and variety of contact tales is considerable; certain motifs repeat themselves, and certain images and symbols.

After Kenneth Arnold reported his historic sighting of nine unidentified flying objects on June 24, 1947, near Mt. Rainier, Washington, reports of contact with alien intelligences suddenly began to multiply. The cult of alien contact flourished in the 1950s, and the "contactee" movement grew up in the shadows of the A-bomb menace and the Cold War.

The case of Orfeo Angelucci, a California employee of Lockheed, illustrates the contactee saga. Carl Jung discussed Orfeo in his book *Flying Saucers: A Modern Myth of Things Seen in the Sky*. Orfeo spoke of an "evolutionary crisis" related to the coming of the saucers. A voice from the saucers sounded in Orfeo's head: "We also hope to give men a deeper knowledge and understanding of their own true nature and a greater awareness of the evolutionary crisis facing them."

As sometimes reported in NDEs, there was a sound of heavenly music, and the voice proclaimed to Orfeo, "Beloved friend of the earth, we baptize you now in the true light of the worlds eternal."

What did the experience feel like? Writes Orfeo:

> A blinding white beam flashed from the dome of the craft. . . .
> Everything expanded into a great shimmering white light. I seemed
> to be projected beyond Time and Space and was conscious only
> of light, light, LIGHT! . . . Every event of my life upon Earth was

crystal clear to me—and the memory of all my previous lives upon Earth returned. In that sublime moment I knew the mystery of life!

Note the similarity to the near-death experience, in which numinous lights are said to shine and panoramic memories of one's life flash on the inward eye. In this 1955 account, we find something else that crops up again in the 1980s. Again, Orfeo:

As I was undressing to go to bed, I remembered again the burning sensation I had on my left side while I was undergoing the profound "initiation" in the saucer. I glanced down and saw what appeared to be a circular "burn" about the size of a quarter directly below my heart. The outer rim of the circle was red—. . . the symbol of the hydrogen atom. I realized that they impressed that mark upon my body to convince me beyond all doubt of the reality of my experiences in the cold light of the coming days.[5]

Both NDEs and UFOs involve the subjective certainty of having contacted an alien *reality;* outsiders, however, are bound to be skeptical. These experiences seem to float in a metaphysical borderland, a place where imagination shades into reality and ordinary reality seems to crumble into elusive images. Some researchers wish to separate sharply the so-called contact encounters from reports of alien abduction. I am skeptical about this separation. Too many reports contain both "abduction" and classic "contactee" motifs.

Alien Abduction

The list of experiences occurring these days that function as catalysts for growth in human consciousness includes some bizarre encounters such as abduction by aliens. Researchers in America have recently focused on such reports. It seems that large numbers of people are telling stories of being kidnapped into spaceships where they are subjected to intrusive medical examinations. Some scientists believe the evidence is strong enough to substantiate these extraordinary claims. As physicist Stanton Friedman has declared in a famous UFO documentary, *"UFOs are real!,"* "real" is meant in a straightforward "nuts-and-bolts" physical sense of reality.

Other researchers are more skeptical about physical flying saucers and prefer psychosocial interpretations, which utilize folklore, mythology, and parapsychology in their interpretation of the phenomenon.[6]

Like the near-death experience, those who have the experience are, for the most part, convinced of its reality. Still, there is such an admixture of mythic and psychic elements, it is hard to take UFO narratives at face value.

Some students think that alien abductions hold the answer to the UFO mystery. One theory is that aliens are kidnapping us because they need our gene pool to reinvigorate their sagging procreative capacities. In this theory, the aliens are parasites and have nothing to do with the contactee pattern of UFO experience, which some investigators dismiss as illusory.

On the other hand, these narratives telling of a dying planet and waning ETs lend themselves rather nicely to a symbolic interpretation. As with any dream, a recurrent collective UFO dream about degeneration may be a comment on the dreamer and *its* problems. In this case, the "dream" would be telling us about our own problems on a dying planet, our own need for "regeneration."

It must be said, however, in fairness to the complexity of the reports on alien abduction, that it would be dangerous to draw any firm conclusions too hastily. Folklorist Thomas Bullard has performed a very detailed analysis of the reports of alien abductions.[7] Bullard finds a stable and coherent narrative that does not yield to any obvious interpretation. Psychiatrist Rima Laibow finds that people who report being kidnapped by aliens show the classic symptoms of traumatic stress disorder, which suggests they have been exposed to a real external experience. That still leaves open the question of what caused the experience. Jenny Randles, a British researcher in the field of anomalies, speculates that alien intelligences are communicating with us via telepathy—creating images which we interpret, for example, as abductions.[8] Again, the conclusion suggests external agency.

Men in Black

Reports of alien contact or abduction often contain associated narratives or subplots: for example, tales of the sinister "Men in Black" (MIB). An example is the report of an ardent student of Sufism. He saw a flying saucer and, being a reporter by profession, decided to investigate further. On the evening he was about to interview another person who saw the same object, he received a strange telephone call. The voice on the line didn't sound human; it spoke in a deep, raspy, mechanical tone and said in no uncertain terms it would not be wise to pursue the story. The intimidating, menacing voice my friend heard is an example of the threat from a so-called "Man in Black."

Psychiatrist Berthold Schwarz combines psychiatric, neurological, parapsychological, and ufological expertise. In a study called *The Men in Black Syndrome*,[9] Schwarz tells an uncanny story. The reader should read the original, but I will summarize.

Herbert Hopkins, a family physician from Maine, was studying the case of a man involved in a UFO incident and an alleged teleportation. On the evening of September 11, 1976, Dr. Hopkins received a visit in his home from a strange man wearing a "black derby, a black jacket, black tie, white shirt, black trousers and shoes." The man had called, not giving his name, but somehow inveigled his way into Dr. Hopkins' home. (He claimed he was from a UFO organization that was found not to exist.) When he took off his hat, he appeared completely hairless, with no eyebrows, and had a dead white complexion. He was wearing bright red lipstick.

The dream-like figure inquired about the UFO case Dr. Hopkins was investigating. The Man in Black was nearly motionless, barely opening a slit-like toothless mouth. He then said that Dr. Hopkins had two coins in his left pocket, which was true; he instructed the doctor to place one of the coins (he chose the penny) on the palm of his hand. The Man in Black told the doctor to keep his eye on the penny, which then gradually faded into a vaporous "blue fuzzy ball" and vanished. "Neither you nor anyone else on this *plane* [not planet] will ever see that coin again," said the Man in Black.

The uncanny visitor then ordered the doctor to destroy any tapes, correspondence, or literature he had on the UFO case he was studying. He said that if Dr. Hopkins failed to comply, he would suffer the fate of Barney Hill—an abductee who died after his experience. The man rose, his voice failing: "My energy is low now—must go now—goodbye." He walked out slowly and unsteadily and vanished. Dr. Hopkins destroyed all his UFO materials.

What can we make of accounts like this? Folklorist Peter Rojcewicz made a study of MIBs and found they have many features in common with traditional accounts of the devil. MIBs seem to slide in and out of reality, behaving like phantoms or nightmares one moment and assuming a daylight actuality the next. Rojcewicz sees the ambiguous ontological status of Men in Black as characteristic of an entire continuum of extraordinary encounters.[10]

Diabolical Attack

Now that we have been exposed to the dark side of the supernatural, we can consider the idea of diabolic attack. Here, of course, is where we are tempted to step back. The modern mind is reluctant to admit the reality of supernatural evil.

Stories of Men in Black seem to blend motifs of UFO abduction and supernatural evil, and all these blend in turn into stories of diabolical attack. Popular media, as well as a semischolarly literature, reinforce the idea that people are having experiences which suggest diabolic assualt. Attacks from diabolic entities were real experiences for Padre Pio (Chapter 10) in the sense that they left physical effects—welts and bruises.

But it is not only saints who report attack by diabolic forces. Ordinary people are said to be victims. I have heard several stories suggestive of diabolic entities. For example, a woman with a photographic memory, Andrea Zona, described to me how she watched a bar of blue flames form a circle around her bed while she was being sexually assaulted by a diabolic personage. Frank de Felitta's novel, *The Entity,* made into a movie of the same name, is based on a story, said to be true, that tells of a similar sexual assault from an invisible "man."

Diabolical attack seems a variation of demoniacal possession, where the alien personality lodges itself in the hapless victim. The possession syndrome may be seen from descriptions in the New Testament (see, for example, Mark 5:2-10) and in contemporary accounts given, for example, in Malachi Martin's *Hostage to the Devil.*

Clearly, diabolical phenomena are in some sense real. But whether they are variations of poltergeist phenomena, emanations of the dark side of ourselves (the Shadow in Jungian terms), or possibly derived from external sources is not a question I can attempt to answer here.

Since I have broached the question of possession, I should point out that among ancient and preliterate societies the state of possession is not inherently evil. Ancient writers held that states of possession and states of enthusiasm and inspiration are akin.

Plato, for example, in the *Phaedrus,* wrote of a "god-given mania," a kind of possession that is the source of the "greatest blessings" to humankind. Plato listed prophetic, artistic, healing, and erotic madness or *mania*. When the soul is possessed by the daimon of Eros, it is lifted up, Plato says, in a kind of out-of-body experience, and granted a vision of the gods. This daimonic exaltation to god consciousness, according to Plato, is the goal of philosophy. It is the agency that mediates between human and divine—an evolutionary accelerator, a way of deepening our consciousness of reality. The daimonic dimension of philosophy has been lost in the Western tradition.

The Old Hag

An important piece of data relevant in this chapter comes under the heading of "the Old Hag." A pioneer study by yet another folklorist, David Hufford, titled *The Terror that Comes in the Night*[11], uses this term to describe the phenomenon also known as the nightmare—waking up to a terrifying presence.

This is a widespread experience. I have had it myself several times. My experience was typical. On several occasions I have become conscious, while lying in bed, of a powerful presence gripping and paralyzing me; I make an effort to move but cannot. My eyes are open. I hear footsteps. The floorboards creak. It seems certain that someone —or something—is in the room with me. I am fully awake, conscious, clear. Suddenly, the weight lifts and the presence is gone.

Once again we find narratives that, while suggesting dreams and unreality, we cannot quite discount as merely subjective. Let me summarize the conclusions of Hufford's remarkable study.

The phenomenon of the "Old Hag" is a distinct, recognizable, and stable pattern of experience that is found in different cultural settings. Hufford believes that the experience validates the empirical core of "numerous traditions of supernatural assault." This is a major assertion. Hufford has found that there is an underlying reality in certain traditions of the supernatural that are usually dismissed as merely legendary or fantastic. Unearthing of the empirical core of the "supernatural" is one of my main concerns in this book.

Hufford found that culture is crucial in the way the experience is interpreted. This is a point I have made several times: a transcendent psi factor appears in our experience, which formally manifests itself through the lens of myth and culture.

Hufford calculated about 15 percent of the population has had the

Old Hag experience. Therefore, it cannot be explained as pathological. Hufford concludes, "The contents of this experience cannot be satisfactorily explained on the basis of current knowledge."

Only further work will establish how the experience of the "Old Hag" figures into the general equation of otherworldly visitation. Suffice to note that some of its features (paralysis and sense of presence) figure in other visitation narratives: Marian visions, out-of-body experiences, mystical trances, alien abductions, and diabolical possession, for instance.

Encounters with the Holy Spirit

Transformative experiences, though quite varied, have in common an ability to stretch our concept of who we are and what is possible. Some have grotesque and disturbing overtones and seem to emanate from the sinister back alleys of the collective unconscious; others, more in line with traditional experiences, seem linked to the ascent and enlightenment of the human spirit.

For example, the twentieth century has witnessed an explosion of born-again, pentecostal, and charismatic Christianity, with millions of people claiming to encounter the Holy Spirit. The Pentecostal revival began as an outgrowth of the Holiness Movement in the late nineteenth century and spread with phenomenal rapidity into mainstream Protestant and Catholic churches in the 1950s and 1960s.

The experience of baptism in the Spirit was first reported at the dawn of Christianity (see Chapter 4). Angels and visitations from the Virgin Mary are part of this syndrome of the outpouring of gifts of the Spirit, and all are linked in religious mythology to the idea of a coming new age—the Millennium. They include prophecy, healing, speaking in tongues, and discernment of spirits. These "charisms" or gifts of the "Holy Spirit" seem part of the continuum of evolutionary accelerators.

According to Luke (23:49), the last words uttered by Jesus before his ascension were: "And now I am sending upon you what the Father has promised. Stay in the city, then, until you are clothed with the power from on high." The Bible states that this power, the power of the Holy Spirit, descended on the disciples soon afterward on the day of Pentecost. We read in the Book of Acts (2:1-2):

> suddenly there came from heaven a sound as if of a violent wind, which filled the entire house in which they were sitting; and there appeared to them tongues as of fire; these separated and came to

rest on the head of each of them. They were all filled with the Holy
Spirit and began to speak different languages as the Spirit gave them
power to express themselves.

The passage from Acts says the disciples spoke in "different
languages." We have no way of knowing if the apostles did or only
seemed to speak in tongues unknown to them. Parapsychology
distinguishes between xenoglossy and glossolalia. Xenoglossy means
literally speaking a foreign language—one that is unknown to the
speaker.

In the charismatic or pentecostal experience today, we find examples
of glossolalia, which usually consists of verbal strings of nonsense
built up from the phonemes of known languages. Glossolalia has been
described as "preconceptual prayer."[12] Others see it as a form of
ecstatic praise. We might think of it as a surrealistic device to summon the energies of the unconscious, a technique for deconstructing
the rules of everyday reason—a kind of linguistic regression in service to the ineffable core of Spirit encounters. One critical but sympathetic commentator describes the pentecostal experience as a "breaking of human barriers and leaping over chasms of alienation."[13]

Holy Spirit encounters trigger other "gifts." Berthold Schwarz has
studied psychosomatic phenomena among the "saints" of the Free
Pentecostal Holiness Church in the mountains of Eastern Kentucky.
Schwarz describes how Kentucky revivalists work themselves up to
a state of mind in which they are seized by "the power of the Lord."
The "saints" hug, kiss, sing, scream, read scripture, and "speak in
tongues," which leads to trance. Thus, in an altered state, they handle
poisonous snakes, become immune to fire, and drink lye and
strychnine.[14]

Transformative experiences of a psychospiritual nature are taking
place both within and outside the context of established traditions.
In China from 1987 to 1989 there was a resurgence of the *Qigong*
movement. *Qi* means "breath, spirit, vital force." Masters of qigong
have demonstrated healing and other psychokinetic abilities.[15] The
qigong experience is like the charismatic experience in that it represents a revival of ancient tradition. Chinese and Western scientists
are presently studying Qigong.

Channeling

Another type of widespread transformative experience being reported
nowadays (though less now than a few years ago) also has its roots

in older traditions, although for the most part practitioners have little awareness of their historical ancestors.

Channeling, as I would roughly define it, is a procedure for trying to obtain information from a higher source. This definition covers a wide range of supposed supernormal communications. Contemporary channeling, especially as practiced in America, differs from mediumship and prophecy. The older Victorian mediumship focused on communication with deceased human beings; it sought "proof" of life after death. Prophecy in the Old Testament "channeled" God; it sought the moral regeneration of a people.

Modern channeling is about communication with personified symbols and sources of "nonphysical," "higher," and "universal" minds whose task is usually not to give proof of discarnate existence but to guide us in our practical lives. Channeled guides—like guardian angels, the Virgin Mary, the Holy Spirit, the Space Brothers and Space Women—all serve as avenues to transcendent sources of information.

One of the most commercially successful experiences of channeling resulted in the publication of *A Course in Miracles,* a huge document written "automatically" from 1965 to 1973 during periods while the "author" was in a dissociated state of consciousness. The "channel" was a New York psychologist, Helen Schucman. This work attracted a following, offering a practical training program of inner transformation, a modern psychology of salvation. Christ was the alleged source.

This is not the place to examine particular channels, their curious styles of discourse, or their specific claims to superior "knowingness"—to use a term they are fond of. Here I want to call attention to channeling as a popular movement with possible evolutionary implications. According to Jon Klimo, thousands of channelers all over the world exist, and hundreds of thousands of people are active in circles, groups, and movements that revolve around channelers.[16] Channeling is a contagious process practiced by ordinary people from all walks of life: housewives, therapists and social workers, laborers and salespeople, people of both sexes and from all economic, social, and educational groups.

We seem to be witnessing the spontaneous emergence of a new myth of transcendence. It is as if there is a collective force redefining the ruling imagery of our human situation. The basic message involves a fantastic enlargement of the concept of self. In revolt against the suffocating dogmas of scientific behaviorism and materialism, the collective imagination keeps reminding us that we can "access"—a popular computerese metaphor—a higher source of unlimited love, intelligence, and creativity. Many believe that source, that divine wellspring, is none other than our own true and deepest selves.

Channeling, however we regard its reality status—bogus, authentic, a mishmash of both, or from the channeler's unconscious—has furnished many a vocabulary of transformation. It has given to popular consciousness a language of higher entities, alternate planes of reality, cosmic schemes of evolution, metaphors of transcendence. Channelers also often perform as they impart higher wisdom offerings. So, for example, J. Z. Knight, a popular channel, takes on the alternate persona of Ramtha, who postures and vociferates as a hoary, wise being from another dimension.

The channelers claim to channel new, strange, and transcendent beings, to have contact with otherworldly entities. In *Agartha*, Meredith Young writes of her encounter with an invisible ally she calls "Mentor." I once asked if Mentor might be a dissociated part of herself, a personified fragment, a symbol for tapping into her own unconscious. Young's reply was emphatic: Mentor was real, an intelligence external to herself.

Modern channeling seems like a spontaneous, democratic process for widening the average consciousness of self. What is interesting is the spontaneous way that people, dead to traditional myths, are personifying their own guides, gods, goddesses—whatever image, form, or scheme they need to break out of the stranglehold of the materialistic worldview. Through this popular remaking of the mythical imagination, we may be preparing ourselves for evolutionary breakthroughs of consciousness.

The Unclassified

As a huge mass of evidence shows, people are having strange encounters with beings said to hail from alien or alternate worlds. Not all of these experiences fall into neatly defined categories, however. I have already noted some odd overlaps, as in the MIBs, which seem to blend diabolic infestation with extraterrestrial encounter. There have been more than a few reports of "big hairy monsters" skulking about in the vicinity of flying saucers. Time forbids us to detail the evidence that implicates flying saucers with visions of the Virgin Mary, for example at Fatima in 1917 and more recently at Medjugorje.[17]

Other hard to classify experiences look like near-death experiences but are triggered by meditation or other states. An example from many I have collected concerns Mark R., an architect living in Brooklyn. He had a transformative experience in 1976 that was triggered by a nightmare. The following account is based on a written account Mark sent me.

Mark dreamt that a human corpse had fallen on his belly, facing him, and woke with a terrifying start. When awake, he found he was paralyzed, and felt the corpse of his nightmare had become a reality. In a violent effort to break his paralysis he fell "through the floor, through the walls of the building, through the earth . . . into outer space, into the gulfs between the stars." He then went "through a glowing tunnel" and heard "millions of voices singing."

Mark then found himself hovering near the ceiling looking down at his body below, still with the corpse on his abdomen. Then a luminous cloud appeared from which a spirit of "gentleness and tranquility" emanated. The light grew and so did the sensation of "blissful warmth and security." The light expanded to encompass a universe of pure golden bliss. A Jesus-like voice communed with him telepathically, and his life passed in review before him. A particular incident of his childhood in which he had behaved selfishly flashed before him.

Mark described the light: "There was something completely disarming about the light, something hardly expected, a childlike quality of freshness and playfulness, it was a fountain of joy, smiling and often bursting with hearty laughter." Reluctantly he returned to his body, but not before the voice in the light assured him they would never part again.

It is remarkable that this experience, which closely resembles the classic near-death experience, was triggered by a nightmare. There are in fact many cases on record in which the sequence associated with the near-death experience is started by an incident that has nothing to do with being literally near death. This suggests that there is a single psychic mechanism, in itself not related to the physiology of being near death, which can be set into motion by a variety of causes. Mark was deeply moved to investigate the nature of his experience which he stated in a letter to me was "growth promoting and accelerating consciousness development."

Monsters and Alien Animals

Let us posit a primal, inherently formless psychic entity—a sheer potential for assuming image and form. Once we consider the "ideoplasticity" of this primal entity—that is, its readiness to materialize in the shape of our thoughts—we will have a handle for grappling with another type in the spectrum of alien visitation.

From the dark side of the psychic continent come reports of monster epiphanies and alien animals. The surprising fact is that there are thousands of reports dealing with so-called lake monsters, large cats that appear out of place, mysterious black dogs, giant birds and bird people, and creatures known as Bigfoot, Yeti, and Sasquatch ("Big Hairy Monsters" or BHMs). For the most part the often puzzling reports of these appearances have not been considered for their symbolic, still less their possible evolutionary, significance. So-called "cryptozoologists" think they may be living organisms that have somehow escaped the notice of science. Others highlight the paranormal side of these reports.[18]

Alien animals like lake monsters and Bigfeet hover tantalizingly on the edge of physical reality, sighted by people and sometimes leaving physical traces, photographs (for instance, of the Loch Ness appearance) or footprints (of Bigfeet and mysterious black dogs); nevertheless, they remain essentially elusive and ambiguous. Are they real or are they phantoms? In their ambiguity, they resemble the other twilight beings described in this chapter.

Indeed, the writers who have looked closely at the evidence incline toward the theory that "monsters" and "alien animals" are on a continuum with other anomalous appearances or entity experiences. For example, Janet and Colin Bord, after a detailed analysis of case histories, conclude, "Our suspicion is that many alien animals are non-physical, in some way linked to the witness, and needing a suitable energy source to help them materialize and to sustain them."[19] They also say, "There are so many similarities between UFOs, UFO entities, and alien animals that there seems a strong possibility that they are part of the same phenomenon."

Another writer who links monsters, flying saucers, ghosts, and UFOs is Ted Holiday in his intriguing book *The Goblin Universe*. Yet another English writer in this field, Jenny Randles, invokes Rupert Sheldrake's morphogenetic fields to account for the mysteries and complexities of what she calls "mind monsters."[20] It is not possible to discuss the detailed arguments of these writers; I mention them only to show how large the family of alien experiences is and how they may form a continuous body of interrelated experiences.

Evolutionary Accelerators

Enough has been said to show there are probably untold thousands of people all over the world today having unusual psychic experiences. We may ask if these experiences are accelerating the evolution of human consciousness. Before trying to answer this question, we should consider the following points:

First, we don't have to explain an experience before we can discuss its evolutionary potential. Scientists disagree on how to explain the near-death experience, though we can examine the way it changes people's lives. Our response to an experience is independent of the mechanism that produces the experience.

Another point is that the evolutionary implications of an experience are not automatic; they are not built into the experience itself. Their meaning, value, and growth potential depend in part on the person who has the experience. The type of evolution being considered is a cocreative process that ultimately rests on human freedom. Therefore, no experience is intrinsically evolutionary. A rigidly skeptical person might have a remarkable near-death experience but not make use of its transformative potential.

The paradigm one holds can determine whether an experience remains merely alien or acquires the potential to become an ally. The paradigm—the model that helps us interpret an experience—must help us find meaning in the experience and provoke us to cooperate with its transformative potential.

In studying the continuum of these potentially transformative experiences, I have more than once hinted that they all derive from a single psychic function. The meaning we get from the experience is inherently individual and depends on social, cultural, and historical variables. Everything seems to point to a general creative ability that lies within our depths. Recognizing this may be the single most crucial thing we have to learn about our evolutionary potential. In speculating on the *means* whereby visions, apparitions, and alien visitors may be produced, Hilary Evans concluded that "our producer is indeed something akin to an autonomous personality, separate from and in many respects superior to our conscious self."[21]

What it is and how this superior creative personality within us "produces" entities is a function of context. To see this more clearly, consider the following. In a lecture on demoniacal possession, William James wrote, "One sees that the type [of demonic possession] is modified by the tradition of the country."[22]

Eugene Taylor, who reconstructed James's Lowell Lectures, says of the lecture on possession that the "demon-possession of old has now been transformed into an optimistic mediumship, related not to devil worship and psychopathology but to personal growth, healing, especially of functional disorders, and to religious or philosophical concerns."[23]

If James is right, this primal blob of neutral psi power tends to "become the more benign and less alarming, the less pessimistically it is regarded." In other words, gods, goddesses, demons, elementals, fairies, and so forth, evolve and change their forms as we change, grow, and evolve. The value of these imaginal forms depends on our interpretation. The observer is inseparable from the observed. In the realm of the sacred, the divine, the supernatural, creation is cocreation.

Experience and Transformation

In reviewing these patterns of alien encounter, we are asking if they have any evolutionary significance. Clearly, there is no simple answer to this question. The significance of any experience is an open matter. But here are four ways the extraordinary encounters described *may* accelerate the evolution of consciousness:

Images and symbols of human potential. The sheer weight of accumulated evidence might force us to confront the idea of our latent potentials. We may become conscious of that superior inner producer that Hilary Evans describes. And this may stir us to take more responsibility for our thoughts, beliefs, and intentions. We may realize more clearly that we are creating our world, however subtly, gradually, and inconspicuously.

The entities described in this book seem in some sense to be objectively real. But because they are partially psychic in origin they are also creatures of symbol and inner significance. Their symbolic outreach is both inward and outward: they point to powers within as well as possible events taking place in the outer world.

A black dog with red eyes or a winged headless man that assaults us on a lonely road is frightening. Yet in a way such visions are merely histrionic gestures that allude to the far greater horrors of actual existence: death squads, serial killers, organized armies and their technologies of murder. Likewise, the vision of Mary is glorious to contemplate, but its deeper significance is the potential for divine compassion that lies within us. The angel that rescues us is also the angel within, our own potential to transcend the possible, our own existential option to be angels to one another.

Again, the important thing is not literal levitation but the world of possibilities that the metaphor of levitation suggests. An endless range of possibilities revolves around the imagery of "levity"—of lightness, detachment, mobility, of liberation from "gravity"—not just the force that yanks us down to earth but the humorless heaviness that weighs on our inner lives.

Alien encounters evoke images of higher worlds, higher intelligences. An image of a higher intelligence at large disposed to help us in our daily lives might provide the stimulus we need to dare things we might otherwise feel too intimidated to attempt. The gods in the Homeric epics seem to work that way: the gods and goddesses are all in Odysseus himself. It is they that draw out his great potential as a human being. They seem to be in the sky drawing him onward, but they are also inside him, propelling him through his adventures.

The energy factor. Many of these experiences stir up, even seem to transmit, a life-enhancing energy. They produce physical effects and aftereffects. Mary irradiates light—through her smile, the palms of her hands, her eyes, her jewelry, her golden gown. She emits the sheer power of a higher radiation that goes to the core of body and soul.

Angels are forms of psychic energy. As he recounts in his autobiography, Benvenuto Cellini was about to commit suicide in prison when a luminous angelic youth appeared to him; the angel hurled Cellini to the ground just as the great artist was about to hang himself on a device he had rigged. Sophie Burnham has collected a wealth of tales of angelic helpers and says that an "angel" even saved her from death on a ski slope.[24]

When people are on the threshold of death, dazzling beings of light appear and pour out their supernormal energies. Experiencers speak in breathless hyperboles of being bathed in a luminous source of unconditional love. This is not a word or a concept or a gray abstraction; it is a burst of superior force, electrifyingly physical. UFO phenomena are nothing if they are not lights that dance and play tricks in space, as if to bewitch us for one moment so that we pause and look up—as Whitman says—in perfect silence at the stars. When UFO contactees speak volubly of solar governments, of light rays of wisdom, of the radiance of love, there is a real psychoenergetic factor at work, an evolutionary accelerator.

According to Hindu tantrism, an energy called *kundalini* lies coiled at the base of the spine. When aroused, it rises through the spine and overflows into the head, inducing ecstatic transformative experiences. Kundalini may produce effects like the Western Platonic Eros—that great daimon whose genius is to lift us from the human to the divine. "Prana" in the yogic tradition, "ki" in the Chinese, "Holy Spirit" in the Christian tradition are names for vital forces that alien contact stories exemplify. This psychoenergetic factor is, I believe, part of the story of how we may be changed by these experiences.

Grappling with the Shadow. We may also be changed by being forced to grapple with the Shadow—the dark challenging corridors we have to pass through at the frontiers of the soul. Clearly, not all alien realities are unqualified in their benignity: there is nastiness afoot in the twilight zone, such as diabolical attack. In spite of all our fantasies of invulnerability, there are red-eyed monsters, suffocating Old Hags, cold-eyed aliens who would strap you down on an operating table. These are the monsters and aliens that lie concealed and repressed in the Shadow. But do they also have an objective reality? It is hard for us rational, light-loving, amiable souls to consider that out there in the world there may be prowling predatory forces of unalloyed evil intent.

Nevertheless, the Shadow can be our best friend. The Shadow—the side in ourselves we dare not look at—can be our best teacher. Terrifying, disorienting experiences may hurt and damage us, but when we are attacked by alien forces, our inner resources are more likely to be awakened. This is true whether the aliens are extraterrestrial or psychoterrestrial. Either way, meeting them can be a way to enlarge our self-understanding.

Dissolving our ordinary sense of reality. Alien adventures turn into allies for transformation when they dissolve our ordinary sense of reality. I think it was Castaneda's don Juan who used to complain that people were too solid, too dense. Finding oneself in bed with a Big Hairy Monster can have a liquefying effect on one's sense of reality. Such an experience can transfigure us by breaking down our habitual sense of what is true, real, and certain.

Socrates, the gadfly, tried to sting people awake from false certainty. Socrates was said to affect people like a torpedo fish, a creature known to cause an electric shock that numbs and paralyzes its victim. Socrates was a dispenser of metaphysical numbing, in which the patient became receptive to new truths.

Is this the way that evolutionary accelerators work? In these encounters at the frontiers of the soul, are we given shocks meant to numb, paralyze, and suspend our normal sense of reality? Socrates awakened his companions to wonder, setting them on the quest for wisdom. Alien contact experiences also inspire philosophical wonder. They force us to question our metaphysical assumptions and to revise our workaday maps of reality.

An extraordinary experience can be an ally or an enemy. In the end, spiritual evolution is a free creation. Whether we advance or retreat in the school of life depends on an act of our imagination, on the way we see the pattern, on the meaning we take from the experience. This is the sticking point of human potential; there are no guarantees, no surefire formulas. Help, grace, miracle—at best they are invitations to awakening. But lacking the right myth, insight, or frame of reference, we are as likely to tumble backward as we are to bolt forward.

14
Beyond the Frontiers

We are upwinging to a posthuman/extraterrestrial zone in evolution.
F. M. Esfandiary

Man is an experiment. The other animals are another experiment.
Time will show whether they were worth the trouble.
Mark Twain

We have been reconnoitering at the frontiers of the soul, exploring possibilities of our psychic evolution. We have looked at religious experience from a psychic perspective—the belief in God, for example, and life after death—and found that, from a psychic perspective, these ancient ideas take on new dimensions of meaning.

Is there anything in the human personality beyond physical existence? This was a critical question, because without a transcendent factor, the higher worldviews founder on the reefs of materialism. Psychic research offers a helping hand—by giving evidence for something within us that exists beyond the limits of space and time.

The psychic approach to God and immortality led to two conclusions: First, the revelations of religious genius are not absolute ends but local beginnings, anticipations of an unfinished process. Second, the divine is interwoven with the human adventure. There is a psi factor at large, a formless potential for transformation; religion is a venture of development, a cocreative process, a partnership between ourselves and a great X luring us beyond ourselves.

The material in these chapters leads to the conclusion that the spiritual is higher than the psychic, as love is greater than power and wisdom superior to intelligence. Still, from an evolutionary perspective, psyche precedes spirit. The soul is the mother of our spiritual capacities, as the earth is the mother of her creatures: earth spawns the rare flower and the poisonous snake, the life-giving stream and the violent tornado. Spirit is rooted in soul, and is helped or hindered by the powers of soul. The line between soul and spirit is drawn perhaps more clearly in our minds and language than in reality.

What then of the prospects of our evolution? Is the human experiment worth the trouble? Are we stations on a yet not fully traveled road? Is there reason to hope, as so many have, that great leaps beyond still await us?

And how will we travel and evolve? Will it always be the few—the rare ones and even then fitfully—who rise to eminence? Or will there come a day when we shall all rise together to a new perfection? Will we complete the circle, come home, return like prodigal children and reclaim our natural birthright?

I doubt that we will all rise together. The myth of Lucifer, the highest angel who turned bad, gives the lie to the fantasy that psychic evolution could ever be as final or complete as was the evolution of sight or the opposable thumb. Lucifer, like every human being, was blessed and cursed with the gift of freedom. The higher we rise, the more headlong the potential fall.

Yet there are grounds for hope for the average human being. It is undeniable that an extraordinary potential is present. Many avenues of investigation suggest that allies of our evolution exist; we just need to recognize and use them. Old beliefs and practices, too, are available—ways to search the god-like sources, ancient mystery rites, cults of angels. As we begin to unmask these obscure practices in light of the new science of the soul, we may hone our skills in harnessing the greater powers.

We also have before us records of extraordinary human beings, ancient and modern, people who demonstrate it is possible to surpass ordinary humanity. Being like ourselves creatures of flesh and blood, they may inspire us to reach beyond our current limitations.

Increasing information suggests that the inner evolution of ordinary human beings may be accelerating in our times. Strange forces seem afoot that are catapulting people to new levels of consciousness, new value systems, new metaphysical outlooks. A growing store of remarkable facts declares the presence of unused faculties in the species and unknown energies awakening in our midst.

There is enough information for speculating on our possible psychic evolution—enough evidence to prove that marvelous breakthroughs are possible. The problem is that we fear breakthrough and are addicted to the known and the familiar.

People like Padre Pio and Sai Baba who are born with rare gifts need a culture to guide their growth and ripening. This is critical to prospects of our higher progress. We need, above all, a revolution in education, a new myth of the human, a belief system that welcomes our higher aspirations. We need to build a new paradigm, a new social milieu open to the seeds of transformation.

And we need to search for the overall pattern in our inward and outward development—the total seamless process of our soul-awakening experiences. It is useless to get bogged down on whether particular items are real, malobserved, or muddled with deceit. These concerns, in the end, are not as important as the whole configuration, the big picture that needs so badly to emerge in consciousness, the energy eager to erupt and goad us to give birth to our future selves.

Our vision must be open to the unexpected. If the history of evolution says anything, it is that novelty is the rule. At the frontiers of the soul, there are no easy landmarks to light the way. The future of our evolution may lurk in shadows of the unforeseen.

It might be that the very things that threaten to destroy us today contain the clues to the next step of our evolution. Take, for one wild example, the greenhouse effect. The greenhouse effect involves an increase in carbon dioxide in the atmosphere. An excess of carbon dioxide, or hypercarbia, is known to produce states of consciousness indistinguishable from the classic near-death and mystical experience. For all we know, the atmosphere may be already changing our brain structure, subtly opening our psychic pores to Mind at Large. One day we might wake up to find we have quietly passed a critical threshold to a new consciousness.

Or consider another supposed menace—overpopulation. Overpopulation may eventually force us to colonize space—and that may be the route to the birth of a new species of humankind.

Judging by accounts of the astronauts, space travel expands the human mind. Jim Irwin of the Apollo 15 lunar mission said he "found God on the moon." Al Worden started channeling poetry when he returned home. Alan Bean said, "Everybody who went to the moon became more like they were deep inside themselves." (Bean became an artist.) Rusty Schweichert, who cried while looking at the stars from outer space, "fell in love with the earth," and found himself asking soul-searching questions like "Who am I?" Edgar Mitchell of the Apollo 14 flight was "overwhelmed with a divine presence," experienced Earth and the universe as "an intelligent system" in a way that was at odds with his scientific training, and founded the Institute of Noetic Sciences.

In destroying the earth we may stumble upon the gates of heaven. In being driven to explore outer space we may discover the secrets of inner space. All the mistakes we have made so far may one day be looked upon as the blunderings of adolescence, the errors we had to make before our childhood's end.

Nobody knows what surprises the future holds. That is what makes time more wonderful than terrible.

Dr. Grosso welcomes accounts of unusual psychic experiences that readers think may bear on themes discussed in this book. Please write Michael Grosso, Ph.D., 26 Little Brooklyn Road, Warwick, NY 10990.

Endnotes

Chapter 1

1. G. S. Kirk, and J. E. Raven, *The Presocratic Philosophers* (Cambridge: University Press, 1957), 163-182.

2. Alfred Russell Wallace, *Miracles and Modern Spiritualism* (London: Spiritualist Press, 1878/1955).

3. H. P. Blavatsky, *The Secret Doctrine* (Wheaton: The Theosophical Publishing House, 1967). See the Preface.

4. For an excellent account, see Alan Gauld, *The Founders of Psychical Research* (London: Routledge, 1968).

5. See, for example, Michael Grosso, *Soulmaker: The Stories from the Far Side of the Psyche* (Norfolk: Hampton Roads, 1992).

6. From the faith-centered point of view, the reader might turn with profit to at least two books: Michael Perry, *Psychic Studies: A Christian's View* (London: Thorsons, 1984) and John Heaney, *The Sacred and the Psychic: Parapsychology and Christian Theology* (New York: Paulist Press, 1984).

7. Rudolf Bultman, *Primitive Christianity* (New York: Meridian, 1956).

Chapter 2

1. The literature is vast. The best sources remain the *Journals and Proceedings for the British and American Societies for Psychical Research.* These publications have been carefully sifting out valid claims of the paranormal for well over a hundred years. For good historical overviews, see Alan Gauld, *The Founders of Psychical Research* (1968); Brian Inglis, *Natural and Supernatural* (1977); Nandor Fodor, *Encyclopaedia of Psychic Science* (1976). For state of the art summaries of research see the series *Advances in Parapsychological Research,* ed. Stanley Krippner, beginning 1977; *Handbook of Parapsychology,* Benjamin Wolman, ed. (1977); *Research in Parapsychology* (various editors) which contain abstracts and papers from annual conventions of the Parapsychological Association; and the annual proceedings of the Parapsychology Foundation in New York City. For philosophical treatment of psi: C. D. Broad, *Religion, Philosophy and Psychical Research* (1953); *Philosophical Dimensions of Parapsychology,* James Wheatley and Hoyt Edge, eds. (1976); Stephen Braude, *The Limits of Influence* (1986). On miracles,

religion, and psi: E. Cobham Brewer, *Dictionary of Miracles* (no date); Herbert Thurston, *The Physical Phenomena of Mysticism* (1952); Scott Rogo, *Miracles* (1977); John Heaney, *The Sacred and the Psychic* (1984); Michael Perry, *Psychic Studies* (1984); Patricia Treece, *The Sanctified Body* (1989); Michael Murphy, *The Future of the Body* (1991).

2. See H. D. Lewis, *The Elusive Mind* (1969) and Stephen Braude, *The Limits of Influence* (1986).

3. There are, of course, many differences between the Platonic *idea* or *eidos* (both words refer to mental images) and archetypal forms of modern imaginal psychology. What they share is the role of psychic dominance and numinosity; Plato's ideas only seem more abstract because they are said to be invisible and seen with the eye of the soul. But Jung too distinguished between the sensible form and the invisible shaping archetype. There is, in fact, a whole Neoplatonic, mystical, and Renaissance tradition of such archetypes; Jung and his followers are the latest empirical students of this world of imaginality.

4. I paraphrase H. H. Price's remark about the nature of speculative philosophy.

5. Hoyt L. Edge, Robert L. Morris, John Palmer, Joseph H. Rush, *Foundations of Parapsychology: Exploring the Boundaries of Human Capability* (New York: Routledge & Kegan Paul, 1986), xvi.

Chapter 3

1. Paul Tillich, *Dynamics of Faith* (New York: Harper, 1957), 1. Tillich defined faith as a "state of being ultimately concerned."

2. William James, *Varieties of Religious Experience* (New York: Longmans, Green, 1913), 458.

3. Randolph C. Byrd, "Positive therapeutic effects of intercessory prayer in a coronary care unit population," *Southern Medical Journal* (July 1988): 826-29.

4. H. H. Price, "Petitionary Prayer and Telepathy," *Essays in the Philosophy of Religion* (Oxford: Clarendon Press, 1972), 37-55.

5. See K. J. Batcheldor, "PK in sitter groups," in *Psychoenergetic Systems*, Vol. 3, (1979): 77-93, and *Psychokinesis, Resistance, and Conditioning* (1966), 21 pages, unpublished manuscript.

6. James Hillman, *Re-Visioning Psychology* (New York: Harper & Row, 1975). See especially Chapter 1, "Personifying or Imagining Things," in which Hillman states: "The world and the Gods are dead or alive according to the condition of our souls. A world view that perceives a dead world or declares the Gods to be symbolic projections derives from a perceiving subject who no longer experiences in a personified way" (16).

7. I. M. Owen, and M. Sparrow, *Conjuring Up Philip* (New York: Pocket Books, 1977), 19.

8. See reference to Thurston *et alia* in note 1 for Chapter 2.

9. Raymond Moody, *Life After Life* (Covington: Mockingbird, 1975).

10. K. Osis, and E. Haraldsson, *At the Hour of Death* (New York: Avon, 1977).

11. Kenneth Ring, *Life At Death* (New York: Coward, McCann, & Geoghegan, 1980).

12. Kenneth Ring, *Heading Toward Omega* (New York: William Morrow, 1984), 162-63.

13. See especially Michael Sabom, *Recollections of Death* (New York: Harper & Row, 1981). This book documents cases of veridical out-of-body episodes during NDEs. The veridical component of the NDE shows that at least part of the experience cannot be viewed as hallucinatory. This feature of NDEs is consistently ignored by so-called skeptics; it clearly qualifies the NDE as a transcendent experience—as defined in Chapter 2.

14. Many examples support the idea that near-death episodes have radically changed people's inner landscapes. Martin Luther decided to become a priest after he was struck by lightning; Thomas Aquinas was virtually struck dumb by a vision he saw in a life-threatening episode, after which he stopped work on his magnum opus, the *Summa Theologica;* Vico records in his autobiography how he fell and cracked his skull when he was a child, went into a coma, and emerged with a "choleric" disposition and melancholy genius; the psychic Croiset was a house painter who fell off a scaffolding and woke in a hospital with suddenly acquired psychic powers. Examples could easily be multiplied.

15. Irwin Rhode, *Psyche: The Cult of Souls and Belief in Immortality Among the Greeks* (New York: Harper & Row, 1966). "At a certain period in Greek history," observes Rhode, "appeared the idea of the divinity, and the immortality implicit in the divinity, of the human soul," Vol. 2, 254.

16. See, for example, D. Scott Rogo, *Mind Beyond the Body* (New York: Penguin, 1978).

17. I use the word "signal" here strictly as a convenient metaphor. There is no intention to liken ESP to radio or any other physical energy transfer system. There is no evidence to support such a view of psi; in fact, evidence and argument are against it.

18. Charles Honorton, "Psi and internal attention states," in B. B. Wolman, *Handbook of Parapsychology* (New York: Van Nostrand, 1977), 435-472.

19. This procedure for limiting sensory input has been studied as a condition for optimizing receptivity to psi. A great deal of experimental work has been done in this field with impressive results. See the Honorton study cited above.

20. Rhea White, "Old and new methods of response in ESP experiments," *Journal of the American Society for Psychical Research* (January, 1964): 21-56.

21. John Palmer, "Extrasensory perception: research findings," in *Advances in Parapsychological Research* (Vol. 2) ed. Stanley Krippner (New York: Plenum Press, 1978), 153.

22. See G. Schmeidler and R. McConnell, *ESP and Personality Patterns* (New Haven: Yale University Press, 1958).

23. See especially Gardner's pamphlet *Thyself Both Heaven and Earth.* (London: Theosophical Publishing House, 1964). I am indebted to Leslie Price, editor of *Theosophical History,* for introducing me to this publication. I am also indebted to Price for the expression "the parapsychology of God." Price, founder of the *Christian Parapsychologist,* is a pioneer in the parapsychology of religion.

24. Ibid., 16-17.

25. W. Y. Evans-Wentz, *The Tibetan Book of the Dead* (New York: Galaxy, 1960). See Jung's psychological commentary, xxxvii.

Chapter 4

1. Kenneth Scott Latourette, *A History of Christianity* (New York: Harper, 1953), 65.

2. Rudolph Bultman, *Jesus Christ and Mythology* (New York: Scribner, 1958).

3. See Jody Brant Smith, *The Image of Guadalupe* (New York: Harper & Row, 1984).

4. See Chapter 10 on Padre Pio.

5. Morton Smith, *Jesus the Magician* (New York: Harper & Row, 1978).

6. See, for example, the chapter on levitation in Thurston, cited in note of Chapter 2. Also, see Eric Dingwall, "St. Joseph of Copertino: The Friar Who Flew," *Some Human Oddities* (New York: University Books, 1962), 9-37.

7. Ibid.

8. From the German, *Quelle,* source.

9. David Williams, *Acts* (New York: Harper & Row, 1976), 21.

10. Walter Cannon, "'Voodoo' death," *American Anthropologist,* Vol. 44, No. 2 (April-June, 1942): 169-181. This is an absorbing study that demonstrates the power of negative placebo to an extreme degree. The words of Cannon merit quotation: "The ethnologists, basing their judgment on a large number of reports, quite independent of one another, admit that there are instances indicating that the belief that one has been subjected to sorcery, and in consequence is inevitably condemned to death, does actually result in death in the course of time.", 175.

11. Bernard Grad, "Some biological effects of the 'laying on of hands': A review of experiments with animals and plants," *Journal of the American Society for Psychical Research* (1965): 59, 95-129.

12. According to Morton Smith (ibid., 109), through all antiquity no one

was credited with more miracles than Jesus: 200 references in the Gospel stories, as compared to 107 in *Philostratus' Life of Apollonius*, 124 in the stories of Moses, and 28 in the stories of Elisha in II Kings.

13. See G. Vico, *The New Science*, sec. 1047.

14. Helmut Schmidt, "PK tests with a high-speed random number generator," *Journal of Parapsychology* (June, 1973): 105-118.

15. F. G. Taylor, "Report on the 'Geller Effect," *Psychoenergetic Systems*, Vol. 2 (1977): 81-88. This issue of *Psychoenergetic Systems* has several papers and commentaries on Geller's metal bending phenomena, some of which are critical.

16. Discussed by B. Grad in paper cited in note 11.

17. This phenomenon has been reported in poltergeist cases. See A. R. G. Owen, *Can We Explain the Poltergeist?* (New York: Garrett Publications, 1964), and A. Gauld and A. D. Cornell, *Poltergeists* (London: Routledge, 1979).

18. Everard Feilding, *Sittings with Eusapia Palladino* (New Hyde Park: University Books, 1963). Palladino's paranormal physical powers were studied by numerous scientists. This book records sittings with her in Naples under carefully controlled conditions, conducted by three veteran researchers, Feilding, W. W. Baggally, and Hereward Carrington. These men knew the conjurer's art and had exposed innumerable fake mediums. Baggally sums up the investigations by stating that 470 phenomena were observed including complete levitation of tables, movements of objects, sounds, breezes, lights, untying of knots, quasi human forms appearing, and countless instances of "grasps and touches by a tangible hand," as well as hands seen. These latter instances of transiently materialized hands were observed while the medium's two hands were visible and controlled in good light by the researchers. See also Anita Gregory, *The Strange Case of Rudi Schneider* (Metuchen: Scarecrow Press, 1985). Essentially the same types of materialization effects were again observed under conditions the author shows are incompatible with fraud or malobservation.

19. In the literature of poltergeist phenomena and in the veridical cases of physical mediumship we find accounts of heavy objects being moved around and sometimes completely levitated.

20. The luminous appearances of the Virgin Mary at Zeitun were photographed. See Francis Johnston, *When Millions Saw Mary* (Chulmleigh, Devon: Augustine Publishing, 1980).

21. See Jule Eisenbud, *The World of Ted Serios* (New York: Pocket Books, 1968), and Cyrill Permutt, *Photographing the Spirit World* (Wellingborough: Aquarian Press, 1988).

22. A widely attested phenomenon. See Owen and Sparrow, *Conjuring Up Philip*, for detailed accounts.

23. Peter Lappin, *Give Me Souls: Life of Don Bosco* (New Rochelle: Don Bosco Publications, 1986), 291-308.

24. Jerome Frank, *Persuasion and Healing* (New York: Schocken Books, 1963).

25. Montague Ullman, "Dream, Metaphor and Psi" (paper delivered at the Parapsychological Convention, 1983).

26. Elizabeth Moltman-Wendel, *The Women Around Jesus* (New York: Crossroad, 1980).

Chapter 5

1. For example, Michael Grosso, "Jung, parapsychology, and the near-death experience," *Anabiosis,* (1983): Vol. 3, No. 1, 3-38.

2. Charles Guignebert, *The Christ* (New Hyde Park: University Books, 1968).

3. Mary Ann Getty, *First Corinthians: Second Corinthians* (Collegeville, MN, 1983).

4. R. P. C. Hanson, *The Second Epistle to the Corinthians* (London: SCM Press, 1961).

5. See Gopi Krishna, *The Biological Basis of Religion and Genius* (New York: Harper & Row, 1971).

6. Richard Kohr, "Near-death experiences, altered states, and psi sensitivity," *Anabiosis,* (1983): Vol. 3, No. 2. 157-176. See also the work of psychiatrist and editor of the *Journal of Near-Death Studies,* Bruce Greyson, "Increase in psychic phenomena following near-death experiences," *Theta,* (1983): II, No. 2, 26-29.

7. This feature has been especially studied by Charles Flynn. See *After the Beyond: Human Transformation and the Near-Death Experience* (Englewood Cliffs: Prentice-Hall, 1986).

8. Robin Lane Fox, *Pagans and Christians* (San Francisco: Harper & Row, 1986), 336-375.

9. Edward Edinger, "Christ as Paradigm for Individuating Ego" in *Ego and Archetype* (Baltimore: Pelican, 1974).

Chapter 6

1. Otto Rank, *The Double* (New York: New American Library, 1971).

2. James Frazer, *The Belief in Immortality* (London: Macmillan, 1913).

3. Jean Paul Sartre, *Being and Nothingness* (New York: Washington Square Press, 1966), 310-370.

4. Herbert Thurston, *The Physical Phenomenon of Mysticism* (London: Burns & Oates, 1953).

5. Giambattista Vico, *Selected Writings,* Leon Pompa, ed., (Cambridge: Cambridge University Press, 1982).

6. Johan Steiner, *Therese Neumann* (New York: Alba House, 1966).

Chapter 7

1. The literature on the subject is extensive. The following should orient the reader. Gardner Murphy, *Three Papers on the Survival Problem* (New York: The American Society for Psychical Research, 1945); James Hyslop, *Psychical Research and Survival* (London: Bell & Sons, 1913); Alan Gould, *Mediumship and Survival* (London: Heineman, 1982); Ian Stevenson, *Children Who Remember Previous Lives* (Charlottesville: University Press of Virginia, 1987); Colin Wilson, *Afterlife* (New York: Doubleday, 1987); David Lorimer, *Survival?* (London: Routledge & Kegan Paul, 1984), D. Scott Rogo, *The Return From Silence* (London: Aquarian Press, 1989).

2. Henri Bergson, *The Two Sources of Mortality and Religion* (New York: Doubleday, 1935), 131.

3. Miguel de Unamuno, *The Tragic Sense of Life* (New York: Dover, 1954).

4. Ernest Becker, *The Denial of Death* (New York: The Free Press, 1973).

5. Norman O. Brown, *Life Against Death* (New York: Vintage Books, 1959).

6. See John Hick, *Death and Eternal Life* (New York: Harper & Row, 1976), especially Chapter 8, "Humanism and Death."

7. Rupert Sheldrake, "The Laws of Nature as Habits: A Postmodern Basis for Science" in David Ray Griffin, ed., *The Reenchantment of Science* (Albany: State University of New York Press, 1985), 79.

8. For a superb critique by a molecular biologist, see Michael Denton, *Evolution: A Theory in Crisis* (Bethesda, Maryland: Adler and Adler, 1985).

9. See Eric Jantsch and Conrad H. Waddington, *Evolution and Consciousness* (Reading, Mass: Addison-Wesley, 1976).

10. See Erwin Edman, ed., *The Philosophy of Schopenhauer* (New York: Modern Library, 1956), especially the essay, "Metaphysics of Love of Sexes," 349, where sexual love is said "to serve the species in the most efficient way, although at the cost of the individual."

11. Richard Dawkins, *The Selfish Gene* (New York: Oxford University Press, 1976).

12. Richard Wilhelm, *The Secret of the Golden Flower* (New York: Harcourt, 1962).

13. Friedrich von Hugel, *Eternal Life* (Edinburgh: T. T. Clark, 1912).

14. William Roll, "A New Look at the Survival Problem," in John Beloff, ed., *New Directions in Parapsychology* (Metuchen: The Scarecrow Press, 1976), 144-164.

15. H. H. Price, "The Idea of Survival in Another World," in J. R. Smythies, ed., *Brain and Mind* (London: Routledge & Kegan Paul, 1965), 1-31.

16. Let us confine the discussion to human imaginal environments, since we have no introspective data on the imaginal life of nonhumans.

17. Frederic W. H. Myers, *Human Personality and its Survival of Bodily Death* (London: Longmans, Green, 1903), 30.

18. Richard C. Lewontin, "Adaptation," *Scientific American* (September, 1978): 212-230.

19. Erich Neumann, *The Origins and History of Consciousness* (New York: Pantheon, 1954), 397-418.

20. Oscar Cullman, "Immortality of the soul or resurrection of the dead?" in Krister Stendhal, ed., *Immortality and Resurrection* (New York: Macmillan, 1965), 9-53.

21. G. R. S. Mead, *The Doctrine of the Subtle Body in Western Tradition* (Wheaton: Theosophical Publishing House, 1967).

22. Kenneth Ring, "Shamanic Initiation, Imaginal Worlds, and Light After Death," in *What Survives*, Gary Doore, ed. (Los Angeles: Tarcher, 1990).

23. Ernest Hartmann, "Dreams and Other Hallucinations: An Approach to the Underlying Mechanism," in *Hallucinations: Behavior, Experience, and Theory*, R. K. Siegel and L. J. West, eds. (New York: John Wiley & Sons, 1975), 71-79.

24. Henri Bergson's phrase.

25. Ronald Siegel, *Intoxication* (New York: E. P. Dutton, 1989).

26. Aldous Huxley, *The Doors of Perception* (New York: Harper & Row, 1954).

27. See, for instance, Isaiah Berlin, *Vico and Herder* (New York: Vintage, 1977), and Leon Pompa, ed., *Vico: Selected Writings* (New York: Cambridge University Press, 1982).

28. Lionello Venturi, *Four Steps Toward Modern Art* (New York: Columbia University Press, 1955), 13.

29. Wassily Kandinsky, *Concerning the Spiritual in Art* (New York: Wittenborn), 10.

30. Alan Bosquet, *Conversations with Dali* (New York: Dutton, 1969).

31. Immanuel Kant, *The Critique of Judgment* (New York: Hafner Publishing, 1961), 157.

32. Herbert Marcuse, "Art as a form of reality," in *On The Future of Art* (New York: The Viking Press, 1970). A few lines will have to indicate the scope of this original, at times perverse, essay by Marcuse: "It seems that the esthetic sublimation is approaching its historical limits. . . . Art, by virtue of its own internal dynamic, . . . wants to be *real*." 129-130.

33. Friedrich Schiller, *On the Esthetic Education of Man* (New York: Frederick Ungar, 1965). Art, for Schiller, is the essence of healing; without the healing that comes from the arts, understood in his sense, no civilization can flourish. "We must continue to regard every attempt at reform as inopportune, and every hope based upon it as chimerical, until the division of the inner man has been done away with.", 46.

34. See Michael Murphy, *Future of the Body* (Los Angeles: Tarcher, 1991).

35. Colin Brookes-Smith, "Recent Research in Psychokinesis," in J. D.

Pearce-Higgins, G. Stanley Whitby, eds., *Life, Death & Psychical Research* (1973), 49-54.

36. For a recent examination of evidence for macro-PK in the golden age of mediumship, see Stephen E. Braude, *The Limits of Influence* (New York: Routledge & Kegan Paul, 1986). Also Camille Flammarion, *Mysterious Psychic Forces* (London: Fisher Unwin, 1907).

Chapter 8

1. J. Finauer, "Divine Gift for Our Time," in R. J. Fox, *Opus Sanctorum Angelorum* (Washington, NJ: AMI Press, 1983).

2. J. Danielou, *The Angels and Their Mission* (Westminster, MD: Christian Classics, Inc., 1987), 80.

3. Both quotations are from a mimeographed sheet from a meeting devoted to the *Opus* in the Church of Saint John's in New York City, April, 1987.

4. A. Parente, *Send Me Your Guardian Angel* (San Giovanni Rotondo: Our Lady of Grace Capuchin Friary, 1984).

5. Ian Stevenson, "Xnoglossy: a review and a report of a case," in *Proceedings of the American Society for Psychical Research*, Vol. 31 (Feb. 1974).

6. See especially John Palmer's monumental study of ESP "Extrasensory Perception: Research Findings," in *Advances in Parapsychological Research 2: Extrasensory Perception*, Stanley Krippner, ed., (New York: Plenum Press, 1978), 59-245.

7. See also Camille Flammarion, *Mysterious Psychic Forces* (London: Fischer Unwin, 1907). This book summarizes many group experiments in the production of telekinetic effects. Chapter 6 and the experiments of Count de Gasparin are particularly relevant.

Chapter 9

1. E. R. Dodds, *Pagan and Christian in an Age of Anxiety* (New York: Norton, 1965).

2. S. Angus, *The Mystery-Religions* (New York: Dover, 1928/1975).

3. George Mylonas, *Eleusis and the Eleusinian Mysteries* (Princeton: Princeton University Press, 1961), 281.

4. All references to Homer are based on *Hesod: The Homeric Hymns and Homerica*, Hugh Evelyn-White, trans., (Cambridge: Harvard University Press, 1959), 288-324.

5. Quoted in Carl Kerenyi, *Eleusis* (New York: Pantheon, 1967) 14.

6. Ibid., 15.

7. Ibid., 15.

8. Ibid., 11-12.

9. For a more detailed discussion of this pattern, which I have called the

archetype of death and enlightenment, see Michael Grosso, *The Final Choice* (Walpole: Stillpoint, 1985).

10. Hypollitos, *The Refutation of all Heresies*, Francis Legge, ed., I, 138.

11. C. G. Jung, *Memories, Dreams, Reflections* (New York: Pantheon Books, 1961), 292-293.

12. Quoted in Mylonas, *Eleusis*, 265.

Chapter 10

1. John McCaffery, in his *Tales of Padre Pio* (New York: Image Books, 1981), confirms the story (see Chapter 11).

2. "Transformation Symbolism in the Mass," in *Psychology and Religion*, Vol. II (London: Routledge, 1958), 203-295.

3. Charles Mortimer Carty, *Padre Pio the Stigmatist* (Rockford, Ill: Tank Books, 1963), 69.

4. All the quotes about the Mass are from Tarciscio Da Cervinara's monograph, *Padre Pio's Mass* (San Giovanni, 1973). This little work collects remarks made in discussions with Padre Pio on the inner nature of his ecstatic masses.

5. McCaffery, *Tales of Padre Pio*, 8.

6. John Schug, *Padre Pio: He Bore the Stigmata* (Huntington, Indiana: Our Sunday Visitor, 1975), 55.

7. Alessio Parente, *Send Me Your Guardian Angel* (San Giovanni Rotondo: Our Lady of Grace Friary, 1983).

8. *The Voice of Padre Pio*, Vol. 5, No. 3 (1975): 14-15.

9. Carty, *Padre Pio the Stigmatist*.

10. Joan C. Cruz, *The Incorruptibles* (Rockford, Illinois: Tan, 1977).

11. Bernard Ruffin, *Padre Pio: The True Story* (Huntington, Indiana: Our Sunday Visitor, 1982).

12. Dorothy Gaudiose, *Prophet of the People* (New York: Alba House, 1974), 137.

13. Giorgio Cruchon, "Padre Pio's Stigmata," in *Padre Pio of Pietrelcina: Acts of the First Congress of Studies on Padre Pio's Spirituality.* (San Giovanni Rotondo: Geraldo Di Flumeri, 1972), 111-140.

14. See accounts in Schug, *Padre Pio*.

15. Patricia Treece, *Nothing Short of a Miracle* (New York: Doubleday, 1988), 177-192.

16. See Schug, *A Padre Pio Profile*, 35.

17. John Neihardt, *Black Elk Speaks* (New York: Pocket Book, 1972). See the postscript.

18. David Barker, "Psi Phenomena in Tibetan Culture," in *Research in Parapsychology 1978* (Metuchen: Scarecrow, 1979), 52-55.

19. See Carty's account, in *Padre Pio the Stigmatist*, 57-58.

Chapter 11

1. Arnold Schulman, *Baba* (New York: Macmillan, 1971), 3.
2. R. S. Mishra, *The Textbook of Yoga Psychology* (New York: Julian Press, 1963).
3. Samuel Sandweiss, *Sai Baba: The Holy Man and the Psychiatrist* (San Diego: Birthday Publishing, 1975).
4. Ibid.
5. Ibid., 12.
6. Howard Murphet, *Sai Baba: Man of Miracles* (York Beach, Maine: Samuel Weiser, 1973), and *Sai Baba: Avatar* (San Diego: Birthday Publishing, 1977).
7. Murphet, *Sai Baba: Avatar,* 32.
8. See Murphet, *Sai Baba: Man of Miracles,* 42-49.
9. Erlendur Haraldsson, *Modern Miracles: An Investigative Report on Psychic Phenomena Associated with Sathya Sai Baba* (New York: Fawcett Columbia, 1987).
10. Ibid., 82.
11. Ibid., 174.
12. Ibid., 128.
13. Murphet, *Man of Miracles.* 156.
14. Haraldsson, *Modern Miracles.* 82.
15. C. T. Chari, "Some Disputable Phenomena Allied to Thought-ography," *Journal of the American Society for Psychical Research* (July, 1969): 273-86.
16. Haraldsson, *Modern Miracles.* 134.
17. Ibid., 124.
18. See Dennis Rawlins in *Starbaby,* a pamphlet published by *Fate Magazine* in October, 1981, and readily available as a reprint.
19. See Murphet, *Sai Baba: Avatar,* 83.

Chapter 12

1. See Michael Grosso, *Soulmaker* (Norfolk: Hampton Roads, 1992), especially Chapter 3, "The Lady of Light."
2. See their *Scientific and Medical Studies on the Apparitions at Medjugorje* (Dublin: Veritas, 1987).
3. Pearl Zaki, *Our Lord's Mother Visits Egypt* (Dar El Alam El Arabi, (no date).
4. Joseph Pelletier, *The Sun Danced at Fatima* (New York: Image Books, 1983).
5. Mikhail Tadros, M.D., *Forty Miracles of the Lady Virgin* (Jersey City: Saint Mark Coptic Church, 1974). An account of healings associated with

the Zeitun appearances of 1968-71. John Dowling, "Lourdes Cures and their Medical Assessment" *Journal of the Royal Society of Medicine,* Vol. 77 (August, 1984): 634-638.

6. E. Dupont, *Catholic Prophecy* (Rockford, Ill.: Tan Books, 1973).

7. F. S. C. Northrop, *Meeting of East and West* (New York: Collier Books), 27.

8. The reports of the alleged locutions of Mary are endlessly particular and precise in their invective against homosexuality, drugs, abortion, and all the other practices religious conservatives denounce.

9. Jody Brant Smith, *The Image of Guadalupe* (New York: Image Books, 1984).

10. See, for example, Edward Whitmont, *The Return of the Goddess* (New York: Crossroad, 1982); Merlin Stone, *When God Was A Woman* (New York: Harvest, 1976); Mary Daly, *Beyond God the Father* (Boston: Beacon Press, 1973).

11. Pablo Antonio Vega, *Apparitions of Our Blessed Mother at Cuapa, Nicaragua* (Washington, NJ: World Apostolate of Fatima, 1982).

12. Caroline Peters, *The Black Madonna* (Paterson, N.J.: St. Anthony Guild Press, 1964), 21.

13. "BVM Visions in Poland." *Fortean Times No. 43. 9.*

14. Colm Toibin, Seeing is Believing (Mountrath, Ireland: Pilgrim Press, 1985).

15. See Albert J. Hebert, *The Tears of Mary and Fatima* (Paulina, LA: no publisher, 1984), for an account of these phenomena. The author is devoid of critical sense but provides enough information to suggest the veracity of the phenomena.

16. L. R. Farnell, *The Evolution of Religion* (New York: Williams and Norgate, 1905), 67.

17. Naomi Goldenberg, *Changing of the Gods* (Boston: Beacon Press, 1979), 75. This is a brilliant book, but I disagree sharply with the author's interpretation of "Mary." See Eileen Power's introduction to *Miracles of the Blessed Virgin Mary: Johannes Herolt,* C. C. Swanton Bland, trans., (London: Routledge, 1928) for an account of the decidedly "bad girl" role of Mary, especially in medieval history.

Chapter 13

1. An excellent source for this chapter are the works of the British writer Hilary Evans, especially his *Visions, Apparitions, and Alien Visitors: A Comparative Study of the Entity Enigma* (Wellingborough: The Aquarian Press, 1984).

2. Kenneth Ring and Christopher Rosing, "The Omega Project: A Psychological Survey of Persons Reporting Abductions and Other UFO Encounters" in *Journal of UFO Studies,* Vol. 2 (1990): 59-98. This study

found that people reporting NDEs and UFOEs afterwards felt heat, tingling, energetic and "deep, ecstatic sensations"—all related to the kundalini syndrome.

3. David Lorimer, *Whole in One* (London: Arkana, 1990).

4. George Gallup, Jr., *Adventures in Immortality* (New York: McGraw-Hill, 1982).

5. Orefeo Angelucci, *The Secret of the Saucers* (Stevens Point, Wisconsin: Amherst Press, 1955), 36.

6. Dennis Stillings, ed., *Cyberbiological Studies of the Imaginal Component in the UFO Contact Experience* (St. Paul: Archaeus Project, 1989).

7. Thomas Bullard, *Comparative Analysis of UFO Abduction Reports* (Washington: Fund For UFO Research, 1987).

8. Jenny Randles, *Alien Abductions: The Mystery Solved* (New Brunswick: Inner Light Publications, 1988).

9. In *UFO Dynamics,* Book I (Moore Haven, FL: Rainbow Books, 1983), 240-272.

10. Peter Rojcewicz, "The 'Men in Black' Experience and Tradition: Analogues with the Traditional Devil Hypothesis," *Journal of American Folklore* (April-June, 1987): 148-160. See also his "Signals of Transcendence: The Human-UFO Equation," *Journal of UFO Studies,* Vol. 1 (1989): 111-127.

11. David Hufford, *The Terror that Comes in the Night* (Philadelphia: Pennsylvania University Press, 1982).

12. George T. Montague, *The Spirit and his Gifts* (New York: Paulist Press, 1974). See Chapter 2 on glossolalia.

13. Ibid., 29.

14. See the chapter "Ordeal by Serpents, Fire and Strychine" in George Montague, *Psychic Nexus* (New York: Van Nostrand, 1980).

15. See Leiping Zha and Tron McConnell, "Parapsychology in the People's Republic of China," *The Journal for the American Society of Psychical Research* (April, 1991): 119-143.

16. Jon Klimo, *Channeling* (Los Angeles: Tarcher, 1987).

17. See Margaret Tabor Millin, "The Message of Medjugorje," *New Realities* (March/April, 1990): 19-26. Millin writes, "I look and see a grey disc to the side of the sun. The disc moves across the sun. . . . All who look see it and all who see it are amazed." What is amazing to me is that this author isn't at all puzzled at seeing a flying disc in the midst of her religious pilgrimage to a Marian vision site.

18. Writers who study anomalous phenomena in the style of Charles Fort include, for example, John Keel, especially his *Mothman Prophecies.* See also *Strange Magazine,* edited by Mark Chorvinsky.

19. Janet and Colin Bord, *Alien Animals* (London: Panther Books, 1980), 196.

20. Jenny Randles, *Mind Monsters: Invaders From Inner Space?* (Wellingborough: Aquarian Press, 1990).

21. Hilary Evans, *Visions, Apparitions, Alien Visitors* (Wellenborough: Aquarian Press, 1984), 301.

22. Eugene Taylor, *William James on Exceptional Mental States* (Amherst: University of Massachusetts Press, 1984).

23. Ibid., 108.

24. Sophie Burnham, *A Book of Angels* (New York: Ballantine Books, 1990).

Index

QUEST BOOKS
are published by
The Theosophical Society in America,
Wheaton, Illinois 60189-0270,
a branch of a world organization
dedicated to the promotion of brotherhood and
the encouragement of the study of religion,
philosophy, and science, to the end that man may
better understand himself and his place in
the universe. The Society stands for complete
freedom of individual search and belief.
In the Classics Series well-known
theosophical works are made
available in popular editions.

NATIVE HEALER

Medicine Grizzlybear Lake

Many claim to be healers and spiritual teachers; the author is both. Here he explains how a person is called to be a medicine man or woman and the trials and tests of a candidate. Lake gives an exciting glimpse into the world of Native American shamanism. He was trained by numerous Native American teachers, including Rolling Thunder, and has conducted hundreds of ceremonies and lectures.

"... very interesting account of a native American Indian healer's apprenticeship and practice..."
— Serge Kahili King
author of *Imagineering for Health* and *Earth Energies*

"... wonderful reading and full of important psychological, anthropological and spiritual information."
— James A. Swan, Ph.D., author of *The Power of Place*

"... it is a joy for me to read this work of Medicine Grizzlybear..."
— Brooke Medicine Eagle

"... a rare opportunity... to learn about shamanism from somebody who has been taught, trained, studied, and practiced in both worlds and societies. I therefore highy recommend it..."
— Rolling Thunder, Inter-tribal Medicine Man

"I highly recommend his book to all those who are feeling the expansion of spiritual awareness in their hearts and those who wish to understand the direct tradition of shamanism whose course is the same throughout many nations of indigenous people."
— Dhyani Ywahoo, Spiritual Director, Sunray Meditation Society

"In Native Healer *we are reminded that healing is a powerful culturally endorsed ritual whose practitioners use skills and wisdom accumulated for centuries to help patients garner their most powerful self-healing responses."*
— Carl A. Hammerschlag, M.D., author of *The Dancing Healers*